# A Writer's Guide to Chicago-Area Publishers

## And Other Freelance Markets

# A Writer's Guide to Chicago-Area Publishers

## And Other Freelance Markets

Compiled and edited by Jerold L. Kellman
and Hilary Richardson Bagnato

**WRITER'S GUIDE PUBLICATIONS**
*A Division of Gabriel House, Inc.*

EVANSTON, ILLINOIS
1994

Printed in the United States of America

ISBN 0-936192-01-1

Library of Congress Catalog Number 93-061808

Design and typography by Troyprint, Highland Park, Illinois

# CONTENTS

Welcome, a Third Time, to Chicago Publishing! .................................ix

## Book Publishers

Abbot, Langer & Associates ..............2
Academy Chicago Publishing..........3
ACTA Publications, Inc. ...................4
African American Images ................5
American Bar Association ..............6
American Catholic Press.................7
American Hospital Publishing, Inc. 8
American Library Association........9
American Technical
    Publishers, Inc. ...........................10
Another Chicago Press...................11
The Art Institute of Chicago .........12
Baha'i Publishing Trust ................13
Bonus Books....................................14
CES Associates ...............................15
Chicago Review Press, Inc. ...........16
Childrens Press ..............................17
Chiron Publications .......................18
Clark Boardman and Callaghan.....19
Contemporary Books......................20
Crossroads Books ...........................21
Crossway Books ..............................22
The Dartnell Corporation..............23
DBI Books, Inc. ...............................24
Ivan R. Dee, Inc. .............................25
Encyclopaedia Britannica, Inc.......26
Evanston Publishing, Inc. .............27
Everyday Learning Corporation ....28
J. G. Ferguson
    Publishing Company .................29
Forest House
    Publishing Company, Inc..........30
Goodheart-Willcox Company, Inc. 31
Great Quotations
    Publishing Company .................32
Harlan Davidson, Inc./
    Forum Press, Inc......................33
InQ Publishing Company .............34
InterVarsity Press ..........................35
Richard D. Irwin, Inc. ...................36
Irwin Professional Publishing .......37
Kazi Publications, Inc. ...................38
Charles H. Kerr
    Publishing Company .................39

Kidsbooks, Inc................................40
Lake View Press .............................41
Loyola University Press .................42
McDougal, Littell
    and Company ...........................43
Moody Press ...................................44
Mosby-Year Book, Inc....................45
Nelson-Hall Publishers .................46
The Noble Press .............................47
Northwestern University Press.....48
NTC Publishing Group .................49
Path Press, Inc................................50
F. E. Peacock Publishing, Inc. .......51
Planning Communications ...........52
P. O. Publishing Company.............53
Polychrome Publishing
    Corporation...............................54
Probus Publishing .........................55
Proteus Enterprises, Inc. ...............56
Publications International Ltd.......57
Quintessence Publishing
    Company....................................58
Real Estate Education
    Company....................................59
Scott Foresman and Company.......60
Harold Shaw Publishers ...............61
Sourcebooks ...................................62
Surrey Books, Inc. ..........................63
Theosophical Publishing House....64
Third Side Press.............................65
Third World Press..........................66
Thorntree Press .............................67
Thunder & Ink Publishers.............68
Tia Chucha Press............................69
Triumph Books ..............................70
Tyndale House Publishers.............71
University of Chicago Press...........72
Urban Research Press.....................73
Victor Books ...................................74
Waveland Press ..............................75
Albert Whitman and Company .....76
Woodall Publishing
    Company, Inc. ...........................77
World Book, Inc. .............................78

# Periodical Publishers

## General Interest

AIM: America's Intercultural
   Magazine.................................80
Air Waves......................................81
American Field ..............................82
Antiques & Collecting Magazine ...83
Auto Racing Digest.........................84
Baseball Digest .............................85
Basketball Digest ..........................86
Bowling Digest ..............................87
The Bulletin of the
   Atomic Scientists .....................88
Campus Life ..................................89
Career World .................................90
Chicago.........................................91
Chicago Computers and Users.......92
Chicago History.............................93
Chicago Life..................................94
Chicago Parent Newsmagazine......95
The Chicago Reporter ...................96
Chicago Schools ............................97
Complete Woman...........................98
Consumers Digest..........................99
Crafts 'n Things ...........................100
Crain's Small Business ................101
The Dartnell Corporation.............102
Dog World ...................................103
Down Beat ...................................104
Ebony...........................................105
The Elks Magazine .......................106
Employee Services Management ..107

Family Safety and
   Health Magazine......................108
Football Digest ............................109
Gay Chicago Magazine.................110
Go Chicago Travel Guide.............111
Hockey Digest...............................112
Illinois Entertainer .......................113
Insider..........................................114
Inside Sports ................................115
In These Times.............................116
Key This Week in Chicago...........117
Lakeland Boating .........................118
The Lion Magazine .......................119
Midwest Outdoors........................120
New Art Examiner ........................121
North Shore..................................122
The Orbit .....................................123
The Original Art Report...............124
P-Form: Performance Art
   Magazine..................................125
Playboy........................................126
PlusVoice......................................127
The Rotarian................................128
Soccer Digest ...............................129
Today's Chicago Woman ..............130
TravelHost....................................131
Vantage........................................132
Vegetarian Times .........................133
Windy City Sports Magazine.......134
Your Money...................................135

## Literary

Another Chicago
   Magazine..................................136
Chicago Review............................137
The Creative Woman ....................138
The Critic.....................................139
New American Writing..................140
Other Voices................................141

Poetry..........................................142
Poetry East..................................143
Primavera ....................................144
Rambunctious Review ..................145
Rhino ...........................................146
TriQuarterly .................................147
Whetstone....................................148

## Religious

AIM: Liturgy Resources ..............149
Anglican Advance.........................150
Brigade Leader ............................151
Chicago Studies............................152
The Christian Century .................153
Christianity & the Arts.................154
Christianity Today .......................155
The Christian Ministry ................156
Church History.............................157
The Covenant Companion ...........158
Daughters of Sarah .....................159
Extension.....................................160

Interlit.........................................161
JUF News.....................................162
The Lutheran................................163
Pioneer Clubs'
   Perspective ..............................164
Probe............................................165
The Sentinel .................................166
Today's Christian Woman ...........167
Urban Ministries, Inc. .................168
Venture.........................................169
World Order .................................170
The Young Crusader ....................171

# Professional

Advertising Age ............................172
American Libraries .......................173
Bank Management.......................174
The Bar Examiner ........................175
Barrister........................................176
Business Insurance ......................177
Business Marketing......................178
Chicago Advertising
  and Media................................179
Chicago Daily Law Bulletin.........180
Chicago Film & Video News........181
Chicago Lawyer............................182
Chicago Purchasor ......................183
Commercial Investment
  Real Estate Journal ..................184
Computerized Investing...............185
Confetti ........................................186
Corporate Legal Times ................187
Curriculum Review......................188
Editor & Publisher.......................189
Employee Benefit Plan Review ...190

Facets............................................191
Fire Chief......................................192
Futures Magazine.........................193
Healthcare Financial
  Management ............................194
Human Rights..............................195
Illinois Legal Times ....................196
Industrial Fire Chief....................197
Inland Architect ..........................198
Journal of Property
  Management ............................199
Lutheran Education .....................200
Marketing Research.....................201
The Neighborhood Works............202
Pensions & Investments...............203
Planning ......................................204
Printing News Midwest................205
Real Estate Business....................206
Restaurants & Institutions...........207
Screen Magazine ..........................208
Student Lawyer ............................209

# Trade

American Clean Car .....................210
American Coin-Op ........................211
American Drycleaner ...................212
American Laundry Digest............213
American Nurseryman.................214
American Printer..........................215
America's Network ......................216
Appliance Service News..............217
Assembly .....................................218
Billiards Digest............................219
Bowlers Journal...........................220
Boxboard Containers...................221
Brewers Digest.............................222
Business Communications
  Review .....................................223
C & D Debris Recycling ...............224
Chef Magazine..............................225
Concrete Products .......................226
Control.........................................227
Distributor ..................................228
Electronic Packaging
  & Production...........................229
Energy Focus ...............................230
Fancy Food...................................231
Fleet Equipment..........................232
Food Business .............................233
Food Industry News.....................234
Food Processing ..........................235
Foodservice Equipment
  & Supplies Specialist ..............236

Gas Industries..............................237
Global Telephony.........................238
Good Cents ..................................239
Grocery Distribution ..................240
Groom & Board............................241
Health Facilities
  Management ............................242
Interior Landscape ......................243
Luxury Homes..............................244
Manufactured Home
  Merchandisers ........................245
Materials Management
  in Health Care.........................246
May Trends ..................................247
Merchandiser/Amoco Jobber.......248
Motor Service ..............................249
Music Inc.....................................250
National Provisioner ...................251
New Product News ......................252
Pet Age.........................................253
PIMA Magazine............................254
Pizza & Pasta ..............................255
P-O-P Times ................................256
Progressive Railroading ..............257
Remodeled Homes ......................258
Successful Dealer ........................259
Telephony ....................................260
3X/400 Systems
  Management ............................261
Transport Fleet News...................262

# Newspaper Publishers

Bolingbrook Metropolitan
   Newspapers, Inc. .....................264
Chicago Reader.............................265
Chicago Sun-Times ......................266
Chicago Tribune Magazine .........267
Crain's Chicago Business .............268
Daily Herald ................................269
Des Plaines Publishing
   Company...................................270
DuPage Business Ledger ..............271
Extra Bilingual Community
   Newspapers ............................272
Hyde Park Herald........................273

Inside .............................................274
Lakeland Publishers, Inc. ............275
Leader Papers, Inc.......................276
Lerner Communications, Inc. ......277
Life Newspapers...........................278
New City ......................................279
Pioneer Press, Inc. .......................280
Press Publications ........................281
Regional News..............................282
Reporter/Progress Newspapers....283
Russell Publications, Inc. ............284
Star Publications ..........................285
Wednesday Journal, Inc. ..............286

# Audio-Visual Producers

AGS & R Communications...........288
Clearvue/eav, Inc. ........................289
Darby Media Group......................290
Gennera, Knab & Company..........291
Goldsholl Design & Film, Inc. .....292
Steve Kalsow Productions, Inc. ...293
Jack Morton Productions, Inc. .....294
Motivation Media, Inc. ................295
Burt Munk and Company ............296

Nystrom .......................................297
OneOnOne Computer Training ...298
Pilot Productions .........................299
Sheppard Productions, Inc. .........300
Rick Simon & Company...............301
Tritel Productions, Inc.................302
United Learning ...........................303
Williams/Gerard
   Productions, Inc. .....................304

# Editorial Services

Ligature, Inc. ...............................306
Mobium .......................................307
Navta Associates .........................308
Publishers Services, Inc..............309

The Quarasan Group....................310
Synthegraphics Corporation ........311
The Wheetley
   Company, Inc. .........................312

# Other Freelance Markets

Gallant Greetings Corporation .....314
Innovisions, Inc............................315
Illinois Theater Center .................316
New Tuners Theatre
   and Workshop .........................317
Northlight Theatre .......................318

The Riverside Publishing
   Company...................................319
Scholastic Testing Service...........320
TPC Training Systems .................321
Universal Training Systems
   Company...................................322

Index...................................................................................................323

# WELCOME, A THIRD TIME, TO CHICAGO PUBLISHING!

Yes, I know it's been a long time. For the better part of the last nine years, I've been asked repeatedly when the third edition of this book would appear. After all, the gap between the first and second editions was a mere six years.

Certainly the need was there. Some firms profiled in the earlier guides no longer publish, or they have moved their publishing operations far from the Chicago area. New firms—many of them splendid markets for freelancers—have come on the scene with phone numbers bearing a 312 or 708 area code (our definition of "Chicago-Area"). A third edition, therefore, was long overdue.

Why the delay? Part of the reason was that old nemesis of freelancers: procrastination. Bringing out a third edition always seemed like a good idea, but it had to compete with other good ideas vying for time and attention. And preparation of this book demands enormous amounts of time and attention. Sources must be scoured to develop lists of eligible firms. Each firm must be contacted by phone to gather the latest information. These lengthy telephone interviews then must be edited into the profile format you see on these pages. Finally, the profiles must be sent out to the companies for their pre-publication inspection and verification.

That the long period of procrastination finally came to an end is largely due to the efforts of Hilary Richardson Bagnato. Agreeing to take on much of the burden of contacting firms and gathering information, she convinced me that a third edition could and should be published. Her diligence is reflected in every profile in this book.

Even Hilary, however, cannot guarantee that the profiles that follow are totally valid at the time you are using this book. Experienced freelancers know that publishing companies often alter their personnel, their identities, and their needs for outside writing. Therefore, Hilary and I offer the following disclaimer: While the following pages are as accurate as we could make them at the time of publication, writers would be well advised to verify names, needs, and other data before submitting queries, proposals, and manuscripts.

I'm also indebted to Hilary for suggesting ways to improve *A Writer's Guide to Chicago-Area Publishers.* As a result of her suggestions, this edition offers the following innovations:

- ◆ "Other Freelance Possibilities"—A new category of information in the book publisher profiles, presenting job leads for editors, proofreaders, indexers, designers, and other freelance publishing professionals.

- ◆ A separate section of literary periodicals, allowing poets, short story writers, essayists, and others to locate more quickly the magazines appropriate to their creative efforts.

- ◆ A separate section of newspaper publishers, containing profiles of a host of neighborhood papers that often are the starting point for a freelance writing career.

These new features, along with old favorites like the standardized profile format and coverage of hundreds of fascinating but little-known firms, make this third edition well worth the long wait. Authors of every variety—novelists, poets, journalists, technical writers, scholars, scriptwriters, playwrights, educators, or simply hobbyists—can find in these pages a multitude of excellent markets. Freelancers, no matter whether they live close to or far from the city, will find at their fingertips a treasure chest of publishing opportunities.

Jerold L. Kellman

# Book Publishers

# ABBOT, LANGER & ASSOCIATES

548 First Street
Crete, Illinois 60417
(708) 672-4200

Established: 1967
Titles in Print:
Total 34; Annual 17

**Contact Person:** Dr. Steven Langer, President.

**Types of Books Published:** How-to, reference, and technical books about human-resources management, salary surveys, security/loss prevention, and sales management.

**Audience:** Human-resource directors, security directors, salary managers, sales managers.

**Recent Titles Published:** *How to Write Job Descriptions; Pay Schedule Developer; Compensation in Nonprofit Organizations.*

**Current Needs:** Manuscripts (96-page minimum) about human-resource management, recruitment/selection, affirmative action, wages and salary.

**Payment Information:**
**Fee or Royalty:** Royalty.
**Advance:** No.

**Rights Policy:** Buys all rights.

**How to Contact:** Send a query.

**What Not to Do:** Phone, drop in without an appointment, or send a complete unsolicited manuscript.

**Time Needed for Reply:** One month.

**Does Author Supply Photos?** Not initially.

**Advice for Authors:** Abbot, Langer & Associates is a very small press, and since most writing is done in house, freelancers are seldom used unless their work can match a certain need. Prospective authors should send a self-addressed, stamped envelope with their work.

# ACADEMY CHICAGO

363 W. Erie Street
Chicago, Illinois 60610
(312) 751-7300

Established: 1975
Titles in Print:
Total 300; Annual: 10-20

**Contact Person:** Dr. Anita Miller, President and Editor; Jordan Miller, Vice President; Blythe Smith, Editorial Assistant.

**Types of Books Published:** Fiction, nonfiction, and occasional reprinting of notable out-of-print works. The emphasis is on mystery titles, feminist works, novels, history, and biography.

**Audience:** Mainly adults.

**Recent Titles Published:** *Murder in Miniature; Threshold of Fire; The Celibacy of Felix Greenspan; Women with Wings.*

**Current Needs:** Good nonfiction (primarily history and biography) and unusual mysteries without gratuitous sex or violence.

**Payment Information:**
    **Fee or Royalty:** Royalty rates vary; those for new authors are based on a book's net price.
    **Advance:** No.

**Rights Policy:** Buys all rights.

**How to Contact:** Send a query with the first three consecutive chapters of a book, or write for manuscript-submission guidelines. Be sure to enclose a self-addressed, stamped envelope.

**What Not to Do:** Phone to attempt to sell the book verbally, or drop in without an appointment.

**Time Needed for Reply:** One or two months.

**Does Author Supply Photos?** Yes, if photographs are an integral part of the book. The company rarely publishes illustrated books.

**Advice for Authors:** Every submission is read. Academy Chicago does not publish self-help books, young adult books, romances, or cookbooks, but the company will consider any other kind of work with merit. Good writing comes first.

*NO FREELANCE EMP.*

# ACTA PUBLICATIONS, INC.

4848 N. Clark Street
Chicago, Illinois 60640
(312) 271-1030

Established: 1958
Titles in Print:
Total 100; Annual: 10

**Contact Person:** Gregory Pierce, Co-Publisher.

**Types of Books Published:** Books, audio cassettes, and videos for the Christian—primarily Catholic—market.

**Audience:** Adults with a Christian outlook. Most material is aimed at an average adult reader.

**Recent Titles Published:** *Daily Meditations (with Scripture) for Moms; Of Human Hands; A Reader in the Spirituality of Work; Kids are Nondivorceable.*

**Current Needs:** Material about spirituality of daily life and about coping with work, family, and community issues.

**Payment Information:**
**Fee or Royalty:** Royalty of 10 percent.
**Advance:** No.

**Rights Policy:** Negotiable.

**How to Contact:** Write to request author guidelines. Enclose a self-addressed, stamped envelope.

**What Not to Do:** Phone or send material without having first read the author guidelines.

**Time Needed for Reply:** Six weeks.

**Does Author Supply Photos?** No.

**Advice for Authors:** ACTA Publications publishes mass-market books. The writing level of manuscripts should reflect this fact. Most books are distributed through churches, schools, and religious bookstores.

# AFRICAN AMERICAN IMAGES

| | |
|---|---|
| 1909 W. 95th Street | Established: 1983 |
| Chicago, Illinois 60643 | Titles in Print: |
| (312) 445-0322 | Total 40; Annual 6 |

**Contact Person:** Jawanza Kunjufu, Ph. D., Editor.

**Types of Books Published:** Africentric books.

**Audience:** Children and adults.

**Recent Titles Published:** *The Power, Passion, and Pain of Black Love; Psychological Storms: The African American Struggle for Identity.*

**Payment Information:**
    **Fee or Royalty:** Royalty.
    **Advance:** No.

**How to Contact:** Send query; may also phone.

**What Not to Do:** Drop in without an appointment.

**Time Needed for Reply:** Ten weeks.

**Does Author Supply Photos?** Not necessarily.

# AMERICAN BAR ASSOCIATION
Department of Publications, Planning and Marketing
750 N. Lake Shore Drive
Chicago, Illinois 60611
(312) 988-6064

Established: 1876
Titles in Print:
Total 600; Annual 100

**Contact Person:** Joseph Weintraub, Director of Publications, Planning and Marketing.

**Types of Books Published:** Books for the legal market with an occasional title or two for the general public.

**Audience:** Lawyers and other professionals involved in legal transactions and related fields.

**Recent Titles Published:** *Trial Notebook: International Estate Planning; The Business of Law; Environmental Litigation; Finding the Right Lawyer; How to Write the Legal Brief; A Lawyer's Guide to Retirement; Managing Partner 101.*

**Current Needs:** Any book of practical interest to those in the legal profession and an occasional book about the legal profession of interest to the general public.

**Payment Information:**
**Fee or Royalty:** Either.
**Advance:** Not usually.

**Rights Policy:** Negotiable.

**How to Contact:** Send query.

**What Not to Do:** Phone or send a manuscript that really belongs in a legal journal.

**Time Needed for Reply:** One month.

**Does Author Supply Photos?** Only if required.

**Other Freelance Possibilities:** Occasional need for copyeditors and indexers familiar with legal technical terms. Send resume to Beverly Loder, Associate Book Editor, Department of Publications, Planning and Marketing.

**Advice for Authors:** The ABA's Department of Publications, Planning and Marketing rarely publishes scholarly or academic books. It also is not interested in memoirs, anecdotal histories, or lay opinions of social, policy, or constitutional issues. It seeks books that will enable lawyers to serve their clients better and enable lawyers and other professionals to understand substantive issues of law and apply that understanding to their practice or profession.

# AMERICAN CATHOLIC PRESS

16160 S. Seton Drive
South Holland, Illinois 60473
(708) 331-5845

Established: 1967
Titles in Print:
Total 15; Annual 6

**Contact Person:** Rev. Michael Gilligan, Editorial Director; Joan Termini, General Manager.

**Types of Books Published:** Books about Catholic liturgy; books of liturgical music.

**Audience:** Priests, deacons, nuns, and lay people interested in liturgy.

**Recent Titles Published:** *American Catholic Hymnbook* (in four editions); *Psalter; Singing the Psalms.*

**Current Needs:** More of the same.

**Payment Information:**
    **Fee or Royalty:** Fee.
    **Advance:** Yes.

**Rights Policy:** Buys all rights.

**How to Contact:** Send query.

**What Not to Do:** Phone.

**Time Needed for Reply:** Two to three months.

**Does Author Supply Photos?** No.

**Advice for Authors:** Authors should be aware that American Catholic Press does not publish poetry or general religious books and that unsolicited manuscripts will not be returned.

# AMERICAN HOSPITAL PUBLISHING, INC.

737 N. Michigan Avenue
Chicago, Illinois 60611
(312) 440-6800

Established: 1979
Titles in Print:
Total 110; Annual 20

**Contact Person:** Marcia Bottoms, Assistant Director, Books Division.

**Types of Books Published:** Books related to hospital administration and health-care issues, not books about clinical medicine.

**Audience:** Hospital CEOs, trustees, managers, and professional staff.

**Recent Titles Published:** *Health Information Management in Hospitals; Service Quality Improvement: The Customer Satisfaction Strategy in Health Care; Food Service Manual for Health Care Institutions* (1994 edition).

**Current Needs:** Books on hospital administration.

**Payment Information:**
**Fee or Royalty:** Individually negotiated.
**Advance:** Possible, but rarely given.

**Rights Policy:** Controls all rights.

**How to Contact:** Send outline, sample chapters, and author's qualifications.

**What Not to Do:** Phone or drop in without an appointment.

**Time Needed for Reply:** One month.

**Does Author Supply Photos?** If necessary.

**Other Freelance Possibilities:** Indexers, developmental editors, and (occasionally) ghost writers.

**Advice for Authors:** American Hospital Publishing, Inc., prefers experienced, practicing professionals who can express themselves clearly and concisely.

# AMERICAN LIBRARY ASSOCIATION

Publishing Services
50 E. Huron Street
Chicago, Illinois 60611
(312) 944-6780

Established: 1876
Titles in Print:
Total 340; Annual 36

**Contact Person:** Herbert Bloom, Senior Editor.

**Types of Books Published:** Library science.

**Audience:** Librarians.

**Recent Titles Published:** *Against Borders: Venture into Cultures; The New Handbook for Storytellers.*

**Current Needs:** Books about management and automation of library service; general-interest reference books; activity and resource-based supplements to topics in school textbooks.

**Payment Information:**
    **Fee or Royalty:** Can be either.
    **Advance:** Yes.

**Rights Policy:** Negotiable.

**How to Contact:** Send query letter.

**What Not to Do:** Send entire manuscript or drop in without an appointment.

**Time Needed for Reply:** One month.

**Does Author Supply Photos?** Yes.

**Other Freelance Possibilities:** Copyeditors, proofreaders, and indexers.

**Advice for Authors:** Although authors need not be librarians, they must possess an interest in configuring information or in teaching with educational resources.

# AMERICAN TECHNICAL PUBLISHERS, INC.

1155 W. 175th Street
Homewood, Illinois 60430
(708) 957-1100

Established: 1898
Titles in Print:
Total 75; Annual 8

**Contact Person:** Thomas E. Proctor, President and Editor-in-Chief.

**Types of Books Published:** Textbooks for vocational and technical education.

**Audience:** Students in secondary and post-secondary vocational programs, and in apprenticeship and trade training.

**Recent Titles Published:** *Printreading for Welders; Metallurgy; Low Pressure Boilers; Troubleshooting Electrical Motors.*

**Current Needs:** Manuscripts about the building and metal trades.

**Payment Information:**
   **Fee or Royalty:** Standard royalty rate.
   **Advance:** Depends on manuscript.

**Rights Policy:** Buys all rights.

**How to Contact:** Phone with idea or send query.

**What Not to Do:** Drop in without an appointment.

**Time Needed for Reply:** Two weeks.

**Does Author Supply Photos?** Not usually.

**Advice for Authors:** American Technical Publishers, Inc. prefers writers with trade and/or teaching experience in the field about which they plan to write. Request a complimentary copy of "Author's Guide—Developing a Proposal."

# ANOTHER CHICAGO PRESS

230 W. Huron Street                    Established: 1985
Chicago, Illinois 60611                Titles in Print:
(312) 943-0947                         Total 30; Annual 3

**Contact Person:** Marie Glazar, Executive Director.

**Types of Books Published:** Fiction (novels) and poetry.

**Audience:** Liberal-minded adults.

**Recent Titles Published:** *The Empty Lot; Noble Rot; Divine Days; Johannesburg and Other Poems.*

**Current Needs:** Manuscripts by authors whose work has already been recognized—either by previous publication or an award.

**Payment Information:**
    **Fee or Royalty:** Royalty of 10 percent.
    **Advance:** Sometimes.

**Rights Policy:** Buys all rights.

**How to Contact:** Send a query with a self-addressed, stamped envelope.

**What Not to Do:** Phone, drop in without an appointment, or send manuscript.

**Time Needed for Reply:** Six months.

**Does Author Supply Photos?** No, the company very rarely publishes illustrated books.

**Advice for Authors:** Another Chicago Press is interested only in material from authors who have had previous work published.

# THE ART INSTITUTE OF CHICAGO
Publications Department

| | |
|---|---|
| 111 S. Michigan Avenue | Established: 1879 |
| Chicago, Illinois 60603 | Titles in Print: |
| (312) 443-3540 | Total 50; Annual 10 |

**Contact Person:** Susan Rossen, Executive Director of Publications.

**Types of Books Published:** Exhibition catalogs and books about the permanent collections of The Art Institute of Chicago.

**Audience:** General adult readership, students and scholars.

**Recent Titles Published:** *Chicago Architecture and Design, 1923-1993: Reconfiguration of an American Metropolis; Asian Art in The Art Institute of Chicago; Textiles in The Art Institute of Chicago; The Ancient Americas: Art from Sacred Landscapes; Italian Paintings before 1600 in The Art Institute of Chicago.*

**Current Needs:** Scholarly articles on works in the collections of The Art Institute of Chicago for publication in a journal entitled Museum Studies.

**Payment Information:**
Fee or Royalty: Flat fee.
Advance: Unlikely.

**Rights Policy:** Retains all rights.

**How to Contact:** Send query or manuscript to the executive director.

**What Not to Do:** Drop in without an appointment.

**Time Needed for Reply:** Six weeks.

**Does Author Supply Photos?** Sometimes.

**Other Freelance Possibilities:** Designers, indexers, and editors (with M. A. in Art History and/or English).

**Advice for Authors:** The Art Institute of Chicago publishes only catalogs and books related to its exhibitions and permanent collections. The Art Institute of Chicago is not a trade publisher of art books or art-historical texts.

# BAHA'I PUBLISHING TRUST

415 Linden Avenue                    Established: 1931
Wilmette, Illinois 60091             Titles in Print:
(708) 251-1854                       Total 189; Annual 4

**Contact Person:** Dr. Betty Fisher, General Editor.

**Types of Books Published:** Sacred writings of the Baha'i Faith, and books and pamphlets about the Faith.

**Audience:** Members of the Baha'i Faith and those interested in the Faith and/or in comparative religion.

**Recent Titles Published:** *Call to Remembrance; Transform My Spirit.*

**Current Needs:** Works about the Baha'i Faith and various aspects of its teachings.

**Payment Information:**
   **Fee or Royalty:** Negotiable.
   **Advance:** Negotiable.

**Rights Policy:** Varies.

**How to Contact:** Send query with outline and two- to three-page summary of the project.

**What Not to Do:** Phone, send manuscript, or drop in without an appointment.

**Time Needed for Reply:** Three months.

**Does Author Supply Photos?** Possibly; it depends upon the work.

**Other Freelance Possibilities:** Indexers.

**Advice for Authors:** The Baha'i Publishing Trust is interested only in works that elucidate the Baha'i Faith or some aspect of its teachings.

# Bonus Books Inc.

160 E. Illinois Street
Chicago, Illinois 60611
(312) 467-0424

Established: 1985
Titles in Print:
Total 200; Annual 25-30

**Contact Person:** Anne Barthel, Associate Editor.

**Types of Books Published:** Professional and general nonfiction, especially sports and health care.

**Audience:** Adults.

**Recent Titles Published:** *Beating the Radar Rap; Shaq Impaq: The Unauthorized Biography of Shaquille O'Neal; Traffic Ticket Defense; Guerrilla Gambling.*

**Current Needs:** General nonfiction.

**Payment Information:**
   **Fee or Royalty:** Negotiable.
   **Advance:** Sometimes.

**Rights Policy:** Buys all rights.

**How to Contact:** Send a query with an outline, proposal, and/or a sample chapter or two.

**What Not to Do:** Phone or drop in without an appointment.

**Time Needed for Reply:** Four to six weeks.

**Does Author Supply Photos?** Yes.

**Other Freelance Possibilities:** Proofreaders, indexers, and (occasionally) graphic artists.

**Advice for Authors:** Enclose a self-addressed, stamped envelope when making submissions to Bonus Books.

# CES ASSOCIATES

| | |
|---|---|
| 112 S. Grant Street | Established: 1973 |
| Hinsdale, Illinois 60521 | Titles in Print: |
| (708) 654-2596 | Total 24; Annual 1-2 |

**Contact Person:** James F. Baker, President.

**Types of Books Published:** Educational texts and programs for business and industry, especially personal and career-development aids for self-directed learning.

**Audience:** Adults reentering the job market or enrolled in continuing-education programs; adolescents interested in career development.

**Recent Titles Published:** *Professional Resume-Writing Techniques; Interpreting Financial Reports for Decision-Making; Job-Search Strategies; Professional Resume-Writing Techniques for Nurses.*

**Current Needs:** Manuscripts by authors who have experience writing about self-directed career or emotional development.

**Payment Information:**
**Fee or Royalty:** Royalty of varying rate if CES publishes the book; fee of varying rate if CES markets the book to another company for publication.
**Advance:** Negotiable.

**Rights Policy:** Varies.

**How to Contact:** Send resume and background material for company to keep on file.

**What Not to Do:** Phone, send manuscript, or drop in without an appointment.

**Time Needed for Reply:** Up to 30 days.

**Does Author Supply Photos?** Yes.

# CHICAGO REVIEW PRESS

814 N. Franklin Street
Chicago, Illinois 60610
(312) 337-0747

Established: 1973
Titles in Print:
Total 200; Annual 15-20

**Contact Person:** Amy Teschner, Editorial Director.

**Types of Books Published:** Nonfiction, specialty cookbooks, various how-to, Chicago guidebooks, activities books for children.

**Audience:** Educated adults and young people 11 years and older.

**Recent Titles Published:** *The Mole People: Life in the Tunnels Beneath New York City; Birthmothers: Women Who Relinquished Babies for Adoption Tell Their Stories.*

**Current Needs:** Good nonfiction manuscripts.

**Payment Information:**
   **Fee or Royalty:** Sliding royalty rate of 7½ to 12½ percent, depending on the number of books sold and whether the book is paper or cloth.
   **Advance:** Between $500 and $3,000.

**Rights Policy:** Holds all rights but splits subsidiary rights.

**How to Contact:** Send query with outline and sample chapter (photocopy OK). Enclose a self-addressed, stamped envelope; Chicago Review Press will not reply to a submission sent without one.

**What Not to Do:** Send fiction (either for adults or children), computer disks, or self-help manuscripts.

**Time Needed for Reply:** Six to eight weeks.

**Does Author Supply Photos?** Yes, if relevant.

**Other Freelance Possibilities:** Copyeditors, proofreaders, and indexers. All must be familiar with the The Chicago Manual of Style.

**Advice for Authors:** Chicago Review Press also assigns writers to prepare manuscripts for book concepts that the company has developed internally. Writers are welcome to submit their resumes.

# CHILDRENS PRESS

5440 N. Cumberland Avenue
Chicago, Illinois 60656
(312) 693-0800

Established: 1946
Titles in Print:
Total 2000; Annual 120-140

**Contact Person:** Joan Downing, Senior Editor; Margrit Fiddle, Creative Director.

**Types of Books Published:** Educational supplementary materials for schools and libraries, primarily nonfiction at the elementary school level (through fourth grade).

**Audience:** Preschool through junior high school.

**Recent Titles Published:** *Sea to Shining Sea series; New True books; The Cornerstones of Freedom.*

**Current Needs:** High interest, low reading level materials.

**Payment Information:**
    **Fee or Royalty:** Can be either.
    **Advance:** Negotiable.

**Rights Policy:** Usually buys all rights.

**How to Contact:** Send query or a photocopy of a partial manuscript. Enclose a self-addressed, stamped envelope.

**What Not to Do:** Phone, drop in without an appointment, or send original copy of manuscript.

**Time Needed for Reply:** Six to eight weeks.

**Does Author Supply Photos?** Not necessary.

**Other Freelance Possibilities:** Copyeditors, proofreaders, and indexers.

**Advice for Authors:** Childrens Press faces a highly competitive market for its books. As a result, proposals are subjected to sales and marketing analyses as well as to editorial reviews. Authors should demonstrate knowledge of the elementary curriculum and be able to develop salable concepts.

# CHIRON PUBLICATIONS

400 Linden Avenue
Wilmette, Illinois 60091
(708) 256-7551

Established: 1984
Titles in Print:
Total 64; Annual 10

**Contact Person:** Siobhan Drummond, Managing Editor.

**Types of Books Published:** Trade books about Jungian psychology, with an occasional book for the general reading public.

**Audience:** Jungian analysts and lay people interested in Jungian psychology.

**Recent Titles Published:** *Psyche and Sports; The Chiron Dictionary of Greek and Roman Mythology; The Call of the Daimon; Jung's Struggle with Freud.*

**Payment Information:**
    **Fee or Royalty:** Royalty.
    **Advance:** No.

**Rights Policy:** Negotiable.

**How to Contact:** Send query and sample chapter.

**What Not to Do:** Phone or send a complete unsolicited manuscript.

**Time Needed for Reply:** Up to four weeks.

**Does Author Supply Photos?** Yes.

**Other Freelance Possibilities:** Occasional need for designers, proofreaders, copyeditors, and indexers.

**Advice for Authors:** Do not send any material that lacks direct relevance to Jungian psychology.

# CLARK BOARDMAN AND CALLAGHAN

155 Pfingsten Road
Deerfield, Illinois 60015
(708) 948-7000

Established: 1863
Titles in Print:
Total 500; Annual 40

**Contact Person:** Elizabeth Berman, Editor-in-Chief.

**Types of Books Published:** Treatises about and practice guides for all areas of law and federal taxation. Fields covered include commercial, corporate, tax, employment, family, and municipal law and litigation.

**Audience:** Attorneys; business leaders of all kinds; state, local, and federal government officials.

**Recent Titles Published:** *The Corporate Compliance Series; Nichols Debtor-Creditor Practice Forms; UCC-SEARCH* (CD-ROM).

**Current Needs:** Subjects of broad and national interest about major law-practice topics. Manuscripts must be suitable for books of at least 500 pages.

**Payment Information:**
**Fee or Royalty:** Can be either; rate is negotiable.
**Advance:** Yes.

**Rights Policy:** Reserves all rights.

**How to Contact:** Send query, tentative outline, and a resume of educational background and professional expertise.

**What Not to Do:** Phone, drop in without an appointment, or send manuscript.

**Time Needed for Reply:** Six to eight weeks.

**Advice for Authors:** Manuscripts should be practical, serving immediately as useful aids to the practicing lawyer. The company is not interested in works of an academic or highly theoretical nature. Professional certification in law or accounting is a virtual prerequisite to writing for this firm.

# CONTEMPORARY BOOKS

Two Prudential Plaza
180 N. Stetson Avenue, Suite 1200
Chicago, Illinois 60601
(312) 782-9181

Established: 1947
Titles in Print:
Total 500; Annual 65

**Contact Person:** Nancy Crossman, Associate Publisher.

**Types of Books Published:** Biographies, cookbooks, how-to, reference, self-help and humor about finance, health, sports, and popular culture.

**Audience:** General adult readership.

**Recent Titles Published:** *Unbelievably Good Deals and Great Adventures That You Absolutely Cannot Get Unless You're Over 50; Lawyers and Other Reptiles; Nasty People; The Art of Cooking for Diabetics.*

**Current Needs:** Reference books.

**Payment Information:**
    **Fee or Royalty:** Varying royalty—5 to 15 percent of retail price.
    **Advance:** Yes.

**Rights Policy:** Generally buys all rights, but negotiable.

**How to Contact:** Phone for general information and then send query.

**What Not to Do:** Drop in without an appointment.

**Time Needed for Reply:** Two to six weeks.

**Does Author Supply Photos?** Depends on the project.

**Other Freelance Possibilities:** Prospective copyeditors, proofreaders, and indexers should send a written query to Kathy Willhoite, Managing Editor.

**Advice for Authors:** Contemporary Books does not publish fiction or children's books.

# CROSSROADS BOOKS

35 N. Western Avenue
Carpentersville, Illinois 60110
(708) 426-0008

**Established: 1983**
**Titles in Print:**
**Total 50; Annual 4-5**

**Contact Person:** D. Ray Wilson, Publisher and Editor.

**Types of Books Published:** Historical tour guides, biographies, business books.

**Audience:** General adult readership.

**Recent Titles Published:** *Organizing the Organization; Indiana Historical Tour Guide; Entertaining Aurora.*

**Current Needs:** Books about the above-mentioned topics.

**Payment Information:**
    **Fee or Royalty:** Negotiable.
    **Advance:** Yes, a small one.

**Rights Policy:** Negotiable.

**How to Contact:** Send query with one or two sample chapters. Enclose a self-addressed, stamped envelope.

**What Not to Do:** Send complete manuscript.

**Time Needed for Reply:** Six weeks.

**Does Author Supply Photos?** Depends on project.

**Other Freelance Possibilities:** Occasional need for designers and illustrators.

**Advice for Authors:** No matter how interesting the history a prospective author may be recounting, Crossroads Books will reject it if it is not well written.

# CROSSWAY BOOKS
**Division of Good News Publishers**
**1300 Crescent Street**
**Wheaton, Illinois 60187**
**(708) 682-4300**

**Established: 1979**
**Titles in Print:**
**Total 250; Annual 50**

**Contact Person:** Leonard G. Goss, Editorial Director.

**Types of Books Published:** Religious books from a conservative evangelical Protestant point of view. Also mainstream fiction, fantasy and science fiction, and children's books—all with a Christian viewpoint.

**Audience:** Clergy, religious educators, and lay leaders.

**Recent Titles Published:** *Tell Me the Secrets; Twice Upon a Time; Ashamed of the Gospel; Disciplines of Grace.*

**Current Needs:** Books addressing the contemporary issues that face Christians informed by an historically orthodox outlook: the church, human sexuality, worship, the relationship of the arts to Christian faith. Also some fiction addressing the same point of view.

**Payment Information:**
    **Fee or Royalty:** Negotiable.
    **Advance:** Only against future royalties.

**Rights Policy:** Buys first North American book rights.

**How to Contact:** Send query or manuscript. Enclose a self-addressed, stamped envelope.

**What Not to Do:** Phone or send ideas for picture books.

**Time Needed for Reply:** Eight to twelve weeks.

**Does Author Supply Photos?** No.

**Advice for Authors:** Manuscripts must be directed at conservative evangelical Christians who are seeking to recover the full heritage of the Christian faith.

# THE DARTNELL CORPORATION

| | |
|---|---|
| 4660 N. Ravenswood Avenue | Established: 1917 |
| Chicago, Illinois 60640 | Titles in Print: |
| (312) 561-4000 | Total 27; Annual 10 |

**Contact Person:** Tracy Butzko, Market Segment Unit Manager for Books and Lists.

**Types of Books Published:** How-to reference books about human resources, marketing, advertising, sales, and business-development subjects.

**Audience:** Management personnel.

**Recent Titles Published:** *Winning with Promotion Power* (for advertising brand managers); *Telephone Terrific* (for telemarketers); *Analyzing Sales Promotion; Marketing Manager's Handbook.*

**Current Needs:** Books that fit the Dartnell line of business how-to reference guides.

**Payment Information:**
   **Fee or Royalty:** Royalty.
   **Advance:** Small advance against future royalties.

**Rights Policy:** Buys all rights.

**How to Contact:** Send query along with outline, resume, and writing samples; may also send complete manuscript (photocopy only) or phone.

**What Not to Do:** Send original material.

**Time Needed for Reply:** One to two months.

**Does Author Supply Photos?** No.

**Advice for Authors:** Writers who intend to submit proposals or manuscripts must keep in mind that Dartnell Corporation publishes exclusively in the areas of business-training information and material for a diverse business audience.

# DBI Books, Inc.

4092 Commercial Avenue
Northbrook, Illinois 60062
(708) 272-6310

Established: 1943
Titles in Print:
Total 50; Annual 8-9

**Contact Person:** Pamela Johnson, Managing Editor.

**Types of Books Published:** Books on individual (i.e., non-team) participant sports such as hunting, fishing, shooting, and camping.

**Audience:** Outdoor-oriented adults.

**Recent Titles Published:** *Trap and Skeet Shooting* (2nd Edition); *Knives '94; The Gun Digest* (annual anthology); *Bow Hunter's Digest; The Complete Survival Guide.*

**Current Needs:** Complete how-to books that will sell in sporting goods stores. Also articles for Digest books.

**Payment Information:**
   **Fee or Royalty:** Negotiable fee.
   **Advance:** Yes.

**Rights Policy:** Buys all rights.

**How to Contact:** Send query.

**What Not to Do:** Phone, send manuscript, or drop in without an appointment.

**Time Needed for Reply:** Two weeks.

**Does Author Supply Photos?** Yes.

**Advice for Authors:** Authors should possess demonstrable expertise in their subject areas, and they must know the market before submitting a query. Subjects outside the field of individual participant sports are not appropriate for DBI Books.

# Ivan R. Dee, Inc.

1332 N. Halsted Street
Chicago, Illinois 60622
(312) 787-6262

Established: 1988
Titles in Print:
Total 125; Annual 25

**Contact Person:** Ivan R. Dee, President.

**Types of Books Published:** Nonfiction dealing with history, literature, politics, biography, and theater.

**Audience:** General intelligent lay audience and college course adoptions.

**Recent Titles Published:** *Molotov Remembers; Grand Opera; Spheres of Influence; From Noon to Starry Night: A Life of Walt Whitman.*

**Current Needs:** Anything in the above-mentioned fields.

**Payment Information:**
Fee or Royalty: Standard royalty.
Advance: Yes, in some cases.

**How to Contact:** Send a query with a one-page outline and at least two sample chapters. Enclose a self-addressed, stamped envelope with the material.

**What Not to Do:** Send a generic query; the company prefers not to receive one of multiple submissions.

**Time Needed for Reply:** One month.

**Does Author Supply Photos?** Depends on the project.

**Advice for Authors:** Send for the company's catalog and become familiar with the list before submitting any ideas.

# ENCYCLOPAEDIA BRITANNICA, INC.

310 S. Michigan Avenue
Chicago, Illinois 60604
(312) 347-7000

Established: 1768
Titles in Print:
Total 50; Annual 10

**Contact Person:** Robert McHenry, Editor-in-Chief.

**Types of Books Published:** General reference encyclopedia, atlases, dictionaries, and educational material.

**Audience:** Curious and intelligent individuals, grade school through adult.

**Current Needs:** For the most part, Britannica relies on specialists in various fields to serve as contributors. But qualified freelancers will be included on the list of potential writers and notified when an appropriate assignment becomes available.

**Payment Information:**
    **Fee or Royalty:** Flat per word fee.
    **Advance:** No.

**Rights Policy:** Reserves all rights.

**How to Contact:** Send query stating areas of expertise.

**What Not to Do:** Phone, send manuscript, or drop in without an appointment.

**Time Needed for Reply:** Two weeks.

**Does Author Supply Photos?** No.

**Advice for Authors:** Encyclopaedia Britannica strives for impeccable authority and accuracy, and it insists on having authors submit sources as verification for facts.

# EVANSTON PUBLISHING, INC.

| | |
|---|---|
| 1571 Sherman Avenue | **Established: 1987** |
| Evanston, Illinois 60201 | **Titles in Print:** |
| (708) 492-1911 | **Total 12; Annual 6-8** |

**Contact Person:** Dorothy Kavka, President.

**Types of Books Published:** General trade books.

**Audience:** General adult readership.

**Recent Titles Published:** *Selling Your Book: The Writer's Guide to Publishing and Marketing; White Man Runs Him: Crow Scout with Custer; Clouds and Rain: A China to America Memoir; Edward Dart, Architect; Meditation: The Book.*

**Payment Information:**
  **Fee or Royalty:** Royalty.
  **Advance:** No.

**How to Contact:** Send query.

**What Not to Do:** Phone or send complete manuscript.

**Time Needed for Reply:** One month.

**Does Author Supply Photos?** Usually.

**Advice for Authors:** Evanston Publishing Company also offers services—i.e., editorial. design, printing—to those interested in self-publishing a book.

# EVERYDAY LEARNING CORPORATION

1007 Church Street, Suite 312
Evanston, Illinois 60201
(708) 866-0702

**Established:** 1988
**Titles in Print:**
**Total 55; Annual 6**

**Contact Person:** Eric Olson, Development Manager.

**Types of Books Published:** Mathematics textbooks for elementary school students and teachers.

**Audience:** Students in kindergarten through sixth grade and their teachers.

**Recent Titles Published:** *Everyday Mathematics; Math Tools for Teachers; Minute Math; Using Mathematics from the Seas to the Stars.*

**Current Needs:** Ideas for textbooks in mathematics and for science and social studies.

**Payment Information:**
    **Fee or Royalty:** Fee.
    **Advance:** Usually not.

**Rights Policy:** Buys all rights.

**How to Contact:** Send query with resume.

**What Not to Do:** Phone.

**Time Needed for Reply:** Indefinite; will reply only when a need arises.

**Does Author Supply Photos?** Usually not.

**Other Freelance Possibilities:** Designers, artists, copyeditors, proofreaders, indexers.

# J. G. FERGUSON PUBLISHING COMPANY

200 W. Madison Street, 3rd Floor
Chicago, Illinois 60606
(312) 580-5480

Established: 1940
Titles in Print:
Total 100; Annual 2-3

**Contact Person:** Carol Summerfield, Editorial Director.

**Types of Books Published:** Home medical books; one-volume encyclopedias; supplemental educational material in career guidance and environmental studies.

**Audience:** Adolescent through adult.

**Recent Titles Published:** *Encyclopedia of Careers and Vocational Guidance* (9th edition); *The New Complete Medical and Health Encyclopedia; Children's Career Discovery Encyclopedia.*

**Current Needs:** Freelancers capable of proofreading, copyediting, indexing, and design.

**Payment Information:**
    **Fee or Royalty:** Fee for editorial/design work, ranging from $15 to $25 an hour.
    **Advance:** No.

**How to Contact:** Send query and resume.

**What Not to Do:** Phone or send unsolicited manuscripts.

**Time Needed for Reply:** Two weeks.

**Does Author Supply Photos?** No.

**Other Freelance Possibilities:** Copyeditors, proofreaders, indexers, and designers.

**Advice for Authors:** J. G. Ferguson Publishing Company looks for good generalists and good researchers.

# FOREST HOUSE PUBLISHING COMPANY, INC.

P. O. Box 738
Lake Forest, Illinois 60045
(708) 295-8287

Established: 1989
Titles in Print:
Total 150; Annual 10-12

**Contact Person:** Dianne Spahr, Co-Publisher and President; Roy Spahr, Publisher and Co-President.

**Types of Books Published:** School and library books—nonfiction, mystery series, and concept books.

**Audience:** Students from kindergarten through grade six.

**Recent Titles Published:** *Every Kid's Guide to Saving the Earth* (series); *Honor the Flag.*

**Current Needs:** Primary science books; series dealing with personal values.

**Payment Information:**
   **Fee or Royalty:** Royalty.
   **Advance:** Yes, small.

**Rights Policy:** Buys all rights.

**How to Contact:** Send query with a very detailed plan for book, or send complete manuscript.

**What Not to Do:** Phone

**Time Needed for Reply:** One to two months.

**Does Author Supply Photos?** Depends on project.

**Other Freelance Possibilities:** Copyeditors, proofreaders, indexers, designers.

**Advice for Authors:** Forest House is not currently seeking fiction manuscripts.

# GOODHEART-WILLCOX COMPANY, INC.

123 W. Taft Drive
South Holland, Illinois 60473
(708) 333-7200

Established: 1921
Titles in Print:
Total 100; Annual 5-6

**Contact Person:** John Flanagan, President.

**Types of Books Published:** Textbooks for vocational and technological education (e.g., automotive and electronics) and home economics. The company also produces videos and software in these fields.

**Audience:** Students in junior high school through college.

**Recent Titles Published:** *Computer-Aided Drafting; Modern Automotive Technology; Digital Circuits; CIM Technology; Building Life Skills; Successful Sewing; Planning Activities for Child Care.*

**Current Needs:** Texts dealing with vocational or industrial/ technical education and careers.

**Payment Information:**
**Fee or Royalty:** Royalty of 10 percent of net income.
**Advance:** Seldom.

**Rights Policy:** Reserves all rights.

**How to Contact:** Send query.

**What Not to Do:** Phone, send manuscript, or drop in without an appointment.

**Time Needed for Reply:** Three weeks.

**Does Author Supply Photos?** Yes.

**Advice for Authors:** Prospective authors should have teaching or industrial experience in the area in which they propose to write. It is imperative that the reading level of each book be appropriate to a particular grade level. Books should include both theory and practice, with a quiz section at the end of each chapter. In addition, all vocational texts should include a chapter on careers in the field.

# GREAT QUOTATIONS PUBLISHING COMPANY

| | |
|---|---|
| 1967 Quincy Court | Established: 1984 |
| Glendale Heights, Illinois 60139 | Titles in Print: |
| (708) 582-2800 | Total 120; Annual 25 |

**Contact Person:** Direct mail submissions to Ringo Suek, President and Editor. Direct phone inquiries to Susanne Starck: (708) 582-2800, ext. 117.

**Types of Books Published:** Gift books and books for special occasions; humor; inspirational works.

**Audience:** General adult readership.

**Recent Titles Published:** *Mrs. Webster's Dictionary; Dear Mr. President; Life's Simple Pleasures.*

**Current Needs:** Uplifting or humorous books; also poetry and children's books.

**Payment Information:**
    **Fee or Royalty:** Negotiable.
    **Advance:** Yes.

**Rights Policy:** Negotiable.

**How to Contact:** Send query and outline; enclose a self-addressed, stamped envelope. May also phone.

**What Not to Do:** Send longer works of fiction, such as novellas or novels.

**Time Needed for Reply:** Within four weeks if not interested.

**Does Author Supply Photos?** Depends on project.

**Other Freelance Possibilities:** Illustrators and proofreaders.

**Advice for Authors:** Great Quotations Publishing Company has two basic book formats: 80 pages and 168 pages. The titles and cover designs are very important in marketing the company's books. Submissions need not be written for the literary-minded reader.

# HARLAN DAVIDSON, INC./FORUM PRESS, INC.

3110 Arlington Heights Road
Arlington Heights, Illinois 60004
(708) 253-9720

Established: 1972
Titles in Print:
Total 400; Annual 7-10

**Contact Person:** Maureen Gilgore Hewitt, Editor-in-Chief and Vice President; Andrew Davidson, Editor and Vice President.

**Types of Books Published:** Primarily college-level textbooks; some high school college-preparatory textbooks.

**Audience:** College and some high school students.

**Recent Titles Published:** *The Cold War: A Post-Cold War History; Charles Sumner and the Northern Conscience; Daughters of Revolution: A History of Women in the U. S. S. R.*

**Current Needs:** Textbooks about U. S. and European history, sociology, psychology, anthropology, philosophy, political science, and literary classics in English.

**Payment Information:**
    **Fee or Royalty:** Individually negotiated.
    **Advance:** Unlikely.

**Rights Policy:** Buys all rights.

**How to Contact:** Send partial manuscript with a query and current academic vitae.

**What Not to Do:** Phone, drop in without an appointment, or submit poetry.

**Time Needed for Reply:** One month.

**Does Author Supply Photos?** Yes, but publisher does final preparation.

**Other Freelance Possibilities:** Occasional need for copyeditors, proofreaders, and indexers.

**Advice for Authors:** High academic qualifications and affiliation are required, and teaching experience is preferred. The company's authors mainly include full professors and writers who have been published frequently, but skilled writers who have not yet been published extensively are encouraged to submit appropriate works.

# InQ Publishing Company

P. O. Box 10
North Aurora, Illinois 60542
(708) 801-0607

Established: 1988
Titles in Print:
Total 8; Annual 5

**Contact Person:** JanaSue Fitting, Publisher.

**Types of Books Published:** Fiction and nonfiction for children and young adults; nonfiction for child-care professionals; some literary annuals.

**Audience:** Children and adults.

**Recent Titles Published:** *Hey Babysitter, Let's Play* (series of workbooks and activity books for child-care professionals to use to teach children); *The Magical Piece of Sand* (fiction for children up to age seven); *Help! Willie's Choking!* (safety instruction for adults to teach children ages three to eight).

**Payment Information:**
Fee or Royalty: Negotiable.
Advance: No.

**Rights Policy:** Negotiable on text; buys all rights to artwork.

**How to Contact:** Send query and one or two photocopied chapters. Enclose a self-addressed, stamped envelope.

**What Not to Do:** Send complete or original manuscript.

**Time Needed for Reply:** Six weeks.

**Does Author Supply Photos?** Depends on project.

**Other Freelance Possibilities:** Occasional need for editors, artists, and designers.

**Advice for Authors:** Authors with manuscripts on computer disk should specify the word-processing software used. Note, also, that InQ Publishing Company will not return submitted materials unless specifically asked to do so.

# INTERVARSITY PRESS

P. O. Box 1400
Downers Grove, Illinois 60515
(708) 964-5700

Established: 1947
Titles in Print:
Total 600; Annual 75

**Contact Person:** Andrew Le Peau, Editorial Director.

**Types of Books Published:** Evangelical Christian.

**Audience:** Christian college students and educated lay people.

**Recent Titles Published:** *Sexual Harassment No More; Philosophers Who Believe; Darwin on Trial.*

**Current Needs:** Christian-oriented manuscripts.

**Payment Information:**
**Fee or Royalty:** Standard royalty contract.
**Advance:** Frequently pays advance, but rate varies.

**Rights Policy:** Buys all rights.

**How to Contact:** Send outline and sample chapters, or send complete manuscript.

**What Not to Do:** Phone, drop in without an appointment, or send manuscript directly to InterVarsity Press.

**Time Needed for Reply:** Two to three months.

**Does Author Supply Photos?** Not necessary.

**Advice for Authors:** Send all material to The Writer's Edge, P. O. Box 1266, Wheaton, IL 60189.

# RICHARD D. IRWIN, INC.

1333 Burr Ridge Parkway
Burr Ridge, Illinois 60521
708) 789-4000

Established: 1933
Titles in Print:
Total 1500; Annual 250

**Contact Person:** John Black, Senior Vice President—College Editorial.

**Types of Books Published:** Business, economics, and engineering textbooks.

**Audience:** Graduate, undergraduate, and continuing education college students.

**Recent Titles Published:** *Managerial Accounting; Economics; Basic Marketing; Principles and Applications of Electrical Engineering; Practical Business Math Procedures.*

**Payment Information:**
   **Fee or Royalty:** Royalty of variable rate.
   **Advance:** Yes.

**Rights Policy:** Usually reserves all rights.

**How to Contact:** Send query with a book idea and author's background.

**What Not to Do:** Phone, send manuscript, or drop in without an appointment.

**Time Needed for Reply:** Two to four weeks.

**Does Author Supply Photos?** Occasionally.

**Other Freelance Possibilities:** Photo researchers, permission editors, copyeditors, proofreaders, indexers, illustrators, photographers, designers.

**Advice for Authors:** Most Irwin authors are professors and have a recognizable name in academia and in the discipline they teach. Irwin insists on accuracy and a responsible point of view.

# IRWIN PROFESSIONAL PUBLISHING
Division of Richard D. Irwin, Inc.

1333 Burr Ridge Parkway
Burr Ridge, Illinois 60521
(708) 789-4000

**Established:** 1965
**Titles in Print:**
**Total 800; Annual 120**

**Contact Person:** Jeffery A. Krames, Editor-in-Chief.

**Types of Books Published:** Professional books for the financial and business world. Topics include finance and investing, management, and banking.

**Audience:** People in business and individual investors.

**Recent Titles Published:** *Bogle on Mutual Funds; The New G. E.; Second to None.*

**Current Needs:** Finance and investing books with a how-to emphasis.

**Payment Information:**
    **Fee or Royalty:** Royalty of variable rate.
    **Advance:** In some cases.

**Rights Policy:** Usually reserves all rights.

**How to Contact:** Phone or send query with an idea and author's background.

**What Not to Do:** Send a manuscript or drop in without an appointment.

**Time Needed for Reply:** Four to six weeks.

**Does Author Supply Photos?** Not necessary.

**Other Freelance Possibilities:** Copyeditors, proofreaders, and indexers.

**Advice for Authors:** An author must have a recognizable name in the field or show expertise and insight in the subject area. Irwin Professional Publishing insists on accuracy and a responsible point of view. References from other authors are valuable, although the right idea presented at the right time stands a good chance of acceptance.

# KAZI PUBLICATIONS, INC.

3023 W. Belmont Avenue
Chicago, Illinois 60618
(312) 267-7002

Established: 1976
Titles in Print:
Total 300; Annual 10

**Contact Person:** Liaquat Ali, President.

**Types of Books Published:** Nonfiction and fiction about Islam and the Middle East.

**Audience:** Children and adults interested in Islam and the Middle East.

**Recent Titles Published:** *A Young Muslim's Guide to the Modern World; God's Will Be Done; What Everyone Should Know About Islam and Muslims.*

**Current Needs:** Translations from Urdu, Persian, and Arabic languages.

**Payment Information:**
   **Fee or Royalty:** Royalty of 10 percent.
   **Advance:** No.

**Rights Policy:** Author has copyright.

**How to Contact:** Send query.

**What Not to Do:** Phone.

**Time Needed for Reply:** One month.

**Does Author Supply Photos?** Yes.

**Other Freelance Possibilities:** Manuscript readers and editors.

**Advice for Authors:** Books need to be very specific in the area of Islam or Islamic culture and civilization.

# CHARLES H. KERR PUBLISHING COMPANY

1740 W. Greenleaf Avenue, Suite 7          Established: 1886
Chicago, Illinois 60626                              Titles in Print:
(312) 465-7774                                          Total 150; Annual 8

**Contact Person:** Laura Valentine, Editor.

**Types of Books Published:** Original works and reprints in the fields of socialism, radical and labor history, popular culture, and women's studies.

**Audience:** Adults and college students.

**Recent Titles Published:** *Progress Without People; Labor Law for the Rank and File.*

**Current Needs:** Original works and translations in the fields of radical, labor, and women's history.

**Payment Information:**
   **Fee or Royalty:** Varies.
   **Advance:** No.

**Rights Policy:** Retains all rights.

**How to Contact:** Send query that includes a detailed description of the proposed publication.

**What Not to Do:** Phone or send manuscript.

**Time Needed for Reply:** Six weeks.

**Does Author Supply Photos?** It depends on the book.

**Other Freelance Possibilities:** Individuals skilled in Word Perfect for word processing; occasional need for substantive editors.

# KIDSBOOKS, INC.

3535 W. Peterson Avenue
Chicago, Illinois 60659
(312) 509-0707

Established: 1987
Titles in Print:
Total 500; Annual 60

**Contact Person:** Dan Blau, President.

**Types of Books Published:** Illustrated children's books (activity and novelty).

**Audience:** Children ages 3 to 12.

**Recent Titles Published:** *Lucky Charm; Eyes on Nature; Dinosaurs; Lost in Time; Too Many Animals Sleep in My Bed.*

**Current Needs:** Illustrated juvenile books.

**Payment Information:**
    **Fee or Royalty:** Flat fee.
    **Advance:** Yes.

**Rights Policy:** Holds copyright.

**How to Contact:** Send manuscript; enclose self-addressed, stamped envelope.

**What Not to Do:** Drop in without an appointment.

**Time Needed for Reply:** Four to six weeks.

**Does Author Supply Photos?** Not necessary.

**Advice for Authors:** Prospective authors are reminded to enclose a self-addressed, stamped envelope when they submit materials to Kidsbooks.

# LAKE VIEW PRESS

P. O. Box 578279
Chicago, Illinois 60657
(312) 935-2694

Established: 1983
Titles in Print:
Total 30; Annual 2

**Contact Person:** Paul Elitzik, Director.

**Types of Books Published:** Fiction and nonfiction about politics and sociology.

**Audience:** Primarily adults.

**Recent Titles Published:** *Political Companion to American Film; Confessions of a Disloyal European; Cinema of Apartheid; Race and Class in South African Film.*

**Current Needs:** Books about film and cultural politics.

**Payment Information:**
Fee or Royalty: Royalty.
Advance: No.

**Rights Policy:** Buys all rights but gives a percentage of subsidiary rights to authors.

**How to Contact:** Send query; enclose a self-addressed, stamped envelope.

**What Not to Do:** Send manuscript.

**Time Needed for Reply:** Two to three weeks.

**Does Author Supply Photos?** Yes.

**Other Freelance Possibilities:** Copyeditors, proofreaders, and indexers.

**Advice for Authors:** Lake View Press wants to publish scholarly books that will also appeal to a general audience.

# LOYOLA UNIVERSITY PRESS

3441 N. Ashland Avenue
Chicago, Illinois 60657
(312) 281-1818

Established: 1912
Titles in Print:
Total 300; Annual 14-15

**Contact Person:** Trade books: Rev. Joseph Downey, Editorial Director; Textbooks: Juanita Raman, Editorial Director; Editorial/Production: Frederick Falkenberg, Production Manager.

**Types of Books Published:** For college-level and older—biographies and textbooks about theology, religious art, church history; for students in kindergarten through eighth grade—religious textbooks; for students in first through eighth grades: English series.

**Audience:** Children through college-educated adults.

**Recent Titles Published:** *Contact with God; The Dissenting Heart; Catholicism, Chicago-Style; Christ Our Life* (series); *Voyages in English* (series).

**Current Needs:** Manuscripts about the above-mentioned topics.

**Payment Information:**
**Fee or Royalty:** 10 percent royalty on net price, retail and wholesale.
**Advance:** Not generally.

**Rights Policy:** Negotiable.

**How to Contact:** Send query or complete manuscript.

**What Not to Do:** Phone.

**Time Needed for Reply:** Two to three months.

**Does Author Supply Photos?** Yes, most of the time.

**Other Freelance Possibilities:** Copyeditors, proofreaders, indexers, and designers. Send query and resume to Frederick Falkenberg, Production Manager.

**Advice for Authors:** Loyola University Press is a Roman Catholic publishing house that also publishes works by and about those belonging to other denominations in the Christian community.

# McDOUGAL, LITTELL & COMPANY

P. O. Box 1667
Evanston, Illinois 60204
(708) 869-2300

**Established: 1969**
**Titles in Print:**
**Total 2500; Annual 235**

**Contact Person:** Susan Schaffrath, Vice President and Editorial Director.

**Types of Books Published:** Educational programs for elementary and secondary students. Disciplines include mathematics, literature, economics, world history, U. S. history, and foreign languages.

**Audience:** Students and teachers in elementary and secondary schools.

**Recent Titles Published:** *The Writer's Craft; Literature and Language; Gateways to Algebra and Geometry.*

**Current Needs:** Writers and editors with experience in el-hi publishing and in multimedia product development.

**Payment Information:**
    **Fee or Royalty:** Project fee or hourly rate of $12 to $30 per hour, depending on task and project.
    **Advance:** Possible, but not typical; never possible for a first project.

**Rights Policy:** Negotiable.

**How to Contact:** Send query and resume.

**What Not to Do:** Phone, send manuscript, or drop in without an appointment.

**Time Needed for Reply:** Varies.

**Does Author Supply Photos?** No.

**Other Freelance Possibilities:** Copyeditors, proofreaders, and designers.

**Advice for Authors:** Writers should be equipped to submit copy on disk. Some projects require temporary in-house status.

# MOODY PRESS

820 N. LaSalle Street
Chicago, Illinois 60610
(312) 329-2101

Established: 1894
Titles in Print:
Total 800; Annual 65-85

**Contact Person:** The Moody Press Editorial Department.

**Types of Books Published:** Christian literature, Bibles, Bible study aids; nonfiction about finances from a Christian perspective.

**Audience:** Primarily an evangelical Christian market of adults and young people, but a general readership as well.

**Recent Titles Published:** *The Coming Economic Earthquake; Power Religion; The Jack Prester Mystery Series.*

**Current Needs:** Good fiction—Christian novels with a biblical message buried in the story and children's adventure stories with a Christian message. Nonfiction—social issues and how Christians deal with them; finance/stewardship.

**Payment Information:**
   **Fee or Royalty:** Royalty.
   **Advance:** Yes.

**Rights Policy:** Buys all rights.

**How to Contact:** Submit either a proposal and one or two sample chapters or a synopsis and cover letter that describe the proposed work's theme and its target audience.

**What Not to Do:** Phone, submit ideas for cookbooks or poetry, send manuscript, or drop in without an appointment to discuss a manuscript.

**Time Needed for Reply:** Up to eight weeks.

**Does Author Supply Photos?** No.

**Advice for Authors:** Research the needs of the marketplace and know both the publisher and the audience.

# MOSBY-YEAR BOOK, INC.

200 N. LaSalle Street
Chicago, Illinois 60601
(312) 726-9733

Established: 1901
Titles in Print:
Total 90; Annual 90

**Contact Person:** Diana Dodge, Associate Managing Editor.

**Types of Books Published:** Some reference books and texts but mostly continuity titles—i.e., those involving abstracts.

**Audience:** Physicians, nurses, medical students, allied health personnel.

**Recent Titles Published:** *Perspectives in Applied Nutrition; Capsules and Comments: in Nursing Management and Leadership; Focus and Opinion in Internal Medicine.*

**Current Needs:** Abstracters of articles. √

**Payment Information:**
**Fee or Royalty:** Fee.
**Advance:** No.

**Rights Policy:** Buys all rights.

**How to Contact:** Send query with resume and samples of previously published work. Enclosed a self-addressed, stamped envelope.

**What Not to Do:** Phone (unless you have previously sent a query and resume) or send unsolicited manuscripts.

**Time Needed for Reply:** Typically four to six weeks.

**Does Author Supply Photos?** No.

**Other Freelance Possibilities:** Copyeditors and proofreaders. For copyediting, contact Fran Perveiler, Production Manager. For proofreading, contact Barbara Kelly, Proofroom Manager.

**Advice for Authors:** A degree in a medical field is not required, but medical knowledge is helpful. Mosby-Year Book is particularly interested in hearing from writers who can translate from French, Spanish, German, Japanese, and/or Swedish.

# NELSON-HALL PUBLISHERS
111 N. Canal Street  
Chicago, Illinois 60606  
(312) 930-9446

Established: 1909  
Titles in Print:  
Total 1100; Annual 30

**Contact Person:** Dorothy Anderson, Senior Editor; Rachel Schick, Associate Editor.

**Types of Books Published:** Primarily college textbooks, some trade nonfiction.

**Audience:** College students, educated adults, libraries.

**Recent Titles Published:** *Understanding Human Behavior; Sociological Theory; Law and Justice.*

**Payment Information:**
**Fee or Royalty:** Fee, either hourly or by the project.
**Advance:** No.

**Rights Policy:** Negotiable.

**How to Contact:** Send query and resume.

**What Not to Do:** Send manuscripts or drop in without an appointment.

**Time Needed for Reply:** Two months.

**Does Author Supply Photos?** Yes.

**Other Freelance Possibilities:** Copyeditors and various production positions. For production assignments, contact Tamara Phelps, Production Manager.

**Advice for Authors:** Most Nelson-Hall authors are academics (with doctoral degrees) and/or experts in their field of business.

# THE NOBLE PRESS, INC.

213 W. Institute Place, Suite 508     **Established: 1988**
Chicago, Illinois 60610     **Titles in Print:**
(312) 642-1168     **Total 35; Annual 12**

**Contact Person:** Douglas Seibold, Executive Editor.

**Types of Books Published:** Nonfiction about social, political, and environmental issues.

**Audience:** Adults interested in progressive nonfiction.

**Recent Titles Published:** *Volunteer Slavery; Sky Burial; The Doctor; The Murder; The Mystery.*

**Current Needs:** Works about African-American, Latino, and women's issues as well as eco-travel.

**Payment Information:**
    **Fee or Royalty:** Conventional royalty.
    **Advance:** Yes.

**Rights Policy:** Negotiable.

**How to Contact:** Send proposal.

**What Not to Do:** Phone with proposal.

**Time Needed for Reply:** Two to eight weeks.

**Does Author Supply Photos?** No.

**Advice for Authors:** Write for the manuscript-submission guidelines and Noble Press catalog. Enclose a 6x9-inch self-addressed envelope with two first-class stamps. Study the guidelines and catalog carefully before sending a book proposal.

# NORTHWESTERN UNIVERSITY PRESS

625 Colfax Street
Evanston, Illinois 60201
(708) 491-5313

Established: 1958
Titles in Print:
Total 275; Annual 60-65

**Contact Person:** Heather Kenny, Editorial Assistant.

**Types of Books Published:** Books of scholarly and general intellectual interest, with an emphasis on literature in translation, literary criticism and theory, law, psychology, philosophy, and theater.

**Audience:** Scholars and other literate, intelligent adults.

**Recent Titles Published:** *The Beneficiary; In the Jaws of Life and Other Stories; Dark Legs and Silk Kisses: The Beatitudes of the Spinners; The Merleau-Ponty Aesthetics Reader.*

**Current Needs:** Eastern European literature.

**Payment Information:**
**Fee or Royalty:** Standard royalty contract.
**Advance:** Yes.

**Rights Policy:** Buys all rights.

**How to Contact:** Send query, resume, and sample chapter(s) with a self-addressed, stamped envelope.

**What Not to Do:** Send complete manuscript or drop in without an appointment.

**Time Needed for Reply:** Six weeks.

**Does Author Supply Photos?** Varies.

**Other Freelance Possibilities:** Occasional need for copyeditors and proofreaders.

**Advice for Authors:** Send for free catalog, and then study the publisher's previously printed titles to get a better idea of the sort of books Northwestern University Press publishes.

# NTC Publishing Group

| | |
|---|---|
| 4255 W. Touhy Avenue | **Established: 1962** |
| Lincolnwood, Illinois 60646 | **Titles in Print:** |
| (708) 679-5500 | **Total 3500; Annual 300** |

**Contact Person:** Foreign Languages/ESL: Keith Fry; Language Arts: John Nolan: Business and Careers: Anne Knudsen; Travel: Dan Spinella.

**Types of Books Published:** Educational textbooks (foreign languages, ESL, language arts, and careers); travel books; business books (advertising, marketing, media, public relations, sales, promotion, and global marketing); dictionaries (English and foreign langauges); how-to books.

**Audience:** For educational books: students from elementary school through college; for trade books: children through adults.

**Recent Titles Published:** *World Literature; World Mythology; Languages for Children* (series); *Just Listen 'n' Learn* (series); *Integrated Marketing Communications.*

**Current Needs:** Literature and language-learning materials; dictionaries; how-to books.

**Payment Information:**
**Fee or Royalty:** Can be either, depending on book.
**Advance:** Yes.

**Rights Policy:** Buys all rights.

**How to Contact:** Send partial manuscript, annotated table of contents, and cover letter explaining purpose and appeal of the book.

**What Not to Do:** Phone, send complete manuscript, or drop in without an appointment. Also, NTC prefers not to receive simultaneous submissions.

**Time Needed for Reply:** Four to six weeks.

**Does Author Supply Photos?** Yes, in most cases.

**Other Freelance Possibilities:** Copyeditors, proofreaders, researchers, indexers, designers (desktop production knowledge a plus), and keyliners.

**Advice for Authors:** NTC carefully evaluates not only how good a book is but also its selling and distributing potential. The process involves many people and thus can take a considerable amount of time to complete. Authors must be patient and must understand that rejection is not necessarily a reflection of the quality of their work but rather a lack of market for the book.

# PATH PRESS, INC.

53 W. Jackson Boulevard, Suite 724
Chicago, Illinois 60604
(312) 663-0167

Established: 1982
Titles in Print:
Total 10; Annual 3

**Contact Person:** Bennett J. Johnson, President; Herman C. Gilbert, Executive Vice President.

**Types of Books Published:** Fiction, nonfiction, and book-length poetry by, for, and about African Americans and peoples of developing nations.

**Audience:** Primarily adults.

**Recent Titles Published:** *Congo Crew* (a novel); *American Diary* (nonfiction)*; Up North Big City Street* (poetry).

**Current Needs:** Hard-hitting manuscripts on political, economic, and social aspects of the life of minorities in the United States and of developing-nations people in their native lands.

**Payment Information:**
  **Fee or Royalty:** Royalty of 10 percent for first 10,000 books sold; 10-15 percent thereafter.
  **Advance:** No.

**Rights Policy:** Standard contract.

**How to Contact:** Send query with resume. Include outline, synopsis, or samples if desired—this is not mandatory.

**What Not to Do:** Drop in without an appointment.

**Time Needed for Reply:** Three months.

**Does Author Supply Photos?** No.

# F. E. PEACOCK PUBLISHERS, INC.

115 W. Orchard Street
Itasca, Illinois 60143
(708) 775-9000

Established: 1967
Titles in Print:
Total 90; Annual 15

**Contact Person:** Richard Lord, Editorial Assistant.

**Types of Books Published:** College textbooks in the social sciences.

**Audience:** Graduate and undergraduate students—and their professors—in the social sciences.

**Recent Titles Published:** *Cultural Anthropology; Theories of Deviance; Human Behavior in the Social Environment; American Political Parties; Basic Interviewing Skills.*

**Current Needs:** College texts in psychology, political science, sociology, social work, and anthropology.

**Payment Information:**
    **Fee or Royalty:** Royalty.
    **Advance:** Yes.

**How to Contact:** Send query.

**What Not to Do:** Phone.

**Time Needed for Reply:** One month.

**Does Author Supply Photos?** No.

**Other Freelance Possibilities:** Copyeditors, researchers, designers, and indexers.

**Advice for Authors:** F. E. Peacock publishes only textbooks and only in the fields of social science.

# PLANNING COMMUNICATIONS

7215 Oak Avenue
River Forest, Illinois 60305
(708) 366-5200

**Established: 1979**
**Titles in Print:**
**Total 5; Annual 3**

**Contact Person:** Daniel Lauber, Publisher.

**Types of Books Published:** Career books.

**Audience:** Adults looking for jobs, entry level and advanced positions.

**Recent Titles Published:** *Professional's Private Sector Job Finder; Government Job Finder; Non-Profits' Job Finder.*

**Current Needs:** How-to books for people looking for work.

**Payment Information:**
    **Fee or Royalty:** Negotiable.
    **Advance:** No.

**Rights Policy:** Negotiable.

**How to Contact:** Send query with table of contents and brief synopsis of each chapter.

**What Not to Do:** Phone or send complete manuscript.

**Time Needed for Reply:** Two months.

**Does Author Supply Photos?** Depends on project.

**Advice for Authors:** Book ideas must offer a new angle on the job-hunting process. We lean towards books that are innovative, graphically pleasing, and a bit entertaining. To get a good idea of what we like, take a look at our three current titles in a bookstore.

# P. O. Publishing Company

P. O. Box 3333
Skokie, Illinois 60076
(708) 329-7929

Established: 1987
Titles in Print:
Total 4; Annual 3

**Contact Person:** Joseph Nykiel, Executive Editor.

**Types of Books Published:** Nonfiction, mostly book-length treatments of reporters' investigative series.

**Audience:** General adult readership.

**Recent Titles Published:** *Issues Confronting City and State Governments; Beginning Journalism; Spanish Fascism* (translation).

**Current Needs:** Politically oriented nonfiction.

**Payment Information:**
    **Fee or Royalty:** Royalty of 5 to 10 percent.
    **Advance:** No.

**Rights Policy:** Negotiable.

**How to Contact:** Send query and sample(s) of previously published work.

**What Not to Do:** Phone.

**Time Needed for Reply:** Four to six weeks.

**Does Author Supply Photos?** Depends on project.

**Other Freelance Possibilities:** Copyeditors and proofreaders.

**Advice for Authors:** Book ideas for P. O. Publishing Company must have national appeal.

# POLYCHROME PUBLISHING CORPORATION

4509 N. Francisco Avenue
Chicago, Illinois 60625
(312) 478-4455

**Established:** 1990
**Titles in Print:**
**Total 6; Annual 4**

**Contact Person:** Sandra Yamate, President.

**Types of Books Published:** Multicultural nonfiction and fiction (with a specialization in Asian American themes) for children; some nonfiction books directed at parents as teaching aids.

**Audience:** Toddlers to adults.

**Recent Titles Published:** *One Small Girl; Blue Jay in the Desert; Almond Cookies and Dragonwell Tea; Ashok by Any Other Name; Nene and the Horrible Math Monster.*

**Current Needs:** Nonfiction and fiction about Asian American children.

**Payment Information:**
**Fee or Royalty:** Nominal fee and then royalty.
**Advance:** Yes.

**Rights Policy:** Buys all rights.

**How to Contact:** Send query and/or complete manuscript.

**What Not to Do:** Send fables, folktales, or animated animal stories.

**Time Needed for Reply:** One to three months.

**Does Author Supply Photos?** Not usually.

**Other Freelance Possibilities:** Copyeditors and graphic designers.

**Advice for Authors:** Polychrome is looking for works with authenticity. Stories and plots must ring true with the cultures they describe.

# PROBUS PUBLISHING

| | |
|---|---|
| 1925 N. Clyborn Avenue | **Established: 1984** |
| Chicago, Illinois 60614 | **Titles in Print:** |
| (312) 868-1100 | **Total 400; Annual 140** |

**Contact Person:** James McNeil, Vice President, Editorial.

**Types of Books Published:** Trade and professional books in business, including such fields as investments, personal financial planning, banking, sales and marketing, and health-care management.

**Audience:** College-educated adults and business professionals.

**Recent Titles Published:** *Bill Griffith's 10 Steps to Financial Prosperity; The Mutual Fund Buyer's Guide.*

**Current Needs:** Trade titles in investments, personal finance, banking, health-care administration, corporate finance, and marketing.

**Payment Information:**
    **Fee or Royalty:** 10 percent on the first 3,000 books sold; 12 percent on all sales over 3,000. Royalty is based on net income received.
    **Advance:** Negotiable, although generally small for first-time authors.

**Rights Policy:** Controls all rights negotiations; income is split with authors.

**How to Contact:** Send outline, prospectus, and personal background information (work history, education, previous publications/articles, etc.).

**What Not to Do:** Drop in without an appointment.

**Time Needed for Reply:** Two weeks.

**Does Author Supply Photos?** Generally not required.

**Other Freelance Possibilities:** Copyeditors, proofreaders, desktop designers/typesetters, and indexers.

**Advice for Authors:** Probus Publishing is primarily interested in quality and usefulness. The goal is to publish for active businesspeople and investors who need timely and accurate information. A responsible point of view is a must. Probus is happy to work with individuals who have limited writing experience but have excellent professional credentials and a unique market position for a new title.

# PROTEUS ENTERPRISES, INC.

226 Northwest Avenue　　　　　　Established: 1976
Elmhurst, Illinois 60126　　　　　Titles in Print:
(708) 530-0300　　　　　　　　　Total 25; Annual 25

**Contact Person:** Andy Hortatsos, Editor and President.

**Types of Books Published:** Nonfiction, reference, and foreign-language books and preschool programs.

**Audience:** Preschool children to adults.

**Recent Titles Published:** *Phonics Factory; Stepping Stones to Knowledge; Three Steps Ahead.*

**Current Needs:** Educational materials for children.

**Payment Information:**
　　**Fee or Royalty:** Negotiable.
　　**Advance:** Yes.

**Rights Policy:** Negotiable.

**How to Contact:** Send idea, outline, or draft.

**What Not to Do:** Phone or drop in without an appointment.

**Time Needed for Reply:** Three weeks.

**Does Author Supply Photos?** No.

**Other Freelance Possibilities:** Occasional need for copyeditors and proofreaders.

**Advice for Authors:** Authors of books for children should send illustrations and an outline so that editors can get a feel for the story.

# PUBLICATIONS INTERNATIONAL, LTD.
# CONSUMER GUIDE® PUBLICATIONS

7373 N. Cicero Avenue
Lincolnwood, Illinois 60646
(708) 676-3470

Established: 1967
Titles in Print:
Total 600; Annual 250

**Contact Person:** Jeff Mintz, Vice President—Acquisitions.

**Types of Books Published:** Books about cooking, crafts, consumer products, sports, health, and entertainment; also books for children.

**Audience:** Adults and children.

**Recent Titles Published:** *Cooking Class* (cookbook series); *Baseball Almanac; Players of Cooperstown; Play-A-Sound* (children's books).

**Current Needs:** Manuscripts of 50,000 words for children's stories (fiction and nonfiction), medical guides, crafts instruction, and automobile books.

**Payment Information:**
   **Fee or Royalty:** Fee of 25 cents per word on acceptance of manuscript, or flat fee based on length of assignment.
   **Advance:** Yes, upon signing of contract.

**Rights Policy:** Buys all rights.

**How to Contact:** Send query with resume.

**What Not to Do:** Phone, send complete manuscript, or drop in without an appointment.

**Time Needed for Reply:** Three weeks.

**Does Author Supply Photos?** Preferably, but not necessary.

**Advice for Authors:** Because most Publications International book concepts are formulated in-house, only authors with demonstrable expertise in areas of company interest should submit queries. The company prefers titles that can be marketed as both books and magazines.

# QUINTESSENCE PUBLISHING COMPANY, INC.

551 N. Kimberly Drive
Carol Stream, Illinois 60188
(708) 682-3223

Established: 1972
Titles in Print:
Total 120; Annual 15

**Contact Person:** Lori Bateman, Editorial Manager.

**Types of Books Published:** Professional and scholarly books and journals about dentistry, medicine, and nutrition.

**Audience:** Primarily dentists and physicians.

**Recent Titles Published:** *Advances in Periodontics; Advanced Osteointegration Surgery: Maxillofacial Applications; Guided Bone Regeneration in Implant Dentistry.*

**Payment Information:**
   **Fee or Royalty:** Royalty.
   **Advance:** In some cases.

**How to Contact:** Send cover letter, resume, sample chapters, and table of contents.

**What Not to Do:** Phone.

**Time Needed for Reply:** Three weeks.

**Does Author Supply Photos?** Yes.

**Other Freelance Possibilities:** Copyeditors, proofreaders, indexers, designers, and medical/technical illustrators.

**Advice for Authors:** Quintessence solicits and publishes only the work of authors who are recognized experts in particular fields of dentistry or medicine.

# REAL ESTATE EDUCATION COMPANY

**Division of Dearborn Financial Publishing**

520 N. Dearborn Street
Chicago, Illinois 60610
(312) 836-4400

Established: 1967
Titles in Print:
Total 90; Annual 40

**Contact Person:** Carol Luitjens, Vice President—Textbooks

**Types of Books Published:** Real estate pre-licensing, continuing education, and professional texts.

**Audience:** Real estate professionals and students.

**Recent Titles Published:** *Modern Real Estate Practice, 13th Edition; Language of Real Estate, 4th Edition; Fundamentals of Real Estate Appraisal, 6th Edition.*

**Current Needs:** Inquire in writing for current needs.

**Payment Information:**
  **Fee or Royalty:** Royalty.
  **Advance:** Rarely.

**Rights Policy:** Buys all rights.

**How to Contact:** Send prospectus, table of contents, and sample chapter (not first chapter).

**What Not to Do:** Phone or drop in without an appointment.

**Time Needed for Reply:** Two to four weeks.

**Does Author Supply Photos?** Yes, if needed.

**Other Freelance Possibilities:** Write to Gerry Lynch-Pinkerton, at the above address, to inquire about other freelance work with the company.

**Advice for Authors:** Be able to discuss the real estate market and competitive books before contacting the company.

*155 N. Wacker Dr. 60606*

# SCOTT FORESMAN & COMPANY
**Subsidiary of HarperCollins Publishers**

| | |
|---|---|
| 1900 E. Lake Avenue | **Established: 1896** |
| Glenview, Illinois 60025 | **Titles in Print:** |
| (708) 729-3000 | **Total 12,000; Annual 1300** |

**Contact Person:** Mary O'Connor, Assistant to the President.

**Types of Books Published:** Textbooks for elementary, high school, and adult education.

**Audience:** Children and adults.

**Recent Titles Published:** Textbooks, activity books, supplementary and other educational materials for all major curriculum areas.

**Current Needs:** Talented, reliable, and responsible writers to participate on authorship teams working in all the major curriculum areas.

**Payment Information:**
**Fee or Royalty:** Primarily royalty at a competitive rate.
**Advance:** Generally not.

**Rights Policy:** Buys all rights.

**How to Contact:** Send query or manuscript to Mary O'Connor, Assistant to the Publisher, who will then route the material to the appropriate division at the company.

**What Not to Do:** Phone or drop in without an appointment.

**Time Needed for Reply:** Four to six weeks; sooner if not interested.

**Does Author Supply Photos?** Author's responsibility for supplying photographs and artwork varies according to the requirements of the particular book project.

**Other Freelance Possibilities:** Copyeditors, proofreaders, and graphic artists.

**Advice for Authors:** For the most part, the School Division first establishes what books it wants to publish and then acquires manuscripts by forming authorship teams. Although each team has one or more active teachers, writers who are not teachers may participate on the teams.

Scott Foresman expects authors to be competent in their academic areas and to know how and be able to write for a particular audience. The company also expects authors to meet agreed-upon schedules and to realize that their work will be edited.

# HAROLD SHAW PUBLISHERS

P. O. Box 567
388 Gundersen Drive
Wheaton, Illinois 60189
(708) 665-6700

Established: 1967
Titles in Print:
Total 250; Annual 35

**Contact Person:** Ramona Cramer Tucker, Director of Editorial Services.

**Types of Books Published:** Primarily general nonfiction. One-quarter of the company's books are Bible study guides.

**Audience:** Evangelical Christian adults.

**Recent Titles Published:** *Working Women, Workable Lives; Renewal on the Run; When You Feel Like Screaming.*

**Current Needs:** Books about the family, parenting, social issues, and spiritual growth—all from an evangelical Christian point of view.

**Payment Information:**
    **Fee or Royalty:** Negotiable; can be either.
    **Advance:** Negotiable.

**Rights Policy:** Author retains copyright unless a work for hire.

**How to Contact:** Send query with cover letter. Can also send outline and sample chapters. Enclose a self-addressed, stamped envelope.

**What Not to Do:** Send material inappropriate for a religious publisher.

**Time Needed for Reply:** Two to four weeks.

**Does Author Supply Photos?** No.

**Advice for Authors:** Harold Shaw Publishers is looking for "mind-stretching" and "spirit-growing" books, not "fluff." In addition, please don't send poetry, literary criticism, or devotions. If you cannot envision at least 5,000 people reading or buying your book, do not send it to Harold Shaw.

# SOURCEBOOKS

P. O. Box 372
Naperville, Illinois 60566
(708) 961-2161

**Established:** 1987
**Titles in Print:**
**Total 50; Annual 15-20**

**Contact Person:** Dominique Raccah, Publisher.

**Types of Books Published:** Financial books and gift books.

**Audience:** General adult readership and business people.

**Recent Titles Published:** *Soft Sell: The New Art of Selling Self-Empowerment; Smart Hiring: The Complete Guide to Hiring the Best Employees; The Smart Business Start-up Guide; 500 Beauty Solutions; The Complete Garage Sale Kit; Something Old, Something New: The Stories Behind Our Favorite Wedding Traditions.*

**Current Needs:** Good books for independent businesses.

**Payment Information:**
**Fee or Royalty:** Can be either.
**Advance:** Usually not.

**Rights Policy:** Prefers to buy all rights.

**How to Contact:** Send query.

**What Not to Do:** Phone or drop in without an appointment.

**Time Needed for Reply:** At least three months.

**Does Author Supply Photos?** Depends on the book project.

**Other Freelance Possibilities:** Occasional need for copyeditors, proofreaders, and indexers. Query to discover current needs.

**Advice for Authors:** Before submitting a query, send for the company's catalog and writer's guidelines. Enclose a self-addressed, stamped envelope.

# SURREY BOOKS, INC.

230 E. Ohio Street, Suite 120
Chicago, Illinois 60611
(312) 751-7334

**Established: 1982**
**Titles in Print:**
**Total 50; Annual 15**

**Contact Person:** Susan Schwartz, Publisher.

**Types of Books Published:** Cookbooks and nonfiction dealing with lifestyle topics.

**Audience:** General adult readership.

**Recent Titles Published:** *Love Your Heart Low Cholesterol Cookbook; Skinny* (series); *How to Get a Job* (series).

**Payment Information:**
   **Fee or Royalty:** Can be either.
   **Advance:** Yes.

**How to Contact:** Send a one-page proposal describing the idea for your book and the niche it will fill. Enclose a self-addressed, stamped envelope.

**What Not to Do:** Phone or send complete manuscript.

**Time Needed for Reply:** Eight weeks.

**Does Author Supply Photos?** Depends on the project.

**Advice for Authors:** Before submitting an idea to Surrey Books, ask yourself whether your book would fit the company's line.

# THEOSOPHICAL PUBLISHING HOUSE

P. O. Box 270
Wheaton, Illinois 60189
(708) 665-0130

**Established:** 1915
**Titles in Print:**
**Total 280; Annual 12**

**Contact Person:** Brenda Rosen, Senior Editor.

**Types of Books Published:** Nonfiction books on theosophy, philosophy, comparative religion, transpersonal psychology, healing and holistic health, meditation, holistic science, self-help, astrology.

**Audience:** Adults interested in theosophy, holistic philosophy, inner growth, New Age thought.

**Recent Titles Published:** *Voices on the Threshold of Tomorrow; Public Like a Frog; Hammering Hot Iron; Jesus Christ, Sun of God; Celebrate the Solstice.*

**Current Needs:** Manuscripts dealing with subjects of contemporary interest from the theosophical point of view.

**Payment Information:**
**Fee or Royalty:** Royalty of variable percentage.
**Advance:** Yes.

**Rights Policy:** Buys all rights.

**How to Contact:** Recognized writers may call or send a query outlining ideas. Others should send a resume with query and outline.

**What Not to Do:** Send fiction or poetry.

**Time Needed for Reply:** Two to four weeks.

**Does Author Supply Photos?** Depends on project.

**Other Freelance Possibilities:** Occasional need for copyeditors.

**Advice for Authors:** Since all texts must deal with the subject matter in a way that harmonizes with theosophical philosophy, writers must have a holistic or spiritually oriented outlook, not necessarily tied to any traditional religion.

# THIRD SIDE PRESS, INC.

2250 W. Farragut Street
Chicago, Illinois 60625
(312) 271-3029

Established: 1991
Titles in Print:
Total 12; Annual 4-6

**Contact Person:** Midge Stocker, President and Publisher.

**Types of Books Published:** Feminist fiction and nonfiction.

**Audience:** Primarily adult women.

**Recent Titles Published:** *Confronting Cancer, Constructing Change* (vol. 2 in the Women/Cancer/Fear/Power series); *Somebody to Love: A Guide to Loving the Body You Have; AfterShocks* (novel); *On Lill Street* (novel).

**Current Needs:** Nonfiction book manuscripts dealing with specific areas of women's health from a feminist perspective; lesbian novels.

**Payment Information:**
    **Fee or Royalty:** Standard royalty.
    **Advance:** No.

**Rights Policy:** Buys all rights and splits some subsidiary rights with author.

**How to Contact:** Send query; enclose a self-addressed, stamped ($0.52) envelope.

**What Not to Do:** Phone or drop in without an appointment.

**Time Needed for Reply:** Six to eight weeks.

**Does Author Supply Photos?** Yes, of self for promotional purposes; rarely, for book interiors.

**Other Freelance Possibilities:** Occasional need for illustrators to prepare cover art.

**Advice for Authors:** Send for writer's guidelines and catalog; enclose a self-addressed, stamped ($0.52) envelope with request, and study these carefully before proceeding further. Third Side Press will read only complete fiction manuscripts.

# THIRD WORLD PRESS

7822 S. Dobson Street
Chicago, Illinois 60619
(312) 651-0700

Established: 1967
Titles in Print:
Total 60; Annual 4

**Contact Person:** Bakari Kitwana, Editorial Director.

**Types of Books Published:** Mainly books by and about African-Americans. Children's fiction and nonfiction (K-12), some preschool readers, picture books, and vocational books. Also adult fiction and nonfiction—primarily politics, cultural history, philosophy, and religion.

**Audience:** General audience, but particularly African-American adults and children.

**Recent Titles Published:** *The Isis Papers; Black Men: Obsolete, Single, Dangerous?; In Search of Serenity.*

**Current Needs:** Well-researched and documented nonfiction books by and about African-Americans.

**Payment Information:**
**Fee or Royalty:** Royalty of 7 percent to 10 percent.
**Advance:** No.

**Rights Policy:** Buys all rights.

**How to Contact:** Currently not accepting unsolicited work.

**What Not to Do:** Phone, send manuscript, or drop in without an appointment.

**Does Author Supply Photos?** Yes.

**Other Freelance Possibilities:** Copyeditors and artists.

**Advice for Authors:** Third World Press is looking for originality in style as well as thoroughness in research and documentation.

# THORNTREE PRESS

547 Hawthorne Lane
Winnetka, Illinois 60093
(708) 446-8099

Established: 1986
Titles in Print:
Total 18; Annual 2

**Contact Person:** Eloise Bradley Fink, President; John Dickson, Treasurer.

**Types of Books Published:** Almost exclusively poetry.

**Audience:** Literate adults who love poetry.

**Recent Titles Published:** *Looking Across; Your Neighborhood Poets; Troika 5; The Literate Person's Guide to Naming a Cat* (nonpoetry).

**Current Needs:** Poetry filled with original metaphors.

**Payment Information:** No financial compensation.

**Rights Policy:** All rights remain with author.

**How to Contact:** Send photocopies of poetry manuscripts; may also phone.

**What Not to Do:** Send original materials; manuscripts will not be returned.

**Time Needed for Reply:** Four months.

**Does Author Supply Photos?** Not unless requested.

**Advice for Authors:** Thorntree Press reads submissions from January 1 through February 14. Authors seeking to be published in Troika should send a $4 entry fee and ten pages of poems.

# THUNDER & INK PUBLISHERS

P. O. Box 7014
Evanston, Illinois 60201
(708) 492-1823

Established: 1988
Titles in Print:
Total 2; Annual 1

**Contact Person:** Tim Burke, Publisher.

**Types of Books Published:** Fiction and nonfiction for children and adults.

**Audience:** Children and adults.

**Recent Titles Published:** *Dark Matter; Cocoa Puppy.*

**Current Needs:** Any kind of children's books.

**Payment Information:**
    **Fee or Royalty:** Negotiable.
    **Advance:** Negotiable.

**Rights Policy:** Buys first North American rights.

**How to Contact:** Send query; enclose self-addressed, stamped envelope.

**What Not to Do:** Send entire manuscript.

**Time Needed for Reply:** Six weeks.

**Does Author Supply Photos?** No.

**Advice for Authors:** Know your audience. Be patient after submitting work.

# TIA CHUCHA PRESS
**Division of the Guild Complex**
P. O. Box 476969                    **Established: 1989**
Chicago, Illinois 60647             **Titles in Print:**
(312) 252-5321                      **Total 11; Annual 3**

**Contact Person:** Luis Rodriguez, Director.

**Types of Books Published:** Poetry.

**Audience:** Educated adults of many cultures.

**Recent Titles Published:** *Open Fist: An Anthology of Young Illinois Poets; Life According to Motown; Rooftop Piper; Double Tongues.*

**Current Needs:** More poetry.

**Payment Information:**
    **Fee or Royalty:** Royalty and book discount for author.
    **Advance:** Negotiable.

**Rights Policy:** Author retains rights; company buys first-time rights.

**How to Contact:** Send manuscript of at least 48 pages to publisher by June 30 of each year. Tia Chucha Press evaluates work over the summer to determine what will appear in its next year's list.

**What Not to Do:** Send manuscripts of less than 48 pages.

**Time Needed for Reply:** Six weeks to six months.

**Does Author Supply Photos?** Depends on project.

**Advice for Authors:** Although its name suggests that the company is a Spanish-language or bilingual publisher, Tia Chucha Press publishes almost exclusively in English.

# TRIUMPH BOOKS

644 S. Clark Street, Suite 2000
Chicago, Illinois 60605
(312) 939-3330

Established: 1990
Titles in Print:
Total 50; Annual 20

**Contact Person:** Mitchell Rogatz, Publisher.

**Types of Books Published:** Record-, fact-, and rulebooks for and about the NCAA, NFL, NHL, NBA, and other sports and other organizations.

**Audience:** General adult readership and professionals.

**Payment Information:**
   **Fee or Royalty:** Negotiable.
   **Advance:** Yes.

**Rights Policy:** Negotiable.

**How to Contact:** Send query.

**What Not to Do:** Phone.

**Time Needed for Reply:** Two weeks.

**Does Author Supply Photos?** Depends on project.

**Other Freelance Possibilities:** Copyeditors, proofreaders, researchers, and indexers.

**Advice for Authors:** All work—manuscript creation and editorial—is done by freelancers.

# TYNDALE HOUSE PUBLISHERS

P. O. Box 80
Wheaton, Illinois 60189
(312) 668-8300

Established: 1962
Titles in Print:
Total 1050; Annual 125

**Contact Person:** Marilyn Dellorto, Manuscript Review Committee.

**Types of Books Published:** General interest books for the evangelical Christian market, including books that fall into the categories of home and family, Christian living, fiction series (biblical, romance, and historical), as well as children's novelty picture books (Bible-based), youth (fiction and nonfiction), and activity, puzzle, and humor books for both adults and children. This all in addition to a full Bible line.

**Audience:** Adults interested in evangelical Christianity.

**Recent Titles Published:** *When God Doesn't Make Sense; The Eleventh Hour; A Voice in the Wind; Family Traditions that Last a Lifetime; My First Bible in Songs.*

**Current Needs:** Books on family life (marriage, parenting); outstanding fiction series for adults and youth; humor and puzzle books.

**Payment Information:**
    **Fee or Royalty:** Royalty of 10 to 18 percent depending on author and book.
    **Advance:** Usually.

**Rights Policy:** Varies.

**How to Contact:** Send query, resume, table of contents, and a detailed synopsis. For fiction, send sample chapter as well. If material is to be returned, enclose a self-addressed, stamped envelope.

**What Not to Do:** Drop in without an appointment, try to explain a book idea over the phone, or send a complete manuscript.

**Time Needed for Reply:** Four to twelve weeks.

**Does Author Supply Photos?** No.

**Other Freelance Possibilities:** Occasional need for substantive editors, copyeditors, and proofreaders.

**Advice for Authors:** Tyndale House Publishers seeks writers who are interested in the spiritual values and needs of the reader.

# UNIVERSITY OF CHICAGO PRESS

5801 S. Ellis Avenue
Chicago, Illinois 60637
(312) 702-7700

Established: 1892
Titles in Print:
Total 4000; Annual 250

**Contact Person:** Penelope Kaiserlian, Associate Director.

**Types of Books Published:** Scholarly books and monographs in all fields and some original poetry by invitation only.

**Audience:** Professional and college-level adults.

**Recent Titles Published:** *A River Runs Through It; Young Men and Fire; Chicago Manual of Style* (14th edition)*; Slim's Table.*

**Current Needs:** Works of substantial and significant scholarship.

**Payment Information:**
    **Fee or Royalty:** Royalty of variable percentage, generally between 10 and 15 percent.
    **Advance:** Yes, but rare.

**Rights Policy:** Buys North American book rights, translation rights abroad, and sometimes quality paperback rights.

**How to Contact:** Send query and outline.

**What Not to Do:** Phone, send complete manuscript, or send unsolicited poetry.

**Time Needed for Reply:** Immediate acknowledgment by postcard; six weeks for substantive reply.

**Does Author Supply Photos?** Sometimes.

**Other Freelance Possibilities:** Occasional need for copyeditors, proofreaders, and indexers.

**Advice for Authors:** Authors must hold professional credentials in the fields about which they propose to write. The University of Chicago Press strongly suggests that, before sending an idea, prospective authors consult the Association of American University Presses Directory for pertinent information regarding submission in general and the University of Chicago Press in particular.

# URBAN RESEARCH PRESS

840 E. 87th Street
Chicago, Illinois 60619
(312) 994-7200

Established: 1969
Titles in Print:
Total 14; Annual 3

**Contact Person:** Dempsey J. Travis, Publisher.

**Types of Books Published:** Biographies of well-known African Americans; books about real estate, finance, social studies; also children's books.

**Audience:** Adults and children.

**Recent Titles Published:** *The Autobiography of Black Jazz; Real Estate Is the Goal in Your Future; Harold: The People's Mayor; The Autobiography of Black Politics; The Autobiography of Black Chicago.*

**Current Needs:** Smaller books about the same topics listed above.

**Payment Information:**
   **Fee or Royalty:** Royalty.
   **Advance:** Possible but not probable.

**Rights Policy:** Author retains rights.

**How to Contact:** Send query.

**What Not to Do:** Send complete manuscript.

**Time Needed for Reply:** Three months.

**Does Author Supply Photos?** Yes, usually.

**Other Freelance Possibilities:** Designers, proofreaders, copyeditors, indexers.

# VICTOR BOOKS

1825 College Avenue
Wheaton, Illinois 60187
(708) 668-6000

Established: 1934
Titles in Print:
Total 425; Annual 100

**Contact Person:** David Horton, Senior Acquisitions Editor.

**Types of Books Published:** Christian books for personal and group study, Christian living, personal growth, Christian ministry, academic and reference works, inspirational books, picture books for children, quality fiction for children and adult readers.

**Audience:** Christians of all ages.

**Recent Titles Published:** *Millennium's Eve; The Puritans; The Power and the Blessing; The Toddler's Bible; Faith on the Line.*

**Current Needs:** Quality Christian fiction, personal growth issues, inspirational, issues facing Christians in contemporary society.

**Payment Information:**
    **Fee or Royalty:** Royalty.
    **Advance:** Yes.

**Rights Policy:** Buys all rights.

**How to Contact:** Send query or brief proposal.

**What Not to Do:** Phone or send complete manuscript.

**Time Needed for Reply:** Six to eight weeks.

**Does Author Supply Photos?** Depends on project.

**Advice for Authors:** Victor typically publishes authors who have a "track record" in the Christian community (i.e., those who are respected for their Bible or ministry expertise). The company does, however, occasionally publish less well-known Christian writers who submit a compelling idea skillfully written.

# WAVELAND PRESS

P. O. Box 400
Prospect Heights, Illinois 60070
(708) 634-0081

Established: 1975
Titles in Print:
Total 500; Annual 75

**Contact Person:** Neil Rowe, Publisher.

**Types of Books Published:** College textbooks and supplements.

**Audience:** College students.

**Recent Titles Published:** *Building Communication Theory* (2nd edition); *A History of the African People* (4th edition); *The Mythology of Crime and Criminal Punishment.*

**Current Needs:** Manuscripts about criminal justice, speech, and anthropology are in particular demand, but the company publishes textbooks in many fields.

**Payment Information:**
   **Fee or Royalty:** Negotiable.
   **Advance:** No.

**Rights Policy:** Negotiable.

**How to Contact:** Write or call with ideas.

**What Not to Do:** Send manuscript before publisher has expressed interest in the project.

**Time Needed for Reply:** Two to four weeks.

**Does Author Supply Photos?** Depends on the project.

**Other Freelance Possibilities:** Occasional need for copyeditors and indexers.

**Advice for Authors:** Have a particular college market (of commercial proportions) in mind when proposing a textbook idea to Waveland Press.

# ALBERT WHITMAN AND COMPANY

6340 Oakton Street
Morton Grove, Illinois 60053
(708) 581-0033

Established: 1919
Titles in Print:
Total 250; Annual 30

**Contact Person:** Kathleen Tucker, Editor.

**Types of Books Published:** Children's fiction and nonfiction.

**Audience:** Children, preschool through eighth grade.

**Recent Titles Published:** *Black, White, Just Right!; Visions: Stories about Women Artists; Someone Was Watching; Two of Everything; The Memory Box.*

**Current Needs:** General children's literature: picture books, easy novels, mysteries, easy biographies.

**Payment Information:**
**Fee or Royalty:** Royalty.
**Advance:** Negotiable.

**Rights Policy:** Buys all rights.

**How to Contact:** Send for writer's guidelines. Enclose a self-addressed, stamped envelope.

**What Not to Do:** Phone.

**Time Needed for Reply:** Two to three months.

**Does Author Supply Photos?** No. The company provides art for its illustrated books.

**Advice for Authors:** Study previous Whitman books before submitting a manuscript.

# WOODALL PUBLISHING COMPANY, INC.

**28167 N. Keith Drive**  **Established: 1934**
**Lake Forest, Illinois 60045**  **Titles in Print:**
**(708) 362-6700**  **Total 18; Annual 8**

**Contact Person:** Barbara Tinucci, Editorial Manager—Annual Publications.

**Types of Books Published:** Directories and guides about camping, recreational vehicles, etc.

**Audience:** Adults and families interested in camping and RVing.

**Recent Titles Published:** *Woodall's Campground Directories; Woodall's Plan It, Pack It, Go; Woodall's RV Buyers' Guide.*

**Current Needs:** Destination articles about various aspects of camping.

**Payment Information:**
**Fee or Royalty:** Fee.
**Advance:** No.

**Rights Policy:** Negotiable.

**How to Contact:** Send query. Enclose a self-addressed, stamped envelope.

**What Not to Do:** Phone.

**Time Needed for Reply:** Two or three weeks.

**Does Author Supply Photos?** Yes, preferably.

**Other Freelance Possibilities:** Occasional need for proofreaders.

**Advice for Authors:** Woodall Publishing Company is not interested in articles about "public" campgrounds; such campgrounds are listed, but the focus is on privately operated parks. For general travel articles, look at previous Woodall publications; the focus is on attractions—what to see and do along the way.

# WORLD BOOK, INC.

525 W. Monroe Street, 20th Floor
Chicago, Illinois 60661
(312) 258-3700

Established: 1917
Titles in Print:
Total 100; Annual 30

**Contact Person:** Lettie Zinnamon, Personnel Department (queries); Janet Peterson, Editorial Administrator and Permissions Editor (all other information).

**Types of Books Published:** Educational reference material: encyclopedias, dictionaries, atlases, CD-ROM.

**Audience:** Children of all ages.

**Recent Titles Published:** *World Book Encyclopedia; Childcraft—The How and Why Library; World Book Health and Medical Annual; Christmas in Today's Germany.*

**Current Needs:** Nonfiction articles and preschool material.

**Payment Information:**
   **Fee or Royalty:** Fee of negotiable rate.
   **Advance:** No.

**Rights Policy:** Buys all rights.

**How to Contact:** Query about current needs. Enclose a resume and a few writing samples.

**What Not to Do:** Phone or send manuscript. All work is done by assignment.

**Time Needed for Reply:** World Book keeps a file of freelance writers. Letters are acknowledged soon after they are received, but a writer may not get an assignment for months or years, depending on the length of time it takes for an appropriate assignment to come up.

**Does Author Supply Photos?** No.

**Other Freelance Possibilities:** Copyeditors, proofreaders, artists, researchers, and indexers.

**Advice for Authors:** World Book is always interested in looking at the credentials of writers skilled at developing clear, concise nonfiction material for students reading at an upper elementary or junior high level. The company is especially interested in hearing from authors who have written textbooks. Medical and science writers are also needed.

# PERIODICAL PUBLISHERS

# AIM—America's Intercultural Magazine

Aim Publications
7308 S. Eberhart Avenue
Chicago, Illinois 60619
(312) 874-6184

Established: 1975
Circulation: 7000

**Contact Person:** Ruth Apilado, Editor; Myron Apilado, Managing Editor.

**Type of Publication:** Nonprofit general circulation magazine.

**Audience:** Adults and children (special section for elementary school students).

**How Frequently Published:** Quarterly.

**Recently Published Articles:** "The Development of Racial Prejudice During Childhood" (nonfiction); "The House of Prayer" (fiction); "Big Mama's House" (fiction).

**Current Needs:** Fiction, nonfiction, and poetry relevant to the magazine's goals of promoting racial harmony and peace and eliminating bigotry.

**Policy on Seasonal Pieces:** Six weeks in advance.

**Usual Length Desired:** Nonfiction—800 words; fiction—3000 words.

**Author Writes on Speculation or Assignment?** Speculation.

**Are Free Sample Copies Available?** No.

**Payment Information:**
    **Rate:** $20 minimum for articles; $3 for poems.
    **Mode:** On publication
    **Advance Possible?** No.

**Rights Policy:** Buys first serial rights.

**How to Contact:** Phone or send manuscript. Photocopy OK. Enclose a self-addressed, stamped envelope.

**What Not to Do:** Send articles about religion or drop in without an appointment.

**Time Needed for Reply:** One month.

**Does Author Supply Photos?** Yes, if appropriate.

**Advice For Authors:** AIM Magazine wants to encourage writers of different cultures to use the periodical as a vehicle for communicating ideas and information that promote racial harmony.

# AIR WAVES
**JB Communications**
**2240 W. 23rd Place**
**Chicago, Illinois 60608**
**(312) 847-4444**

**Established: 1993**
**Circulation: 20,000**

**Contact Person:** Joe Brar, Editor and Publisher.

**Type of Publication:** Magazine that covers local radio industry news and trends.

**Audience:** Disc jockeys, sound engineers, and other radio station personnel as well as listeners.

**How Frequently Published:** Monthly.

**Recently Published Articles:** Articles about programming and stations; profiles of local radio personalities.

**Current Needs:** More of the same.

**Policy on Seasonal Pieces:** One week to one month in advance.

**Usual Length Desired:** 500 to 2000 words.

**Author Writes on Speculation or Assignment?** Assignment.

**Are Free Sample Copies Available?** Yes.

**Payment Information:**
    **Rate:** Negotiable.
    **Mode:** On publication.
    **Advance Possible?** No.

**Rights Policy:** Negotiable.

**How to Contact:** Send query and clips, or phone with idea.

**What Not to Do:** Send manuscript or drop in without an appointment.

**Time Needed for Reply:** Up to three weeks.

**Does Author Supply Photos?** Not usually.

**Advice for Authors:** Please don't include Air Waves as part of a multiple submission or share information with other reporters after agreeing to do a story for this magazine.

# AMERICAN FIELD

542 S. Dearborn Street
Chicago, Illinois 60605
(312) 663-9797

Established: 1874
Circulation: 10,000

**Contact Person:** B. J. Matthys, Managing Editor.

**Type of Publication:** General circulation magazine reporting field trials of sporting breeds of dogs.

**Audience:** Adults interested in outdoor sporting pastimes, such as hunting and fishing.

**How Frequently Published:** Weekly.

**Recently Published Articles:** Mostly field trials, but some articles.

**Current Needs:** American Field is interested in three categories of articles: summer conditioning, training, and breeding of dogs; genealogical studies of dogs that do well in competition; and anything in the veterinary line (e.g., new ailments, effective treatments).

**Usual Length Desired:** 1500 to 3000 words.

**Author Writes on Speculation or Assignment?** Speculation.

**Are Free Sample Copies Available?** Yes.

**Payment Information:**
Rate: $50 to $200 per article.
Mode: On acceptance.
Advance Possible? No.

**Rights Policy:** Author retains rights.

**How to Contact:** Phone, send query with synopsis, or send manuscript. Photocopy OK. Enclose a self-addressed, stamped envelope.

**What Not to Do:** Drop in without an appointment.

**Time Needed for Reply:** Three to four weeks.

**Does Author Supply Photos?** Occasionally; author usually specifies which illustrations the publisher should include.

**Advice for Authors:** Articles about hunting bird-dogs appear from time to time, but the magazine is devoted primarily to reporting field trials.

# ANTIQUES & COLLECTING MAGAZINE

**Lightner Publishing Corporation**
**1006 S. Michigan Avenue**
**Chicago, Illinois 60605**          **Established: 1931**
**(312) 939-4767**          **Circulation: 20,000**

**Contact Person:** Dale Graham, Publisher.

**Type of Publication:** General circulation magazine.

**Audience:** Collectors, 15 years old and up.

**How Frequently Published:** Monthly.

**Recently Published Articles:** Articles about Dorchester pottery, collectible shoes, toy theaters, fish decoys, antique bird cages, and Lassie memorabilia.

**Current Needs:** In-depth articles about specific antiques or companies for both the novice and veteran collector.

**Policy on Seasonal Pieces:** Three months in advance.

**Usual Length Desired:** 2,000 words maximum.

**Author Writes on Speculation or Assignment?** Can be either.

**Are Free Sample Copies Available?** Yes.

**Payment Information:**
   **Rate:** $100 to $250 per article.
   **Mode:** On publication.
   **Advance Possible?** No.

**Rights Policy:** Buys first rights and receives credit on reprint.

**How to Contact:** Send query or manuscript; photocopy OK. Enclose a self-addressed, stamped envelope.

**What Not to Do:** Phone or drop in without an appointment.

**Time Needed for Reply:** Ten days to two weeks.

**Does Author Supply Photos?** Yes.

**Advice for Authors:** All material must be well-researched, and all information must be accurate.

# AUTO RACING DIGEST

**Century Publishing Company**
**990 Grove Street**
**Evanston, Illinois 60201**
**(708) 491-6440**                    **Established: 1972**

**Contact Person:** Larry Burke, Senior Editor; James O'Connor, Managing Editor.

**Type of Publication:** Magazine covering the world of auto racing.

**Audience:** General adult readership (mostly men).

**How Frequently Published:** Bimonthly.

**Recently Published Articles:** "The Self-Made Sabates Is a Mover and Shaker"; "Biofile: Bobby Rahal"; "The Race I'll Never Forget"; "Why Karts? The Reasons Are Endless."

**Current Needs:** Features and previews of the IndyCar, Winston Cup, and Formula One circuits.

**Policy on Seasonal Pieces:** Six weeks in advance.

**Usual Length Desired:** 1500 words.

**Author Writes on Speculation or Assignment?** Can be either.

**Are Free Sample Copies Available?** No.

**Payment Information:**
    **Rate:** Negotiable.
    **Mode:** On acceptance.
    **Advance Possible?** No.

**How to Contact:** Send written query or complete manuscript. Enclose a self-addressed, stamped envelope.

**What Not to Do:** Phone or include Auto Racing Digest as part of a simultaneous submission.

**Time Needed for Reply:** Four weeks.

**Does Author Supply Photos?** No.

**Advice for Authors:** Please do not query the magazine about obvious ideas. Auto Racing Digest focuses on features and previews more than on event coverage.

# BASEBALL DIGEST

**Century Publishing Company**
**990 Grove Street**
**Evanston, Illinois 60201**          **Established: 1942**
**(708) 491-6440**          **Circulation: 300,000**

**Contact Person:** John Kuenster, Editor; Bob Kuenster, Managing Editor.

**Type of Publication:** Magazine covering professional baseball.

**Audience:** General adult readership (mostly men).

**How Frequently Published:** Monthly.

**Recently Published Articles:** "Veteran Scout Says Style of Play Has Changed in Majors"; "Baseball Profile: Outfielder Rickey Henderson"; "Here's a Recap of a Few Zany Moments from Last Season."

**Current Needs:** Features about professional baseball—e.g., profiles of personalities, timeless themes about the game.

**Policy on Seasonal Pieces:** Two months in advance.

**Usual Length Desired:** 1500 words, but more if needed.

**Author Writes on Speculation or Assignment?** Can be either.

**Are Free Sample Copies Available?** No.

**Payment Information:**
    **Rate:** Negotiable.
    **Mode:** On acceptance.
    **Advance Possible?** No.

**How to Contact:** Send written query or complete manuscript. Be sure to include phone number. Enclose a self-addressed, stamped envelope.

**What Not to Do:** Phone or include Baseball Digest as part of a simultaneous submission.

**Time Needed for Reply:** Four weeks.

**Does Author Supply Photos?** No.

**Advice for Authors:** Please do not query the magazine about obvious ideas. Baseball Digest focuses on features and previews more than on event coverage.

# BASKETBALL DIGEST
Century Publishing Company
990 Grove Street
Evanston, Illinois 60201
(708) 491-6440                              Established: 1973

**Contact Person:** Larry Burke, Senior Editor; James O'Connor, Managing Editor.

**Type of Publication:** Magazine covering professional and college basketball.

**Audience:** General adult readership (mostly men).

**How Frequently Published:** Eight times per year (monthly November through May, combined June/July issue).

**Recently Published Articles:** "When Rebuilding, Just Follow the Sun(s)"; "No Kidding: Cal's Superstar May Fly"; "Miracle Workers of the College Hardwood."

**Current Needs:** Features about personalities and trends in professional and college basketball.

**Usual Length Desired:** 1500 words.

**Author Writes on Speculation or Assignment?** Can be either.

**Are Free Sample Copies Available?** No.

**Payment Information:**
    **Rate:** Negotiable.
    **Mode:** On acceptance.
    **Advance Possible?** No.

**How to Contact:** Send written query or complete manuscript. Enclose a self-addressed, stamped envelope.

**What Not to Do:** Phone or include Basketball Digest as part of a simultaneous submission.

**Time Needed for Reply:** Four weeks.

**Does Author Supply Photos?** No.

**Advice for Authors:** Please do not query the magazine about obvious ideas. Basketball Digest focuses on features and previews more than on event coverage.

# BOWLING DIGEST
**Century Publishing Company**
**990 Grove Street**
**Evanston, Illinois 60201**
**(708) 491-6440**                                        **Established: 1983**

**Contact Person:** Larry Burke, Senior Editor; James O'Connor, Managing Editor.

**Type of Publication:** Magazine covering the world of bowling.

**Audience:** General adult readership.

**How Frequently Published:** Bimonthly.

**Recently Published Articles:** "A Pro's Approach: Equipped with All the Answers"; "Bowling Digest Interview: Kim Couture"; "The Inside Angle: Let the Lanes Be Your Guide."

**Current Needs:** Features about personalities and trends in bowling; also instructional pieces.

**Usual Length Desired:** 500 to 4000 words.

**Author Writes on Speculation or Assignment?** Can be either.

**Are Free Sample Copies Available?** No.

**Payment Information:**
    **Rate:** Negotiable.
    **Mode:** On acceptance.
    **Advance Possible?** No.

**How to Contact:** Send written query or complete manuscript. Enclose a self-addressed, stamped envelope.

**What Not to Do:** Phone or include Bowling Digest as part of a simultaneous submission.

**Time Needed for Reply:** Four weeks.

**Does Author Supply Photos?** No.

**Advice for Authors:** Please do not query the magazine about obvious ideas. Bowling Digest focuses on features more than on event coverage.

# THE BULLETIN OF THE ATOMIC SCIENTISTS

**Educational Foundation for Nuclear Science**
**6042 S. Kimbark Avenue**
**Chicago, Illinois 60637**          **Established: 1945**
**(312) 702-2555**                        **Circulation: 15,000**

**Contact Person:** Mikle Moore, Editor.

**Type of Publication:** A magazine of science and public affairs for the well-educated reader.

**Audience:** Professional scientists and others interested in the impact of science and technology on public affairs.

**How Frequently Published:** Every other month.

**Recently Published Articles:** Articles about several former Soviet states, North Korea's nuclear capability, and the feasibility of imposing sanctions.

**Current Needs:** Articles covering a broad range of topics dealing with the relationship between science and society.

**Usual Length Desired:** 2500 to 3000 words, but will consider a longer article if appropriate.

**Author Writes on Speculation or Assignment?** Mostly on assignment.

**Are Free Sample Copies Available?** Yes.

**Payment Information:**
    **Rate:** Negotiable.
    **Mode:** On publication.
    **Advance Possible?** No.

**Rights Policy:** Varies.

**How to Contact:** Send query or manuscript. Photocopy OK.

**What Not to Do:** Phone or drop in without an appointment.

**Time Needed for Reply:** Four to six weeks.

**Does Author Supply Photos?** Yes, if possible; also other illustrations if appropriate.

**Advice for Authors:** The Bulletin is a prestigious publication featuring internationally recognized authorities—including Nobel laureates. It will consider material only of the highest professional quality, but it does encourage submissions from young writers who are concerned with the subject matter covered by the Bulletin.

# CAMPUS LIFE MAGAZINE

**Christianity Today, Inc.**
**465 Gundersen Drive**
**Carol Stream, Illinois 60188**          **Established: 1944**
**(708) 260-6200**                        **Circulation: 120,000**

**Contact Person:** Chris Lutes, Senior Editor.

**Type of Publication:** Youth magazine.

**Audience:** Young adults of high school and college age.

**How Frequently Published:** Ten times per year, once in May/June and July/August.

**Recently Published Articles:** Articles about friendship, dating, and resolution of problems facing teens.

**Current Needs:** First-person accounts of situations involving topics mentioned above.

**Policy on Seasonal Pieces:** Three months in advance.

**Usual Length Desired:** 1000 to 2000 words.

**Author Writes on Speculation or Assignment?** Can be either.

**Are Free Sample Copies Available?** No, but free writer's guidelines are.

**Payment Information:**
　　**Rate:** Nonfiction—$150 to $300; fiction—$250 to $400.
　　**Mode:** On acceptance.
　　**Advance Possible?** No.

**Rights Policy:** Buys first rights and requests that material not be reprinted elsewhere for at least 60 days after it appears in Campus Life.

**How to Contact:** Send query and clips.

**What Not to Do:** Phone or send complete manuscript.

**Time Needed for Reply:** Four to six weeks.

**Does Author Supply Photos?** No.

**Advice For Authors:** Interested writers should request the writer's guidelines and study the magazine to get an understanding of the audience and the style.  For seasonal pieces, keep in mind that Campus Life needs a lead time of three months for production purposes.

# CAREER WORLD
**General Learning Corporation**
**60 Revere Drive, Suite 200**
**Northbrook, Illinois 60062**          **Established: 1971**
**(708) 205-3000**                       **Circulation: 85,000**

**Contact Person:** Carole Rubenstein, Managing Editor.

**Type of Publication:** Magazine with occupation and career-guidance information.

**Audience:** Junior and senior high school students.

**How Frequently Published:** Seven times per year (September through May; combined issues November/December and April/May).

**Recently Published Articles:** "Making Today's Economic Forces Work for You"; "AIDS in the Workplace"; also career-specific articles and occupational guidance information.

**Current Needs:** Articles featuring high-profile professionals; pieces about career and industry trends; interviews with people that describe the work they do and how it affects their lives.

**Policy on Seasonal Pieces:** Six to nine months in advance.

**Usual Length Desired:** 1000 to 1200 words.

**Author Writes on Speculation or Assignment?** Assignment.

**Are Free Sample Copies Available?** Yes. Enclose a self-addressed, stamped ($.75) envelope.

**Payment Information:**
   **Rate:** $100 to $150 per article.
   **Mode:** On publication.
   **Advance Possible?** No.

**Rights Policy:** Buys all rights.

**How To Contact:** Send query, clips, and resume.

**What Not To Do:** Phone or send manuscripts.

**Time Needed For Reply:** Six weeks.

**Does Author Supply Photos?** Not necessary.

**Advice For Authors:** Articles must be clearly written and directed to the younger high school students. They must have an upbeat style that is oriented more toward magazines than textbooks.

# CHICAGO
Chicago Publishing, Inc.
414 N. Orleans Street, Suite 800
Chicago, Illinois 60610          Established: 1970
(312) 222-8999                   Circulation: 165,000

**Contact Person:** Shane Tritsch, Managing Editor.

**Type of Publication:** General circulation magazine.

**Audience:** Adults living in and around Chicago.

**How Frequently Published:** Monthly.

**Recently Published Articles:** Articles about Chicago history, government, and sports; profiles of local personalities; service pieces.

**Current Needs:** More of the same.

**Usual Length Desired:** 3000 to 5000 words.

**Author Writes on Speculation or Assignment?** Assignment.

**Are Free Sample Copies Available?** No.

**Payment Information:**
   **Rate:** Varies according to length and type of article.
   **Mode:** On acceptance.
   **Advance Possible?** No.

**Rights Policy:** Buys first serial rights.

**How to Contact:** If time permits, send query. Phone only if article topic requires immediate coverage. Can also send manuscript; photocopy OK. Enclose a self-addressed, stamped envelope.

**What Not to Do:** Drop in without an appointment.

**Time Needed for Reply:** Three weeks.

**Does Author Supply Photos?** No.

**Advice for Authors:** Articles should involve some aspect of Chicago and should be knowledgeable, well-written, interesting, and fair.

# CHICAGO COMPUTERS AND USERS
JB Communications
2240 W. 23rd Place
Chicago, Illinois 60608      Established: 1991
(312) 847-4444      Circulation: 20,000

**Contact Person:** Joe Brar, Editor and Publisher.

**Type of Publication:** Computer magazine.

**Audience:** Local users—both professional and amateur—of various kinds of computers.

**How Frequently Published:** Monthly.

**Recently Published Articles:** Articles about new products and national computer news; profiles of area companies.

**Current Needs:** Reader-friendly (i.e., not too technical) articles relevant to the focus of the magazine.

**Usual Length Desired:** 500 to 2000 words.

**Author Writes on Speculation or Assignment?** Assignment.

**Are Free Sample Copies Available?** Yes.

**Payment Information:**
     **Rate:** Negotiable.
     **Mode:** On publication.
     **Advance Possible?** No.

**Rights Policy:** Negotiable.

**How to Contact:** Send query and clips, or phone with an article idea.

**What Not to Do:** Send manuscript or drop in without an appointment.

**Time Needed for Reply:** Up to three weeks.

**Does Author Supply Photos?** Not usually.

**Advice for Authors:** Please don't include Chicago Computers and Users as part of a multiple submission or share information with other reporters after agreeing to do a story for this magazine.

# CHICAGO HISTORY
**Chicago Historical Society**
**Clark Street at North Avenue**
**Chicago, Illinois 60614**  **Established: 1945**
**(312) 642-4600**  **Circulation: 10,000**

**Contact Person:** Claudia Wood, Acting Editor.

**Type of Publication:** Popular-audience magazine specializing in Chicago and urban history.

**Audience:** Professional historians and interested lay readers from high school through adult.

**How Frequently Published:** Three times per year.

**Recently Published Articles:** Articles about the 1893 and 1933 worlds fairs and about gambling in Chicago.

**Current Needs:** Articles dealing with any aspect of Chicago history up to recent past. Analytical, informative articles of cultural, political, economic, social, architectural, or institutional significance directed at a popular—but informed—audience.

**Policy on Seasonal Pieces:** Three months to one year in advance.

**Usual Length Desired:** 2500 to 4000 words.

**Author Writes on Speculation or Assignment?** Primarily assignment.

**Are Free Sample Copies Available?** No.

**Payment Information:**
    **Rate:** $150 to $250 per article.
    **Mode:** On publication.
    **Advance Possible?** Generally not.

**Rights Policy:** Retains all rights.

**How to Contact:** Send manuscript (photocopy OK); enclose a self-addressed, stamped envelope. Enquiries welcome.

**Time Needed for Reply:** Immediate acknowledgment of receipt of manuscript; two months for substantive reply.

**Does Author Supply Photos?** Can submit, but photos frequently come from the Society's graphic collection.

**Advice for Authors:** Articles must consist of material not previously published—i.e., not a rehash of other people's writings. Consequently, authors should not undertake to write an article without considerable knowledge of the subject and a willingness to perform detailed research. Although it does not publish citations, Chicago History expects all manuscripts to be fully footnoted.

# CHICAGO LIFE
P. O. Box 11131
Chicago, Illinois 60611          Established: 1984
(312) 528-2737                   Circulation: 60,000

**Contact Person:** Paula Lyon, Editor.

**Type of Publication:** Lifestyles/issues magazine.

**Audience:** Affluent baby boomers.

**How Frequently Published:** Six times per year.

**Recently Published Articles:** "Investment Trends"; "Protecting Your Privacy"; "Headache Relief."

**Current Needs:** Articles about finance, health, important political issues, trends. Also book and art critiques.

**Usual Length Desired:** 300 to 2000 words.

**Author Writes on Speculation or Assignment?** Mostly on speculation, but can be either.

**Are Free Sample Copies Available?** Yes; enclose a self-addressed, stamped envelope with request.

**Payment Information:**
   **Rate:** $30 per article.
   **Mode:** Can be either on acceptance or publication.
   **Advance Possible?** No.

**Rights Policy:** Buys first-time rights.

**How to Contact:** Send manuscript. Enclose a self-addressed, stamped envelope.

**What Not to Do:** Phone or drop in without an appointment.

**Time Needed for Reply:** Two weeks.

**Does Author Supply Photos?** Sometimes.

**Advice for Authors:** Please read the magazine before submitting an article or article idea.

# CHICAGO PARENT NEWSMAGAZINE

**The Wednesday Journal, Inc.**
**141 S. Oak Park Avenue**
**Oak Park, Illinois 60302**          **Established: 1984**
**(708) 386-5555**                    **Circulation: 85,000**

**Contact Person:** Mary Haley, Editor.

**Type of Publication:** Free tabloid featuring child-related articles and a comprehensive calendar of events.

**Audience:** Parents with children of all ages (focus is on younger children).

**How Frequently Published:** Monthly.

**Recently Published Articles:** "Handguns and Our Kids"; "Inclusion: Learning to Really Listen"; "What Happens When Mom's in Jail?"

**Current Needs:** Good how-to features about any aspect of parenting—from how to get your child a Social Security card to how to get the kids to bed on time; also essays for the "My Family" column.

**Policy on Seasonal Pieces:** Two to three months in advance.

**Usual Length Desired:** Features—1500 to 2500 words; column—650 words.

**Author Writes on Speculation or Assignment?** Mostly on assignment.

**Are Free Sample Copies Available?** Yes.

**Payment Information:**
    **Rate:** $75 to $200 per article.
    **Mode:** On publication.
    **Advance Possible?** On rare occasions.

**Rights Policy:** Buys first-time, one-time rights.

**How to Contact:** Send query and clips; can also send complete manuscript.

**What Not to Do:** Phone.

**Time Needed for Reply:** Four to six weeks.

**Does Author Supply Photos?** Depends on article.

**Advice for Authors:** Be sure to put your name, address, and phone number on the actual manuscript, not just in the query or cover letter.

# THE CHICAGO REPORTER

**332 S. Michigan Avenue, Suite 500**
**Chicago, Illinois 60604**            **Established: 1972**
**(312) 427-4830**                     **Circulation: 10,000**

**Contact Person:** Laura Washington, Editor.

**Type of Publication:** Investigative publication covering racial issues and public affairs.

**Audience:** Media, top executives, city government officials, educators, community leaders.

**How Frequently Published:** Monthly.

**Recently Published Articles:** "Aldermen Keep Firm Hold on Bronzeville"; "The Black Belt Remembered"; "Race in Review"; "To Preserve and Protect"; "The Cost of Racism."

**Current Needs:** Feature articles or profiles of individual leaders in the city; coverage of Chicago events and programs; pieces on social and public policy; original ideas for investigative stories.

**Usual Length Desired:** 2500 to 3000 words.

**Author Writes on Speculation or Assignment?** Assignment.

**Are Free Sample Copies Available?** Yes.

**Payment Information:**
    **Rate:** $300 per article.
    **Mode:** On acceptance.
    **Advance Possible?** No.

**Rights Policy:** Buys all rights.

**How to Contact:** Send query and clips.

**What Not to Do:** Phone or drop in without an appointment.

**Time Needed for Reply:** Two weeks.

**Does Author Supply Photos?** No.

**Advice for Authors:** Know the audience for whom you are writing. Place the emphasis on racial issues.

# CHICAGO SCHOOLS

**JB Communications**
**2240 W. 23rd Place**
**Chicago, Illinois 60608**       **Established: 1990**
**(312) 847-4444**                 **Circulation: 20,000**

**Contact Person:** Joe Brar, Editor and Publisher.

**Type of Publication:** Magazine covering higher education and career information.

**Audience:** High school juniors and seniors, junior college students, and college freshmen and sophomores.

**How Frequently Published:** Monthly.

**Recently Published Articles:** Articles about career choices and how to obtain financial aid for college.

**Current Needs:** More of the same.

**Policy on Seasonal Pieces:** One week to one month in advance.

**Usual Length Desired:** 500 to 2000 words.

**Author Writes on Speculation or Assignment?** Assignment.

**Are Free Sample Copies Available?** Yes.

**Payment Information:**
　　**Rate:** Negotiable.
　　**Mode:** On publication.
　　**Advance Possible?** No.

**Rights Policy:** Negotiable.

**How to Contact:** Send query and clips, or phone with article idea.

**What Not to Do:** Send manuscript or drop in without an appointment.

**Time Needed for Reply:** Up to three weeks.

**Does Author Supply Photos?** Not usually.

**Advice for Authors:** Please don't include Chicago Schools as part of a multiple submission or share information with other reporters after agreeing to do a story for this magazine.

# COMPLETE WOMAN
**1165 N. Clark Street, Suite 607**
**Chicago, Illinois 60610**        **Established: 1981**
**(312) 266-8680**        **Circulation: 500,000**

**Contact Person:** Jean Iversen, Assistant Editor.

**Type of Publication:** Women's general interest magazine.

**Audience:** Women ages 18 to 35, married and single.

**How Frequently Published:** Every two months.

**Recently Published Articles:** "Sex Survey"; "How to Cope with Divorce"; "Getting Slim for Summer."

**Current Needs:** Articles about relationships with men and friends, focusing on women's total well-being in all aspects of life—especially love and sex.

**Policy on Seasonal Pieces:** Four to six months in advance.

**Usual Length Desired:** 900 to 2000 words.

**Author Writes on Speculation or Assignment?** Can be either.

**Are Free Sample Copies Available?** No.

**Payment Information:**
    **Rate:** Negotiable.
    **Mode:** Negotiable.
    **Advance Possible?** Negotiable.

**Rights Policy:** Buys one-time rights.

**How to Contact:** Send query.

**What Not to Do:** Phone.

**Does Author Supply Photos?** Not usually.

**Advice for Authors:** Familiarize yourself with Complete Woman's content and style before submitting an article idea. Articles must have a lively tone and take a unique slant on the subject.

# CONSUMERS DIGEST

**5705 N. Lincoln Avenue**
**Chicago, Illinois 60659**          **Established: 1961**
**(312) 275-3590**          **Circulation: 1.2 million**

**Contact Person:** John Manos, Editor-in-Chief.

**Type of Publication:** General circulation magazine.

**Audience:** Adults.

**How Frequently Published:** Every other month.

**Recently Published Articles:** "Domestic Car Preview"; "Walking Shoes"; "Carry-On Bags."

**Current Needs:** Articles that provide information about a variety of consumer goods and services.

**Policy on Seasonal Pieces:** Four months in advance.

**Usual Length Desired:** 2000 to 3000 words.

**Author Writes on Speculation or Assignment?** Mostly on assignment.

**Are Free Sample Copies Available?** Yes. Enclose six first-class stamps with request.

**Payment Information:**
   **Rate:** 30 to 50 cents per word.
   **Mode:** On acceptance.
   **Advance Possible?** Yes, but not likely.

**Rights Policy:** Negotiable.

**How to Contact:** Send query and clips.

**What Not to Do:** Phone, send complete manuscript, or drop in without an appointment.

**Time Needed for Reply:** One to two months.

**Does Author Supply Photos?** Not usually.

**Advice for Authors:** Articles must be very subject specific. Authors should be experts in the subjects they cover and should remember that, in this case, subject knowledge is more important than writing skill.

# CRAFTS 'N THINGS
**Clapper Communications Company**
**701 Lee Street, Suite 1000**
**Des Plaines, Illinois 60016**          **Established: 1975**
**(708) 297-7400**          **Circulation: 303,000**

**Contact Person:** Julie Stephani, Editor; Lora Wintz, Projects Editor.

**Type of Publication:** Subscription and newsstand magazine about crafts of all types.

**Audience:** Craft hobbyists and professionals.

**How Frequently Published:** Ten times a year (once each in June/July and December/January).

**Recently Published Articles:** Pieces about cross-stitch, cut-and-glue projects, knitting, painting, and clay.

**Current Needs:** How-to craft projects with clear instructions and full-size patterns.

**Policy on Seasonal Pieces:** Six months in advance.

**Usual Length Desired:** No length restriction.

**Author Writes on Speculation or Assignment?** Speculation.

**Are Free Sample Copies Available?** Yes.

**Payment Information:**
    **Rate:** $50 to $250 per article.
    **Mode:** 30 days after acceptance.
    **Advance Possible?** No.

**Rights Policy:** Negotiable.

**How to Contact:** Send finished item or a photo of item or full-size pattern along with full directions. Enclose a self-addressed, stamped envelope. Only original work will be published.

**What Not to Do:** Phone, send query, or drop in without an appointment.

**Time Needed for Reply:** One month.

**Does Author Supply Photos?** Yes, either a photo or an accurate drawing (need not be camera-ready artwork) of finished item.

**Advice for Authors:** Crafts 'n Things wants authors to possess demonstrable expertise and originality in the particular craft. Instructions must be clear and simple.

# CRAIN'S SMALL BUSINESS

**Crain Communicications, Inc.**
**740 N. Rush Street**
**Chicago, Illinois 60611**          **Established: 1993**
**(312) 649-5411**                    **Circulation: 50,000**

**Contact Person:** Bob Reed, Editor.

**Type of Publication:** Newsmagazine covering business and finance issues for Chicago-area small businesses (i.e., those with fewer than 100 employees).

**Audience:** Owners and managers of small businesses.

**How Frequently Published:** Ten times per year (monthly with combined issues in July/August and December/January).

**Recently Published Articles:** "The Business of Baseball" (impact of baseball on small business); "Fear and Loathing of the EPA"; "ISA Direct Inc." (profile of a suburban printer.)

**Current Needs:** Profiles of small businesses and owners of small businesses; also management how-to articles.

**Policy on Seasonal Pieces:** Four to five weeks in advance.

**Usual Length Desired:** Cover article—800 to 900 words; inside article—500 words.

**Author Writes on Speculation or Assignment?** Assignment.

**Are Free Sample Copies Available?** Yes.

**Payment Information:**
    **Rate:** $13.20 per column inch.
    **Mode:** On acceptance.
    **Advance Possible?** No.

**Rights Policy:** Buys all rights.

**How to Contact:** Send query and one or two samples of best writing—preferably of a financial nature.

**What Not to Do:** Phone.

**Time Needed for Reply:** Two weeks.

**Does Author Supply Photos?** No, but suggestions for relevant photos are appreciated.

**Advice for Authors:** Read and get to know Crain's Small Business before querying with article ideas. The publication tries to humanize business and prefers writers who are comfortable (i.e., not intimidated) when profiling and reporting on businesses and business people.

# THE DARTNELL CORPORATION

**4660 N. Ravenswood Avenue**
**Chicago, Illinois 60640**
**(312) 561-4000**                    **Established: 1917**

**Contact Person:** Susan Elliott, Editorial Assistant.

**Type of Publications:** Four-page business newsletters, 24-page booklets, and a large bulletin.

**Audience:** Business professionals—managers, salespeople, supervisors, and secretaries.

**How Frequently Published:** Newsletters—biweekly; booklets and bulletin—monthly.

**Recently Published Articles:** "New Account Selling"; "Production Team"; "Quality First"; "The Effective Executive"; "What A Supervisor Should Know About . . . ."

**Current Needs:** Articles of interest to office and sales personnel; how-to articles for people in management; new trends in a particular industry.

**Policy on Seasonal Pieces:** Three months in advance.

**Usual Length Desired:** Newsletters—600 words maximum; booklets—5000 words maximum.

**Author Writes on Speculation or Assignment?** Can be either.

**Are Free Sample Copies Available?** Yes.

**Payment Information:**
    **Rate:** Varies by publication.
    **Mode:** On acceptance.
    **Advance Possible?** No.

**Rights Policy:** Varies.

**How to Contact:** Send query or manuscript and writing samples.

**What Not to Do:** Drop in without an appointment.

**Time Needed for Reply:** One week.

**Does Author Supply Photos?** Occasionally.

**Advice for Authors:** Writers must be experts in their fields or be willing to perform a great deal of research. All material must be clearly written and straightforward in approach.

# DOG WORLD

**Maclean Hunter Publishing Company**
**29 N. Wacker Drive**
**Chicago, Illinois 60606**          **Established: 1921**
**(312) 726-2802**                   **Circulation: 56,000**

**Contact Person:** Donna Marcel, Editor.

**Type of Publication:** Magazine about all aspects of dog owning and breeding.

**Audience:** Dog breeders and exhibitors, animal clinics, and pet suppliers.

**How Frequently Published:** Monthly.

**Recently Published Articles:** Pieces about veterinary medicine, training, dog sports, updated technology for breeding.

**Current Needs:** Articles about dog sports, field trials, and medical news.

**Policy on Seasonal Pieces:** Two months in advance.

**Usual Length Desired:** 1500 to 2500 words.

**Author Writes on Speculation or Assignment?** Can be either.

**Are Free Sample Copies Available?** Yes.

**Payment Information:**
> **Rate:** $200 to $900.
> **Mode:** On publication.
> **Advance Possible?** Rarely, if ever.

**Rights Policy:** Buys first North American serial rights and reserves the right to reprint material for promotional purposes.

**How to Contact:** Send query and samples and pay history.

**What Not to Do:** Send complete manuscript.

**Time Needed for Reply:** Three to four months.

**Does Author Supply Photos?** Yes.

**Advice for Authors:** Please present as much pertinent information as possible in the query.

# DOWN BEAT

**Maher Publications, Inc.**
**180 W. Park Avenue**
**Elmhurst, Illinois 60126**          **Established: 1934**
**(708) 941-2030**                    **Circulation: 90,000**

**Contact Person:** Frank Alkyer, Editorial Director/Associate Publisher.

**Type of Publication:** Jazz/blues magazine.

**Audience:** Practicing musicians, serious album collectors, and music lovers in general.

**How Frequently Published:** Monthly.

**Recently Published Articles:** "41st Annual International Critics Poll"; "Sun Ra's Sunset"; "Woody Allen's Blues"; "Why Jelly Roll Morton Still Counts."

**Current Needs:** Performance reviews and interesting interviews with musicians.

**Policy on Seasonal Pieces:** Three months in advance.

**Usual Length Desired:** 2500 to 3000 words.

**Author Writes on Speculation or Assignment?** On assignment.

**Are Free Sample Copies Available?** No.

**Payment Information:**
   **Rate:** Varies.
   **Mode:** On publication.
   **Advance Possible?** No.

**Rights Policy:** Buys all rights.

**How to Contact:** Send query.

**What Not to Do:** Phone, send complete manuscript, or drop in without an appointment.

**Time Needed for Reply:** Two weeks.

**Does Author Supply Photos?** No.

**Advice for Authors:** Down Beat usually works with professional writers. The competition is tough for newcomers, but submissions are welcome.

# EBONY

**Johnson Publishing Company, Inc.**
**820 S. Michigan Avenue**
**Chicago, Illinois 60605**      **Established: 1945**
**(312) 322-9200**      **Circulation: 2 million**

**Contact Person:** Hans Massaquoi, Managing Editor.

**Type of Publication:** General circulation magazine.

**Audience:** Blacks in the United States, the Caribbean, Africa, and Europe.

**How Frequently Published:** Monthly.

**Recently Published Articles:** "President Clinton and Other Whites Tell 'What King Means to Me'"; "The Michael Jordan Nobody Knows"; "Black Presidents in Fortune 500 Companies."

**Current Needs:** Profiles, interviews, historical pieces, and human interest stories.

**Policy on Seasonal Pieces:** Two months in advance.

**Usual Length Desired:** 2500 words minimum.

**Author Writes on Speculation or Assignment?** Speculation.

**Are Free Sample Copies Available?** No.

**Payment Information:**
    **Rate:** Varies.
    **Mode:** On publication.
    **Advance Possible?** No.

**Rights Policy:** Buys all rights.

**How to Contact:** Send query and clips.

**What Not to Do:** Phone, send complete manuscript, or drop in without an appointment.

**Time Needed for Reply:** One to two weeks.

**Does Author Supply Photos?** Yes, with captions. Prefers negatives or contact sheets, but will accept black-and-white glossies. Also uses color transparencies.

**Advice for Authors:** Stories and articles should concern and be of interest to a wide range of black readers.

# THE ELKS MAGAZINE

425 W. Diversey Parkway
Chicago, Illinois 60614          Established: 1922
(312) 528-4500                   Circulation: 1.3 million

**Contact Person:** Fred Oakes, Editor/Marketing Director; Judith Keogh, Managing Editor.

**Type of Publication:** General interest organization magazine.

**Audience:** Members of the Elks and their families.

**How Frequently Published:** Ten times a year (combined July/August and December/January issues).

**Recently Published Articles:** "Joys of Winter Camping"; "The Great Ferris Wheel of 1893"; "Optimal Friendships: How to Get the Most Out of Your Relationships."

**Current Needs:** Articles about leading-edge technology as it applies to the average reader's lifestyle.

**Policy on Seasonal Pieces:** Five to six months in advance.

**Usual Length Desired:** 1250 to 3000 words.

**Author Writes on Speculation or Assignment?** Speculation.

**Are Free Sample Copies Available?** Yes, as are writer's guidelines. Enclose a self-addressed, stamped envelope with request.

**Payment Information:**
> **Rate:** $150 to $500 per article depending on length and the author's relationship with the magazine.
> **Mode:** On acceptance.
> **Advance Possible?** No.

**Rights Policy:** Buys first North American rights.

**How to Contact:** Send query. Enclose a self-addressed, stamped envelope.

**What Not to Do:** Phone, send manuscript, or drop in without an appointment.

**Time Needed for Reply:** Four to six weeks.

**Does Author Supply Photos?** Yes, when possible.

**Advice for Authors:** The Elks Magazine looks for articles that educate readers and entertain them with a fresh approach. Articles should provoke interest but not controversy.

# EMPLOYEE SERVICES MANAGEMENT

**National Employee Services and Recreation Association**
**2211 York Road, Suite 207**
**Oak Brook, Illinois 60521**          **Established: 1950**
**(708) 368-1280**                    **Circulation: 5000**

**Contact Person:** Cynthia Helson, Editor.

**Type of Publication:** Special-interest association magazine.

**Audience:** Members and directors of employee recreation, fitness, and service enterprises in business, industry, and government.

**How Frequently Published:** Ten times a year (combined issues for December/January and May/June).

**Recently Published Articles:** "Is Work Coming Home or Home Coming to Work?"; "Do Wellness Incentives Work?"; "Computerized Sports League Scheduling: Is It Right for You?"

**Current Needs:** Each issue has a single theme, including such topics as sports, travel, communications, and progressive management.

**Policy on Seasonal Pieces:** Two months.

**Usual Length Desired:** 2500 words maximum, although occasionally longer articles serialized.

**Author Writes on Speculation or Assignment?** Assignment.

**Are Free Sample Copies Available?** Yes.

**Payment Information:** No monetary payment.

**How to Contact:** Phone or send query, resume, and outline.

**What Not to Do:** Send manuscript or drop in without an appointment.

**Time Needed for Reply:** One to two weeks.

**Does Author Supply Photos?** Yes.

**Advice for Authors:** Employee Services Management needs writers with knowledge of employee relations, personnel policies, fitness, and recreation. The style is informal and nonacademic.

# FAMILY SAFETY AND HEALTH MAGAZINE

National Safety Council
1121 Spring Lake Drive
Itasca, Illinois 60143       **Established: 1961**
(708) 285-1121       **Circulation: 1.5 million**

**Contact Person:** Debra Fleischman, Associate Editor.

**Type of Publication:** Subscription-only magazine covering off-the-job safety and health.

**Audience:** Employees of member companies of the National Safety Council.

**How Frequently Published:** Quarterly.

**Recently Published Articles:** "Learn About Food Fads"; "Say Goodbye to Your Aching Back"; "Glide Through a Cross-Country Ski Lesson"; "First Aid and CPR—Don't Be Afraid to Help."

**Current Needs:** Articles about accident prevention in sports and recreation, the car, and the home; also articles about health- and fitness-related topics.

**Policy on Seasonal Pieces:** Three months in advance.

**Usual Length Desired:** 600 to 1200 words.

**Author Writes on Speculation or Assignment?** Can be either.

**Are Free Sample Copies Available?** Yes.

**Payment Information:**
     **Rate:** Varies according to quality and length and reputation of writer.
     **Mode:** On acceptance.
     **Advance Possible?** No.

**Rights Policy:** Buys all rights, but author can receive reprint rights.

**How to Contact:** Send resume and clips.

**What Not to Do:** Phone or send complete manuscript.

**Time Needed for Reply:** Up to two months.

**Does Author Supply Photos?** Yes. The magazine pays extra for color transparencies.

**Advice for Authors:** Articles should be concrete and to the point, not a rehash of widely available information. They must be thoroughly researched but written in an easy-to-read, creative style.

# FOOTBALL DIGEST
**Century Publishing Company**
**990 Grove Street**
**Evanston, Illinois 60201**
**(708) 491-6440**                    **Established: 1971**

**Contact Person:** Larry Burke, Senior Editor; James O'Connor, Managing Editor.

**Type of Publication:** Magazine covering professional and college football.

**Audience:** General adult readership (mostly men).

**How Frequently Published:** Ten times per year (monthly September through April, combined issues in May/June and July/August).

**Recently Published Articles:** "NFL to TV Viewers: Never Fear, Fox is Here!"; "Can FSU's Star Ward Off the Heisman Jinx?"; "Mike Morris: What Dimension is He From?"

**Current Needs:** Features about personalities and trends in professional and college football.

**Usual Length Desired:** 500 to 1500 words.

**Author Writes on Speculation or Assignment?** Can be either.

**Are Free Sample Copies Available?** No.

**Payment Information:**
   **Rate:** Negotiable.
   **Mode:** On acceptance.
   **Advance Possible?** No.

**How to Contact:** Send written query or complete manuscript. Enclose a self-addressed, stamped envelope.

**What Not to Do:** Phone or include Football Digest as part of a simultaneous submission.

**Time Needed for Reply:** Four weeks.

**Does Author Supply Photos?** No.

**Advice for Authors:** Please do not query the magazine about obvious ideas. Football Digest focuses on features and previews more than on event coverage.

# GAY CHICAGO MAGAZINE
Gernhardt Publishing, Inc.
3121 N. Broadway
Chicago, Illinois 60657      Established: 1976
(312) 327-7271      Circulation: 22,000

**Contact Person:** Ralph Paul Gernhardt, Publisher.

**Type of Publication:** Controlled circulation (free) magazine to gay bars, gay bookstores, gay restaurants, and other entertainment establishments on Chicago's North Side.

**Audience:** Gays/lesbians 18 years and older.

**How Frequently Published:** Weekly.

**Recently Published Articles:** Columns about the law and taxes, features, point-of-view articles, reviews, calendar of events.

**Current Needs:** Articles of interest to the gay community: news, entertainment, book reviews, commentaries.

**Policy on Seasonal Pieces:** Six to eight weeks in advance for features.

**Usual Length Desired:** Up to three typed (double-spaced) pages.

**Author Writes on Speculation or Assignment?** Speculation.

**Are Free Sample Copies Available?** Yes.

**Payment Information:**
    **Rate:** $25 to $50 per article.
    **Mode:** On publication.
    **Advance Possible?** No.

**Rights Policy:** Author retains all rights.

**How to Contact:** Send query.

**What Not to Do:** Phone.

**Time Needed for Reply:** Three weeks.

**Does Author Supply Photos?** Not usually.

**Advice for Authors:** Gay Chicago Magazine's interest is in articles that depict the varied aspects of gay life and lifestyles. The emphasis is on Chicago, but material need not be restricted to the local area.

# Go Chicago Travel Guide

**JB Communications**
**2240 W. 23rd Place**
**Chicago, Illinois 60608**
**(312) 847-4444**

**Established: 1992**
**Circulation: 20,000**

**Contact Person:** Joe Brar, Editor and Publisher.

**Type of Publication:** Guide to local, national, and international travel.

**Audience:** Adults interested in travel.

**How Frequently Published:** Monthly.

**Recently Published Articles:** Articles dealing with travel tips and local, national, and international destinations.

**Current Needs:** More of the same.

**Policy on Seasonal Pieces:** One week to one month in advance.

**Usual Length Desired:** 500 to 2000 words.

**Author Writes on Speculation or Assignment?** Assignment.

**Are Free Sample Copies Available?** Yes.

**Payment Information:**
    **Rate:** Negotiable.
    **Mode:** On publication.
    **Advance Possible?** No.

**Rights Policy:** Negotiable.

**How to Contact:** Send query and clips, or phone with article idea.

**What Not to Do:** Send manuscript or drop in without an appointment.

**Time Needed for Reply:** Up to three weeks.

**Does Author Supply Photos?** Not usually.

**Advice for Authors:** Please don't include Go Chicago Travel Guide as part of a multiple submission or share information with other reporters after agreeing to do a story for this magazine.

# HOCKEY DIGEST
**Century Publishing Company**
**990 Grove Street**
**Evanston, Illinois 60201**
**(708) 491-6440**                    **Established: 1972**

**Contact Person:** Larry Burke, Senior Editor; James O'Connor, Managing Editor.

**Type of Publication:** Magazine covering professional and college hockey.

**Audience:** General adult readership (mostly men).

**How Frequently Published:** Eight times per year (monthly November through May, combined Summer issue).

**Recently Published Articles:** "A True Hockey Temple Takes One Last Bow"; "Courtenay's Comeback is Cause for Celebration"; "There's a New Game in Town Down in Charlotte."

**Current Needs:** Features about personalities and trends in NHL, college, and junior-level hockey.

**Usual Length Desired:** 1500 words.

**Author Writes on Speculation or Assignment?** Can be either.

**Are Free Sample Copies Available?** No.

**Payment Information:**
    **Rate:** Negotiable.
    **Mode:** On acceptance.
    **Advance Possible?** No.

**How to Contact:** Send written query or complete manuscript. Enclose a self-addressed, stamped envelope.

**What Not to Do:** Phone or include Hockey Digest as part of a simultaneous submission.

**Time Needed for Reply:** Four weeks.

**Does Author Supply Photos?** No.

**Advice for Authors:** Please do not query the magazine about obvious ideas. Hockey Digest focuses on features and previews more than on event coverage.

# ILLINOIS ENTERTAINER

**Roberts Publishing, Inc.**
**2250 E. Devon Avenue, Suite 150**
**Des Plaines, Illinois 60018**
**(708) 298-9333**

**Established: 1974**
**Circulation: 80,000**

**Contact Person:** Michael Harris, Editor.

**Type of Publication:** Free music and entertainment magazine.

**Audience:** Teens to adults.

**How Frequently Published:** Monthly.

**Recently Published Articles:** Pieces about jazz, blues, and rock music on the local, national, and international level; also reviews, profiles, and columns about theater and film.

**Current Needs:** Articles covering topics listed above.

**Policy on Seasonal Pieces:** Six to seven weeks in advance.

**Usual Length Desired:** Reviews—250 words; cover stories—2500 words.

**Author Writes on Speculation or Assignment?** Can be either, but usually on assignment.

**Are Free Sample Copies Available?** Yes.

**Payment Information:**
    **Rate:** Reviews—$8; cover story—$100
    **Mode:** On publication.
    **Advance Possible?** Rarely.

**Rights Policy:** Buys first North American serial rights.

**How to Contact:** Send query and clips.

**What Not to Do:** Phone or send query without clips.

**Time Needed for Reply:** Two to six weeks.

**Does Author Supply Photos?** Sometimes, but not necessary.

**Advice for Authors:** Illinois Entertainer is looking for good music-oriented writers with diverse capabilities.

# INSIDER

Innate Graphics, Inc.
4124 Oakton Street
Skokie, Illinois 60076          **Established: 1984**
(708) 673-3458                  **Circulation: 750,000**

**Contact Person:** Sarah Fister, Managing Editor.

**Type of Publication:** Entertainment/career information magazine.

**Audience:** College-age (i.e., 18-27) young adults.

**How Frequently Published:** Monthly.

**Recently Published Articles:** Stories and profiles of young people poised for successful careers in business, sports, and entertainment fields; music and book reviews; new products; campus life; career tips.

**Current Needs:** Articles with a national focus of interest to this audience.

**Policy on Seasonal Pieces:** Two months in advance.

**Usual Length Desired:** Features—1000 words; reviews—300 words.

**Author Writes on Speculation or Assignment?** Assignment, usually.

**Are Free Sample Copies Available?** Yes.

**Payment Information:**
    **Rate:** 1 cent per word, minimum.
    **Mode:** On publication.
    **Advance Possible?** Not usually.

**Rights Policy:** Buys all rights.

**How to Contact:** Send query, clips, and resume.

**What Not to Do:** Phone or send first-person essays.

**Time Needed for Reply:** One month.

**Does Author Supply Photos?** Yes, if possible.

**Advice for Authors:** Send for free writer's guidelines. Also, knowledge of AP style is very important.

# INSIDE SPORTS

**Century Publishing Company**
**990 Grove Street**
**Evanston, Illinois 60201**  **Established: 1978**
**(708) 491-6440**  **Circulation: 677,000**

**Contact Person:** Larry Burke, Senior Editor; James O'Connor, Managing Editor.

**Type of Publication:** Consumer magazine for those interested in professional and college sports.

**Audience:** General adult readership (mostly men).

**How Frequently Published:** Monthly.

**Recently Published Articles:** "Interview: Dennis Rodman"; "Sports Salaries: Rocketing Out of Control?"; "Baseball Preview."

**Current Needs:** Features about sports-related topics, emphasizing personalities and trends. Most articles deal with baseball, basketball, hockey, and professional and college football.

**Usual Length Desired:** 500 to 4000 words.

**Author Writes on Speculation or Assignment?** Can be either.

**Are Free Sample Copies Available?** No.

**Payment Information:**
　　**Rate:** Negotiable.
　　**Mode:** On acceptance.
　　**Advance Possible?** No.

**How to Contact:** Send written query or complete manuscript. Enclose a self-addressed, stamped envelope.

**What Not to Do:** Phone or include Inside Sports as part of a simultaneous submission.

**Time Needed for Reply:** Four weeks.

**Does Author Supply Photos?** No.

**Advice for Authors:** Please do not query the magazine about obvious ideas. Inside Sports concentrates on feature coverage and previews more than on event coverage.

# In These Times

**2040 N. Milwaukee Avenue, 2nd Floor**
**Chicago, Illinois 60647**       **Established: 1977**
**(312) 772-0100**                **Circulation: 20,000**

**Contact Person:** James Weinstein, Editor.

**Type of Publication:** National political news magazine.

**Audience:** Intellectuals, people on the left, and people involved in progressive activities.

**How Frequently Published:** 26 times per year.

**Recently Published Articles:** Articles about U. S. politics, budget, and defense; also Europe, women, minorities, culture.

**Current Needs:** Articles about issues pertaining to the American left.

**Usual Length Desired:** 500 to 2000 words.

**Author Writes on Speculation or Assignment?** Can be either.

**Are Free Sample Copies Available?** Yes.

**Payment Information:**
    **Rate:** Negotiable.
    **Mode:** Negotiable.
    **Advance Possible?** Negotiable.

**Rights Policy:** Buys first-time rights.

**How to Contact:**  Send query; may also phone.

**What Not to Do:** Drop in without an appointment.

**Time Needed for Reply:** Two weeks.

**Does Author Supply Photos?** Sometimes.

**Advice for Authors:** Read the magazine before querying.

# KEY THIS WEEK IN CHICAGO

**904 W. Blackhawk Street**
**Chicago, Illinois 60622**      **Established: 1920**
**(312) 943-0838**      **Circulation: 20,000**

**Contact Person:** Walter West, Publisher.

**Type of Publication:** Free visitors' guide distributed in area hotels.

**Audience:** Adult visitors to the Chicago area.

**How Frequently Published:** Weekly.

**Recently Published Articles:** Information about dining, nightlife, and shopping in Chicago.

**Current Needs:** Articles relevant to topics listed above.

**Policy on Seasonal Pieces:** At least 30 days in advance.

**Usual Length Desired:** 300 to 450 words.

**Author Writes on Speculation or Assignment?** Assignment.

**Are Free Sample Copies Available?** Yes.

**Payment Information:**
    **Rate:** Negotiable.
    **Mode:** Negotiable.
    **Advance Possible?** No.

**Rights Policy:** Negotiable.

**How to Contact:** Phone first to discuss current needs.

**What Not to Do:** Send complete manuscript without first discovering current needs.

**Time Needed for Reply:** Two to three weeks.

**Does Author Supply Photos?** Sometimes.

**Advice for Authors:** Articles should be either advertiser related or of interest to visitors to Chicago.

# LAKELAND BOATING

O'Meara-Brown Publications, Inc.
1560 Sherman Avenue, Suite 1220
Evanston, Illinois 60201                    Established: 1945
(708) 869-5400                              Circulation: 40,000

**Contact Person:** Randy Hess, Managing Editor.

**Type of Publication:** Magazine about recreational power boating in the Great Lakes region.

**Audience:** Adults interested in power boating.

**How Frequently Published:** 11 times per year (combined November/December issue).

**Recently Published Articles:** Destination articles, equipment analyses, weather stories, nostalgia pieces.

**Current Needs:** More of the same.

**Policy on Seasonal Pieces:** Two months in advance.

**Usual Length Desired:** 100 to 2500 words.

**Author Writes on Speculation or Assignment?** Can be either.

**Are Free Sample Copies Available?** No.

**Payment Information:**
  **Rate:** Negotiable.
  **Mode:** On publication.
  **Advance Possible?** No.

**Rights Policy:** Buys first North American serial rights.

**How to Contact:** Send query and clips.

**What Not to Do:** Phone.

**Time Needed for Reply:** Six to eight weeks.

**Does Author Supply Photos?** Yes, if possible.

**Advice for Authors:** Lakeland Boating covers power boating only. Writers should either be boaters or people who write like boaters.

# THE LION MAGAZINE

**Lions Clubs International**
**300 22nd Street**
**Oakbrook, Illinois 60521**
**(708) 571-5466**

**Established: 1918**
**Circulation: 600,000**

**Contact Person:** Robert Kleinfelder, Editor.

**Type of Publication:** Controlled circulation magazine filled with Lions Club news for service-minded people.

**Audience:** Members of Lions clubs; civic-minded businesspeople.

**How Frequently Published:** Ten times a year (once each in July/August and December/January.

**Recently Published Articles:** "Communicating with Children Under Six"; "Who Needs Whom the Most."

**Current Needs:** Articles about sight conservation (Lions Clubs' emphasis), social awareness, and the environment.

**Usual Length Desired:** 400 to 2500 words.

**Author Writes on Speculation or Assignment?** Assignment mostly.

**Are Free Sample Copies Available?** Yes.

**Payment Information:**
    **Rate:** $100 to $500 per article depending on length and quality.
    **Mode:** On acceptance.
    **Advance Possible?** No.

**Rights Policy:** Buys all rights.

**How to Contact:** Queries preferred but phone calls accepted.

**What Not to Do:** Send complete manuscript or drop in without an appointment.

**Time Needed for Reply:** Two to four weeks.

**Does Author Supply Photos?** Yes, with caption information; color transparencies or prints preferred.

**Advice for Authors:** The Lion Magazine publishes only one or two general interest articles in each issue. Investigate large-scale Lions' club service projects in your area. Avoid subjects with political or religious implications.

# MIDWEST OUTDOORS

**Midwest Outdoors, Ltd.**
**111 Shore Drive**
**Burr Ridge, Illinois 60521**       **Established: 1967**
**(312) 887-7722**       **Circulation: 48,000**

**Contact Person:** Gene Laulunen, Publisher.

**Type of Publications:** Magazine for outdoor enthusiasts in the region.

**Audience:** People interested in hunting, fishing, camping, and other outdoor sports.

**How Frequently Published:** Monthly.

**Recently Published Articles:** Articles about where and how to hunt, fish, and camp in the Midwest.

**Current Needs:** More of the same.

**Policy on Seasonal Pieces:** Two months in advance.

**Usual Length Desired:** 1000 to 1500 words.

**Author Writes on Speculation or Assignment?** Speculation.

**Are Free Sample Copies Available?** No, but free writer's guidelines are.

**Payment Information:**
   **Rate:** $20 to $30 per article.
   **Mode:** On publication.
   **Advance Possible?** No.

**Rights Policy:** Buys all rights.

**How to Contact:** Send manuscript or phone.

**What Not to Do:** Send query or drop in without an appointment.

**Time Needed for Reply:** Within three weeks.

**Does Author Supply Photos?** Yes; submit captions with photos.

**Advice for Authors:** Midwest Outdoors does not want new product information, book reviews, or articles like "My First Fishing Trip with Grandpa" or "How to Clean and Repair Equipment."

# NEW ART EXAMINER

**The Chicago New Art Association**
**1255 S. Wabash Avenue, 4th Floor**
**Chicago, Illinois 60605**          **Established: 1973**
**(312) 786-0200**          **Circulation: 5000**

**Contact Person:** Ann Wiens, Editor.

**Type of Publication:** Magazine about the visual arts.

**Audience:** Artists, dealers, critics, educators.

**How Frequently Published:** Ten times per year (September through June).

**Recently Published Articles:** "The End of Creative Imagination"; stories about artist-dealer contracts and legal rights; special crafts issue.

**Current Needs:** Reviews of exhibitions from all over the country; articles about current issues in the visual arts.

**Policy on Seasonal Pieces:** Three months in advance.

**Usual Length Desired:** 1500 words.

**Author Writes on Speculation or Assignment?** Can be either.

**Are Free Sample Copies Available?** No.

**Payment Information:**
    **Rate:** Reviews—$40; articles—$75 to $300.
    **Mode:** On publication.
    **Advance Possible?** No.

**Rights Policy:** Negotiable.

**How to Contact:** Send query with resume and writing sample.

**What Not to Do:** Phone or send unsolicited exhibition reviews.

**Time Needed for Reply:** Six to eight weeks.

**Does Author Supply Photos?** Yes, usually.

**Advice for Authors:** New Art Examiner is looking for good writers with an extensive knowledge of the art world.

# NORTH SHORE

**PB Communications**
**874 Green Bay Road**
**Winnetka, Illinois 60093**
**(708) 441-7892**

**Established: 1978**
**Circulation: 54,000**

**Contact Person:** Karen Titus, Managing Editor.

**Type of Publication:** General interest city/metro-area magazine.

**Audience:** Adults living in Chicago and its northern and northwestern suburbs.

**How Frequently Published:** Monthly.

**Recently Published Articles:** "Chicagoland Dining Guide"; "Doing Good: Volunteers of the Year"; "Suburban Grandparents"; "Realtors Views: How Much Is Your Home Worth Today?"

**Current Needs:** Articles about newsworthy people and subjects of current social significance—all relating to communities in Chicago's northern and northwestern suburbs.

**Policy on Seasonal Pieces:** Three months in advance.

**Usual Length Desired:** 1000 to 2000 words.

**Author Writes on Speculation or Assignment?** Assignment.

**Are Free Sample Copies Available?** Not usually.

**Payment Information:**
    **Rate:** $50 to $400 (average $200) per article.
    **Mode:** On publication.
    **Advance Possible?** No.

**Rights Policy:** Buys first North American serial rights.

**How to Contact:** Send query with a brief cover letter, resume, and clips. Enclose a self-addressed, stamped envelope.

**What Not to Do:** Send photocopied manuscript or drop in without an appointment.

**Time Needed for Reply:** Two months.

**Does Author Supply Photos?** Sometimes.

**Advice for Authors:** North Shore prefers writers who are thoroughly familiar with Chicago and its northern/ northwestern suburbs. Articles should contain plenty of anecdotal material and interesting quotes.

# THE ORBIT
**The Hadley School for the Blind**
**700 Elm Street, Box 299**
**Winnetka, Illinois 60093**
**(708) 446-8111** **Circulation: 9000**

**Contact Person:** Dawn Turco, Vice President/Educational Services.

**Type of Publication:** Magazine with news coverage and feature articles of interest to the blind.

**Audience:** Students, both present and past, of the school; also professionals in fields related to blindness.

**How Frequently Published:** Twice per year (January and July).

**Recently Published Articles:** "Senior Citizen Exemplifies Lifelong Learning"; "Hadley Student Studies in the Wilderness"; "'Good Morning, Hadley School.'"

**Current Needs:** Any material with reference or of interest to the blind.

**Policy on Seasonal Pieces:** Two months in advance.

**Usual Length Desired:** 200 words.

**Author Writes on Speculation or Assignment?** Assignment.

**Are Free Sample Copies Available?** Yes.

**Payment Information:** Pays in copies of the issue in which contributor's work appears.

**Rights Policy:** Author retains rights.

**How to Contact:** Send query; may also phone.

**What Not to Do:** Drop in without an appointment.

**Time Needed for Reply:** Two months.

**Does Author Supply Photos?** No.

**Advice for Authors:** The Hadley School is interested in any material about the blind.

# THE ORIGINAL ART REPORT

P. O. Box 1641
Chicago, Illinois 60690
(312) 588-6897                              Established: 1967

**Contact Person:** Frank Salantrie, Editor and Publisher.

**Type of Publication:** Six-page newsletter about the visual arts condition.

**Audience:** Persons involved with various aspects of the visual arts.

**How Frequently Published:** Irregularly.

**Recently Published Articles:** Pieces about the political, economic, and social conditions affecting artists and society.

**Current Needs:** More of the same, all based on thorough investigation and displaying the writer's interpretive analysis and personal convictions.

**Usual Length Desired:** 500 words maximum.

**Author Writes on Speculation or Assignment?** Can be either.

**Are Free Sample Copies Available?** Yes. Enclose a self-addressed, stamped envelope with request.

**Payment Information:**
    **Rate:** 1 cent per word.
    **Mode:** On publication.
    **Advance Possible?** No.

**Rights Policy:** Author can retain rights.

**How to Contact:** Send query or manuscript. In your letter, mention how you first heard about The Original Art Report.

**What Not to Do:** Phone or drop in without an appointment.

**Time Needed for Reply:** Two weeks.

**Does Author Supply Photos?** No; publication does not use photos.

**Advice for Authors:** Queries are always welcome. The Original Art Report is looking for original writers with strong interests or background in the visual arts.

# P-Form: Performance Art Magazine

**756 N. Milwaukee Avenue**
**Chicago, Illinois 60622**  **Established: 1986**
**(312) 666-7737**  **Circulation: 2000**

**Contact Person:** Kenneth Thompson, Managing Editor.

**Type of Publication:** Art magazine.

**Audience:** Artists and people who appreciate performance art.

**How Frequently Published:** Quarterly.

**Recently Published Articles:** Pieces about performance-art forms, installations, video art; also interviews, national reviews, and special issues about music, performance art, and pedagogy.

**Current Needs:** Anything about conceptually based art forms.

**Policy on Seasonal Pieces:** Two months in advance.

**Usual Length Desired:** 1000 to 4000 words.

**Author Writes on Speculation or Assignment?** Can be either.

**Are Free Sample Copies Available?** Yes. Enclose a self-addressed, stamped envelope with request.

**Payment Information:** Two copies of the issue in which writer's work appears.

**Rights Policy:** Author retains rights.

**How to Contact:** Send query and clips; can also phone with story idea(s).

**What Not to Do:** Send poetry.

**Time Needed for Reply:** Three months maximum.

**Does Author Supply Photos?** Appreciated if possible, but not mandatory.

**Advice for Authors:** P-Form offers a national forum to writers who are just starting out.

# PLAYBOY

680 N. Lake Shore Drive
Chicago, Illinois 60611          **Established: 1953**
(312) 751-8000                   **Circulation: 3.4 million**

**Contact Person:** Nonfiction—Peter Moore or Stephen Randall; fiction—Alice K. Turner, Fiction Editor.

**Type of Publication:** Men's entertainment magazine.

**Audience:** Primarily men.

**How Frequently Published:** Monthly.

**Recently Published Articles:** "All Eyes on Court TV"; "Calvin Klein"; "Literary Golf."

**Current Needs:** Articles on politics, music, personalities, business, sports, and science. Also timely humor, exposes, and fiction.

**Policy on Seasonal Pieces:** Five to six months in advance.

**Usual Length Desired:** 4000 to 6000 words.

**Author Writes on Speculation or Assignment?** On assignment for nonfiction; on speculation for fiction.

**Are Free Sample Copies Available?** No, but writer's guidelines are.

**Payment Information:**
　　**Rate:** $3,500 for a standard nonfiction article.
　　**Mode:** On acceptance.
　　**Advance Possible?** Yes, if writer is working on assignment.

**Rights Policy:** Buys all rights.

**How to Contact:** For nonfiction article, send brief query with a writing sample to nonfiction department; for fiction, send complete manuscript to fiction editor; send filler items to Upfront After Hours. Enclose a self-addressed, stamped envelope.

**What Not to Do:** Phone, fax, or send multiple or simultaneous submissions.

**Time Needed for Reply:** Four to six weeks.

**Does Author Supply Photos?** No.

**Advice for Authors:** Read a current issue for insight into Playboy's tastes and judgment. Extremely experimental stories and outright pornography have their place but not in Playboy.

# PLUSVOICE

**29 S. LaSalle Street, Suite 1150**
**Chicago, Illinois 60603**  **Established: 1993**
**(312) 357-0200**  **Circulation: 75,000**

**Contact Person:** Brett Grodeck, Editor.

**Type of Publication:** Nonprofit health and lifestyle magazine for and about people infected with—and affected by—the HIV virus.

**Audience:** HIV-positive people and those who support them.

**How Frequently Published:** Bimonthly.

**Recently Published Articles:** Profile of Ann Copeland (co-founder of the advocacy group Women at Risk); medical advice about choosing an HIV specialist; interview with national AIDS policy coordinator Kristine Gebbie.

**Current Needs:** Profiles and articles regarding policy issues and HIV.

**Policy on Seasonal Pieces:** Six weeks to two months in advance.

**Usual Length Desired:** 1000 to 1500 words.

**Author Writes on Speculation or Assignment?** Can be either.

**Are Free Sample Copies Available?** Yes, but only to qualified individuals who submit queries.

**Payment Information:**
    **Rate:** Negotiable.
    **Mode:** Negotiable.
    **Advance Possible?** No.

**Rights Policy:** Negotiable.

**How to Contact:** Send resume and writing samples; may also send complete manuscript.

**What Not to Do:** Phone or drop in without an appointment.

**Time Needed for Reply:** One month.

**Does Author Supply Photos?** Depends on the piece.

**Advice for Authors:** Stories should have a positive spin, neither too morose nor too technical. As a nonprofit magazine, PlusVoice appreciates pro bono stories and story ideas.

# THE ROTARIAN

Rotary International
1560 Sherman Avenue
Evanston, Illinois 60201
(708) 866-3000

**Established: 1911**
**Circulation: 530,000**

**Contact Person:** Charles Pratt, Managing Editor.

**Type of Publication:** Official publication of Rotary International, a worldwide service organization.

**Audience:** Mostly, but not exclusively, members of Rotary clubs.

**How Frequently Published:** Monthly.

**Recently Published Articles:** "The Windy World of Kites"; "Can the City Survive?"; "A Portrait of Norway"; "Telephones of Tomorrow."

**Current Needs:** Articles about aspects of business (especially management), travel, and medical breakthroughs.

**Usual Length Desired:** Departments—800 to 1000 words; features— 1200 to 1700 words.

**Policy on Seasonal Pieces:** Three months in advance.

**Author Writes on Speculation or Assignment?** Speculation, generally.

**Are Free Sample Copies Available?** Yes.

**Payment Information:**
    **Rate:** $100 to $1,000, depending on article length.
    **Mode:** On acceptance.
    **Advance Possible?** No.

**Rights Policy:** Negotiable, although the magazine prefers to buy all rights.

**How to Contact:** Send a detailed query. Specify any connection with Rotary.

**What Not to Do:** Phone.

**Time Needed for Reply:** Two to three weeks.

**Does Author Supply Photos?** Yes, usually.

**Advice for Authors:** The main reason for rejecting a story or story idea is that it is too U. S. oriented to be of interest to Rotary's international audience. In addition, writers must stay away from political, religious, and one-sided controversial issues since the publication's audience includes all races, religions, and nationalities.

# SOCCER DIGEST
**Century Publishing Company**
**990 Grove Street**
**Evanston, Illinois 60201**
**(708) 491-6440**                    **Established: 1978**

**Contact Person:** Larry Burke, Senior Editor; James O'Connor, Managing Editor.

**Type of Publication:** Magazine covering professional soccer.

**Audience:** General adult readership (mostly men).

**How Frequently Published:** Bimonthly.

**Recently Published Articles:** "The U. S. Defense Rests—Uneasily"; "Romania is Out for Revenge"; "World Cup Qualifying Was Electric"; "Colombia Joins the South American Hierarchy."

**Current Needs:** Features about personalities and trends in soccer.

**Usual Length Desired:** 500 to 1500 words.

**Author Writes on Speculation or Assignment?** Can be either.

**Are Free Sample Copies Available?** No.

**Payment Information:**
    **Rate:** Negotiable.
    **Mode:** On acceptance.
    **Advance Possible?** No.

**How to Contact:** Send written query or complete manuscript. Enclose a self-addressed, stamped envelope.

**What Not to Do:** Phone or include Soccer Digest as part of a simultaneous submission.

**Time Needed for Reply:** Four weeks.

**Does Author Supply Photos?** No.

**Advice for Authors:** Please do not query the magazine about obvious ideas. Soccer Digest focuses on features and previews more than on event coverage.

# TODAY'S CHICAGO WOMAN

**Leigh Communications, Inc.**
**233 E. Ontario Street, Suite 1300**
**Chicago, Illinois 60611**          **Established: 1982**
**(312) 951-7600**          **Circulation: 160,000**

**Contact Person:** Pam Levy, Managing Editor.

**Type of Publication:** Feature oriented magazine.

**Audience:** Professional women in the Chicago area.

**How Frequently Published:** Monthly.

**Recently Published Articles:** Personality profiles and articles on fashion, health, and politics.

**Current Needs:** More of the same.

**Usual Length Desired:** 750 words.

**Author Writes on Speculation or Assignment?** Assignment.

**Are Free Sample Copies Available?** Yes.

**Payment Information:**
    **Rate:** Varies.
    **Mode:** Within 30 days of acceptance.
    **Advance Possible?** No.

**Rights Policy:** Buys all rights.

**How to Contact:** Send query and clips.

**What Not to Do:** Phone or drop in without an appointment.

**Time Needed for Reply:** Ten days.

**Does Author Supply Photos?** Yes, if possible.

**Advice for Authors:** Today's Chicago Woman is interested in seeing work from good journalistic-style writers.

# TravelHost

1 E. Wacker Drive
Chicago, Illinois 60601      **Established: 1977**
(312) 828-9112               **Circulation: 20,000**

**Contact Person:** Thomas Higgins, Editor.

**Type of Publication:** In-the-guest-room hotel magazine for the greater Chicago area.

**Audience:** Travelers staying in Chicago-area hotels and motels.

**How Frequently Published:** Weekly.

**Recently Published Articles:** "Spotlight" (show previews); "Chicago: Your Kind of Town" (column); restaurant reviews.

**Current Needs:** Articles that tell visitors what to do and see in the area.

**Policy on Seasonal Pieces:** Ten days in advance.

**Usual Length Desired:** 800 to 1100 words.

**Author Writes on Speculation or Assignment?** Assignment.

**Are Free Sample Copies Available?** Yes.

**Payment Information:**
    **Rate:** Varies on a per article basis depending on quality and length.
    **Mode:** On acceptance.
    **Advance Possible?** Yes, for expenses incurred.

**Rights Policy:** Negotiable.

**How to Contact:** Send query and clips; may also phone first.

**What Not to Do:** Send complete manuscript or drop in without an appointment.

**Time Needed for Reply:** Two to four weeks.

**Does Author Supply Photos?** Yes.

**Advice for Authors:** TravelHost needs writers whose style is light and entertaining, with a touch of humor.

# VANTAGE
**The Signature Group/Cade Communications**
**70 W. Hubbard Street, Suite 201**

| | |
|---|---|
| **Chicago, Illinois 60610** | **Established: 1984** |
| **(312) 644-4485** | **Circulation: 500,000** |

**Contact Person:** Ann Cade, Editor-in-Chief.

**Type of Publication:** Magazine for active senior citizens.

**Audience:** People 55 years of age and older.

**How Frequently Published:** Every other month.

**Recently Published Articles:** Articles about food, health, entertainment, gardening, sports, leisure activities, and ways to save money.

**Current Needs:** Articles about clever, unusual, totally honest ways to make money—e.g., as an artisan.

**Policy on Seasonal Pieces:** Six months in advance.

**Usual Length Desired:** 1000 words.

**Author Writes on Speculation or Assignment?** Can be either.

**Are Free Sample Copies Available?** Yes.

**Payment Information:**
    **Rate:** $250 to $350 per article.
    **Mode:** On publication.
    **Advance Possible?** No.

**Rights Policy:** Buys first rights.

**How to Contact:** Send query and clips.

**What Not to Do:** Phone.

**Time Needed for Reply:** Six to eight weeks.

**Does Author Supply Photos?** Yes, if possible. Vantage occasionally pays extra for photos, depending upon the circumstances.

**Advice for Authors:** Vantage is looking for articles that relate unusual experiences of people 55 and older and that provide personal and practical money-saving advice for people on fixed incomes.

# VEGETARIAN TIMES

P. O. Box 570
Oak Park, Illinois 60303          **Established: 1974**
(708) 848-8100                    **Circulation: 310,000**

**Contact Person:** Terry Christofferson, Editorial Assistant.

**Type of Publication:** Consumer magazine covering health and all aspects of vegetarianism.

**Audience:** Adults interested in health and vegetarianism.

**How Frequently Published:** Monthly.

**Recently Published Articles:** "Basics of Vegetarian Cooking"; "The Politics of Nutrition"; "What's the Score on Osteoporosis?"

**Current Needs:** Articles about animal rights, fitness, nutrition, and the environment.

**Policy on Seasonal Pieces:** Three months in advance.

**Usual Length Desired:** 2000 to 3000 words.

**Author Writes on Speculation or Assignment?** Can be either.

**Are Free Sample Copies Available?** No.

**Payment Information:**
    **Rate:** Negotiable.
    **Mode:** On publication.
    **Advance Possible?** Negotiable.

**Rights Policy:** Buys all rights.

**How to Contact:** Send query and clips.

**What Not to Do:** Phone or drop in without an appointment.

**Time Needed for Reply:** Usually about four weeks.

**Does Author Supply Photos?** No.

**Advice for Authors:** Study the magazine before sending material.

# WINDY CITY SPORTS MAGAZINE

Chicago Sports Resources, Inc.
1450 W. Randolph Street
Chicago, Illinois 60607
(312) 421-1551

**Established: 1986**
**Circulation: 100,000**

**Contact Person:** Shelley Berryhill, Editor.

**Type of Publication:** Magazine covering amateur sports in the Chicago area.

**Audience:** General adult readership.

**How Frequently Published:** Monthly.

**Recently Published Articles:** Articles and columns about running, cycling, triathalons, health clubs, volleyball, climbing, kayaking, and skiing.

**Current Needs:** Shorter pieces about nutrition, women in amateur sports, sports medicine.

**Policy on Seasonal Pieces:** Two months in advance.

**Usual Length Desired:** 500 to 1200 words.

**Author Writes on Speculation or Assignment?** Usually assignment.

**Are Free Sample Copies Available?** Yes. Enclose a self-addressed, stamped envelope ($2 worth of stamps) with request.

**Payment Information:**
> **Rate:** Usually 10 cents a word.
> **Mode:** On acceptance for assignment; on publication for work submitted on speculation.
> **Advance Possible?** No.

**Rights Policy:** Buys first-time, one-time rights.

**How to Contact:** Send query stating very specific story idea(s); include clips.

**What Not to Do:** Suggest stories about professional sports.

**Time Needed for Reply:** Two weeks.

**Does Author Supply Photos?** Photos are appreciated, and writers who supply publishable photos receive additional compensation.

**Advice for Authors:** Please keep in mind that Windy City Sports is a magazine about amateur sports *only.* An editorial calendar is available upon request.

# YOUR MONEY

**Consumers Digest**
**5707 N. Lincoln Avenue**
**Chicago, Illinois 60659**            **Established: 1979**
**(312) 275-3590**                     **Circulation: 350,000**

**Contact Person:** Dennis Fertig, Editor.

**Type of Publication:** Magazine about personal finance and investments.

**Audience:** Individual investors.

**How Frequently Published:** Every two months.

**Recently Published Articles:** Articles about mutual funds, stocks, charitable giving, taxes, insurance products, and college and retirement planning.

**Current Needs:** Coverage of business opportunities and information for the neophyte investor.

**Policy on Seasonal Pieces:** Three months in advance.

**Usual Length Desired:** 2000 to 2500 words.

**Author Writes on Speculation or Assignment?** Assignment.

**Payment Information:**
    **Rate:** 35 cents a word, minimum.
    **Mode:** 30 days after acceptance.
    **Advance Possible?** No.

**Rights Policy:** Buys first North American serial rights.

**How to Contact:** Send query and/or outline with cover letter and credentials.

**What Not to Do:** Phone or send complete manuscript (paper or disk).

**Time Needed for Reply:** Three months.

**Does Author Supply Photos?** Sometimes.

**Advice for Authors:** Your Money is interested in stories that focus on real people and offer helpful suggestions.

# ANOTHER CHICAGO MAGAZINE
3709 N. Kenmore Avenue
Chicago, Illinois 60613          **Established: 1977**
(312) 248-7665                   **Circulation: 10,000**

**Contact Person:** Barry Silesky, Senior Editor.

**Type of Publication:** Literary magazine that includes interviews, essays, and poetry.

**Audience:** Poets, short-story writers, critics, and anyone who appreciates literature.

**How Frequently Published:** Twice a year.

**Recently Published Articles:** Works by Diane Wakoski, Charles Simic, Sesshu Foster, Sharon Dubiago, Sydney Chadwick, and Albert Goldbarth, among others.

**Current Needs:** Fiction, poetry, translations, and features that live in the world.

**Usual Length Desired:** Prose—5,000 words; poetry—no length restrictions.

**Author Writes on Speculation or Assignment?** Mostly on speculation.

**Are Free Sample Copies Available?** No.

**Payment Information:**
    **Rate:** Ranges from $5 to $50 plus one year's subscription.
    **Mode:** On acceptance.
    **Advance Possible?** No.

**Rights Policy:** Rights revert to author on publication with the understanding that Another Chicago Magazine receives a first publication acknowledgment with all future use.

**How to Contact:** Send manuscript.

**What Not to Do:** Phone.

**Time Needed for Reply:** Average of two to three months.

**Does Author Supply Photos?** No.

**Advice for Authors:** Before submitting a manuscript, request a copy of the writer's guidelines and examine back issues.

# CHICAGO REVIEW
**University of Chicago**
**5801 S. Kenwood Avenue**
**Chicago, Illinois 60637**              **Established: 1946**
**(312) 702-0887**                        **Circulation: 2500**

**Contact Person:** David Nicholls, Editor.

**Type of Publication:** General circulation contemporary literary magazine.

**Audience:** College students and adults.

**How Frequently Published:** Quarterly.

**Recently Published Articles:** Works by Luis Rodriguez, Paula Gunn Allen, Meena Alexander, Billy Collins, among others.

**Current Needs:** Reviews, poetry, fiction, interviews, drama, translations, and essays on contemporary culture.

**Policy on Seasonal Pieces:** Two to three months in advance.

**Usual Length Desired:** 20 typed (double-spaced) pages maximum.

**Author Writes on Speculation or Assignment?** Speculation, usually.

**Are Free Sample Copies Available?** No.

**Payment Information:** Three copies of the Review and a one-volume subscription.

**Rights Policy:** Chicago Review holds the copyright for the author, returning it upon request.

**How to Contact:** Send query or manuscript. Photocopy OK, but indicate if multiple submission. Enclose a self-addressed, stamped envelope.

**What Not to Do:** Phone or drop in without an appointment.

**Time Needed for Reply:** Two to three months.

**Does Author Supply Photos?** Rarely.

**Advice for Authors:** Chicago Review is known for mixing the work of unknowns with that of established authors. Writers whose works are engaged in interpreting contemporary life are especially encouraged.

# THE CREATIVE WOMAN
The TAPP Group
126 East Wing Street, Suite 288
Arlington Heights, Illinois 60004      Established: 1977
(708) 255-1232                        Circulation: 475

**Contact Person:** Margaret Choudhury, Editor.

**Type of Publication:** A magazine of women's achievements in many areas.

**Audience:** Mainly women, but some men, too.

**How Frequently Published:** Quarterly.

**Recently Published Articles:** Fiction, poetry, and nonfiction (book reviews, article about women inventors, film directors, and producers), and original artwork.

**Current Needs:** More of the same.

**Policy on Seasonal Pieces:** Six months in advance.

**Usual Length Desired:** Generally 2000 words for prose pieces.

**Author Writes on Speculation or Assignment?** Can be either.

**Are Free Sample Copies Available?** No.

**Payment Information:**
   **Rate:** Negotiable.
   **Mode:** On acceptance.
   **Advance Possible?** No.

**Rights Policy:** Buys first publication rights.

**How to Contact:** Send query and manuscript. If submitting artwork, send copies only.

**What Not to Do:** Include The Creative Woman as part of a simultaneous submission.

**Time Needed for Reply:** Six weeks.

**Does Author Supply Photos?** Sometimes.

**Advice for Authors:** Don't be discouraged if your work is rejected. A rejection may merely indicate a backlog of material, not that your work wasn't liked.

# THE CRITIC

TMA
**205 W. Monroe Street**
**Chicago, Illinois 60606**          **Established: 1985**
**(312) 609-8880**                    **Circulation: 2000**

**Contact Person:** Julie Bridge, Editor.

**Type of Publication:** Literary magazine.

**Audience:** College-educated Catholics.

**How Frequently Published:** Quarterly.

**Recently Published Articles:** Author profiles, critical commentary, poetry, short fiction, essays, short humor pieces, cartoons.

**Current Needs:** Good short fiction.

**Policy on Seasonal Pieces:** Four months in advance.

**Author Writes on Speculation or Assignment?** Can be either. Usually speculation for fiction and assignment for nonfiction.

**Are Free Sample Copies Available?** No.

**Payment Information:**
    **Rate:** Negotiable.
    **Mode:** On acceptance.
    **Advance Possible?** No.

**Rights Policy:** Buys first-time rights; rights then revert to author.

**How to Contact:** Send manuscript for fiction; send query for nonfiction. Enclose a self-addressed, stamped envelope.

**What Not to Do:** Phone.

**Time Needed for Reply:** Two months.

**Does Author Supply Photos?** Depends on material.

**Advice for Authors:** The Critic is not currently seeking poetry. Although published works need not pertain directly to some aspect of Catholicism, authors should keep the magazine's readership in mind.

# NEW AMERICAN WRITING

2920 W. Pratt Boulevard
Chicago, Illinois 60645          **Established: 1986**
(312) 764-1048                   **Circulation: 4000**

**Contact Person:** Paul Hoover and Maxine Chernoff, Editors.

**Type of Publication:** Literary journal with an emphasis on poetry.

**Audience:** General adult readership.

**How Frequently Published:** Twice a year.

**Recently Published Articles:** Works by Michael Palmer, Charles Simic, Ann Lauterbach, Wanda Coleman, and Robert Creeley.

**Current Needs:** Poetry, essays, translations, and short stories.

**Usual Length Desired:** Poetry—three to five pages; prose—no limit.

**Author Writes on Speculation or Assignment?** Can be either.

**Are Free Sample Copies Available?** No.

**Payment Information:**
   **Rate:** $5 to $10 per page plus two copies of the journal in which the work appears.
   **Mode:** On publication.
   **Advance Possible?** No.

**Rights Policy:** Buys all rights but will readily reassign on request.

**How to Contact:** Send query.

**What Not to Do:** Phone.

**Time Needed for Reply:** One to three weeks.

**Does Author Supply Photos?** No.

**Advice for Authors:** Primarily a poetry magazine, New American Writing is a good freelance market for poets. Since the magazine has a specific taste, potential authors would be wise to examine a past issue before proceeding.

# OTHER VOICES
Department of English (M/C 162)
University of Illinois at Chicago
Chicago, Illinois 60607

Established: 1984
Circulation: 1200

**Contact Person:** Sharon Fiffer, Co-Editor; Lois Hauselman, Co-Editor.

**Type of Publication:** Literary journal of fiction only: short stories and excerpts from novels.

**Audience:** Literate adults.

**How Frequently Published:** Semiannually (spring and autumn).

**Recently Published Articles:** Fiction by Melissa Banks, Edith Pearlman, and Elaine Palencia.

**Current Needs:** Short stories. Ineptitude and murkiness are the only taboos.

**Policy on Seasonal Pieces:** Works are read between October 1 and April 1.

**Usual Length Desired:** Preferably under 5000 words.

**Author Writes on Speculation or Assignment?** Speculation.

**Are Free Sample Copies Available?** No.

**Payment Information:** Two copies of issue in which contributor's work appears.

**Rights Policy:** Copyright reverts to author upon publication.

**How to Contact:** Send manuscript; enclose a self-addressed, stamped envelope.

**What Not to Do:** Send work between April 1 and October 1; manuscripts submitted during that time will be returned unread.

**Time Needed for Reply:** Ten to twelve weeks.

**Does Author Supply Photos?** No.

**Advice for Authors:** An interesting market for quality fiction, Other Voices is dedicated to publishing original, fresh, diverse stories and novel excerpts by new—as well as recognized—talent.

# POETRY

**Modern Poetry Association**
**60 W. Walton Street**
**Chicago, Illinois 60610**          **Established: 1912**
**(312) 280-4870**          **Circulation: 7500**

**Contact Person:** Joseph Parisi, Editor.

**Type of Publication:** Poetry magazine.

**Audience:** Anyone interested in reading poetry.

**How Frequently Published:** Monthly.

**Current Needs:** Verse of all forms and subject themes.

**Policy on Seasonal Pieces:** Six months in advance.

**Usual Length Desired:** From one to four poems.

**Author Writes on Speculation or Assignment?** Speculation.

**Are Free Sample Copies Available?** No.

**Payment Information:**
    **Rate:** $2 per line.
    **Mode:** On publication.
    **Advance Possible?** No.

**Rights Policy:** Buys all rights, but will transfer rights back to author on request.

**How to Contact:** Send original manuscript. Enclose a self-addressed, stamped envelope.

**What Not to Do:** Phone or drop in without an appointment.

**Time Needed for Reply:** Three months.

**Does Author Supply Photos?** Not necessary.

**Advice for Authors:** Poetry consistently publishes the work of new people. It also awards prizes for the best verse published in the magazine, with awards ranging from $100 to $1000. Poets should submit neatly typed verse never before published.

# POETRY EAST

**DePaul University, Department of English**
**802 W. Belden Avenue**
**Chicago, Illinois 60614**          **Established: 1980**
**(312) 362-5114**          **Circulation: 1800**

**Contact Person:** Richard Jones, Editor; Marilyn Woitel, Managing Editor.

**Type of Publication:** Poetry and arts journal.

**Audience:** Poets and other people who love poetry.

**How Frequently Published:** Twice annually, spring and autumn.

**Recently Published Articles:** "Praises": prose commentary by contemporary poets about those poets whose work inspired them; art portfolio in the one open issue per year.

**Current Needs:** Poetry and art are always encouraged.

**Policy on Seasonal Pieces:** 18 months in advance.

**Usual Length Desired:** No limits on poetry.

**Author Writes on Speculation or Assignment?** Speculation.

**Are Free Sample Copies Available?** No.

**Payment Information:** Two copies of the issue in which contributor's work appears.

**Rights Policy:** Rights revert to the contributor, with the understanding that Poetry East will receive credit on any reprints.

**How to Contact:** Send manuscript.

**What Not to Do:** Send long (e.g., 30-page) prose manuscripts.

**Time Needed for Reply:** Three months.

**Does Author Supply Photos?** Yes, if appropriate.

**Advice for Authors:** Poetry East is a politically informed and aware journal. Writers should submit work that is as timely as possible. Keep in mind, too, that a few fine works will be better received than many mediocre ones.

# PRIMAVERA

P. O. Box 37-7547
Chicago, Illinois 60637          **Established: 1975**
(312) 324-5920                    **Circulation: 800**

**Contact Person:** Board of Editors.

**Type of Publication:** Literary and arts anthology reflecting women's experiences.

**Audience:** Primarily women, but some men as well.

**How Frequently Published:** Annually.

**Recently Published Articles:** "Poetry in Translation" (works from India, Poland, Bangladesh, and Pakistan); "Playing the Titanic" (story); "In the Backyard" (poem); five collages by Carol Padberg (art).

**Current Needs:** Stories and poems expressing women's outlooks.

**Policy on Seasonal Pieces:** Three months in advance.

**Usual Length Desired:** 3000 words maximum for fiction; no more than six poems per submission.

**Author Writes on Speculation or Assignment?** Speculation.

**Are Free Sample Copies Available?** No.

**Payment Information:** Two volumes in which contributor's work appears.

**Rights Policy:** Buys first-time rights which then revert to author.

**How to Contact:** Send manuscript; enclose a self-addressed, stamped envelope.

**What Not to Do:** Phone.

**Time Needed for Reply:** One week to four months.

**Does Author Supply Photos?** Yes, if appropriate.

**Advice for Authors:** Primavera needs original and well-crafted pieces. Though the anthology is about women's viewpoints, men are encouraged to send relevant work. No simultaneous submissions, please.

# RAMBUNCTIOUS REVIEW
**Rambunctious Press, Inc.**
**1221 W. Pratt Boulevard**
**Chicago, Illinois 60626**

**Established: 1982**
**Circulation: 500**

**Contact Person:** Mary Dellutri, Richard Goldman, Beth Hausler, and Nancy Lennon, Co-Editors.

**Type of Publication:** Literary magazine featuring fiction, poetry, photography, and graphic arts.

**Audience:** Readers interested in literary forms.

**How Frequently Published:** Once per year.

**Recently Published Articles:** Poetry by Pam Miller and Dick Calisch; fiction by Hugh Fox.

**Current Needs:** Short fiction, poetry, photography, and graphic arts.

**Usual Length Desired:** One to five poems; fiction no longer than 12 typed (double-spaced) pages.

**Author Writes on Speculation or Assignment?** Speculation.

**Are Free Sample Copies Available?** No.

**Payment Information:** Two copies of issue in which contributor's work appears.

**Rights Policy:** Rights revert to author following initial publication.

**How to Contact:** Send manuscript anytime between the beginning of September until the end of May. Enclose a self-addressed, stamped envelope.

**What Not to Do:** Submit work in June, July, or August; drop in without an appointment.

**Time Needed for Reply:** Three months.

**Does Author Supply Photos?** No.

**Advice for Authors:** Rambunctious Review welcomes work of high literary quality from both established and unpublished authors.

# RHINO

**8403 W. Normal Avenue**
**Niles, Illinois 60648**       **Established: 1976**
**(708) 823-6721**       **Circulation: 300**

**Contact Person:** Kay Meier, Co-Editor (address above); Don Hoffman, Co-Editor (1808 N. Larrabee Street, Chicago, Illinois 60614).

**Type of Publication:** Literary journal, consisting primarily of poetry with some short fiction.

**Audience:** People interested in poetry and literary prose.

**How Frequently Published:** Once per year.

**Recently Published Articles:** Poetry by Debra Bruce, John Jacob, and John Dickson.

**Current Needs:** Poetry and short prose.

**Usual Length Desired:** Three to five poems; three typed (double-spaced) pages for short prose.

**Author Writes on Speculation or Assignment?** Speculation.

**Are Free Sample Copies Available?** No, but writer's guidelines are.

**Payment Information:** One copy of issue in which contributor's work appears.

**Rights Policy:** All rights remain with author.

**How to Contact:** Send manuscript between October 1 and April 1.

**What Not to Do:** Submit work between April 1 and October 1.

**Time Needed for Reply:** Six months.

**Does Author Supply Photos?** No.

**Advice for Authors:** Rhino is looking for poems with a fresh point of view. They should show authentic insight and emotion and be carefully crafted. The magazine is not interested in submissions of sentimental pieces.

To enter Rhino's annual poetry contest, send poems, entry fee ($3 per poem for up to three poems, $10 for four poems), and a self-addressed, stamped envelope by April 1. First prize—$100; second prize—$50; honorable mention (two)—$25 each.

# TriQuarterly

**Northwestern University**
**2020 Ridge Avenue**
**Evanston, Illinois 60208**          **Established: 1964**
**(708) 491-7614**                    **Circulation: 2500**

**Contact Person:** Reginald Gibbons and Susan Hahn, Editors.

**Type of Publication:** An international journal of arts, writing, and cultural inquiry.

**Audience:** Adults with strong literary interests.

**How Frequently Published:** Three times a year (winter, spring/summer, autumn).

**Recently Published Articles:** Works by Janet Kauffman, Sterling Plumpp, Robert Pinsky, Alberto Savinio, and Wislawa Szymborska.

**Current Needs:** Short stories, poetry, novellas, essays of a general cultural nature.

**Usual Length Desired:** No length limitations.

**Author Writes on Speculation or Assignment?** Speculation.

**Are Free Sample Copies Available?** No.

**Payment Information:**
    **Rate:** Varies.
    **Mode:** On publication.
    **Advance Possible?** No.

**Rights Policy:** Buys first North American serial rights.

**How to Contact:** For essays, query first; for prose and poetry, send manuscript. Send photos or slides of artwork.

**What Not to Do:** Phone or send original artwork.

**Time Needed for Reply:** Eight to twelve weeks.

**Does Author Supply Photos?** Depends on piece.

**Advice for Authors:** TriQuarterly welcomes both known and unknown authors. The magazine is most interested in fiction and poetry; it is not looking for scholarly works, literary criticism, or complete novels.

# WHETSTONE
**Barrington Area Arts Council**
**P. O. Box 1266**
**Barrington, Illinois 60303**

**Established: 1982**
**Circulation: 600**

**Contact Person:** Jean Tolle, Co-Editor.

**Type of Publication:** Literary journal.

**Audience:** Adults with literary interests.

**How Frequently Published:** Annually.

**Recently Published Articles:** Works by Anne Brashler, Eleanore Devine, John Dickson, Tom Grimes, Edith Pearlman, and Alice Ryerson.

**Current Needs:** Quality poetry, short fiction, memoir, and parts of novels.

**Usual Length Desired:** Poetry—three to seven poems; prose—up to 25 typed (double-spaced) pages.

**Author Writes on Speculation or Assignment?** Speculation.

**Are Free Sample Copies Available?** No.

**Payment Information:**
    **Rate:** Varies.
    **Mode:** On publication.
    **Advance Possible?** No.

**Rights Policy:** Holds first North American serial rights; then rights revert to author.

**How to Contact:** Send manuscript; enclose a self-addressed, stamped envelope.

**Time Needed for Reply:** Three to four months.

**Does Author Supply Photos?** No.

**Advice for Authors:** Whetstone is the winner of eight Illinois Arts Council awards in the last six years. Work submitted for publication must meet a like standard. Authors must write from the heart.

# AIM: LITURGY RESOURCES

**J. S. Paluch Company, Inc.**
**3825 N. Willow Road**
**Schiller Park, Illinois 60176**
**(708) 678-9300**                              **Circulation: 16,000**

**Contact Person:** Alan Hommerding, Editor.

**Type of Publication:** Magazine about liturgy, pastoral planning, and parish ministry—primarily in the Roman Catholic Church.

**Audience:** Priests and ministers.

**How Frequently Published:** Quarterly.

**Recently Published Articles:** Themed issues focused on church music, Scriptures, and worship with children.

**Current Needs:** Short articles on religion, especially worship and liturgy in the Roman Catholic Church.

**Policy on Seasonal Pieces:** Six weeks in advance.

**Usual Length Desired:** 1000 words.

**Author Writes on Speculation or Assignment?** Assignment.

**Are Free Sample Copies Available?** Yes; enclose a self-addressed, stamped envelope with request.

**Payment Information:**
   **Rate:** $250.
   **Mode:** On acceptance.
   **Advance Possible?** No.

**Rights Policy:** Author retains rights.

**How to Contact:** Phone, send query, or send manuscript. Enclose a self-addressed, stamped envelope.

**What Not to Do:** Drop in without an appointment.

**Time Needed for Reply:** One month.

**Does Author Supply Photos?** Yes; submit black-and-white prints that relate to the text.

**Advice for Authors:** AIM wants articles of a practical—rather than theoretical—nature.

# ANGLICAN ADVANCE
**Episcopal Diocese of Chicago**
**65 E. Huron Street**
**Chicago, Illinois 60611**          **Established: 1885**
**(312) 751-4207**                    **Circulation: 48,000**

**Contact Person:** David Skidmore, Editor.

**Type of Publication:** Twenty-page tabloid.

**Audience:** Lay persons and clergy.

**How Frequently Published:** Seven times per year.

**Recently Published Articles:** Articles about sexual misconduct, church voluntary giving; interviews with significant leaders; coverage of the Parliament of World Religions; book reviews.

**Current Needs:** More of the same.

**Policy on Seasonal Pieces:** Two months in advance.

**Usual Length Desired:** 1500 words (features).

**Author Writes on Speculation or Assignment?** Can be either.

**Are Free Sample Copies Available?** Occasionally.

**Payment Information:** Two copies of issue in which contributor's work appears.

**Rights Policy:** Buys first rights.

**How to Contact:** Send query and outline.

**What Not to Do:** Send complete manuscript.

**Time Needed for Reply:** One month.

**Does Author Supply Photos?** Yes.

**Advice for Authors:** Anglican Advance does not actively solicit work from freelancers. Writers must be familiar with the Episcopal denomination and its current issues.

# BRIGADE LEADER

**Christian Service Brigade**
**P. O. Box 150**
**Wheaton, Illinois 60189**          **Established: 1960**
**(708) 665-0630**          **Circulation: 9000**

**Contact Person:** Deborah Christenson, Managing Editor.

**Type of Publication:** Magazine for Christian Service Brigade leaders.

**Audience:** Adult men—pastors and lay workers—who lead boys.

**How Frequently Published:** Quarterly.

**Recently Published Articles:** Theme issues about finances, prayer, sexual abuse of children.

**Current Needs:** Practical, family oriented articles about how men can relate to boys.

**Policy on Seasonal Pieces:** Three months in advance.

**Usual Length Desired:** 1500 words for nonfiction.

**Author Writes on Speculation or Assignment?** Mostly assignment.

**Are Free Sample Copies Available?** No.

**Payment Information:**
**Rate:** 5 to 10 cents per word.
**Mode:** On publication.
**Advance Possible?** No.

**Rights Policy:** Buys first rights or second reprint rights.

**How to Contact:** Send writing samples. Request writer's guidelines. Enclose a self-addressed, stamped envelope.

**What Not to Do:** Phone.

**Time Needed for Reply:** One week.

**Does Author Supply Photos?** Usually not.

**Advice for Authors:** Brigade Leader mostly works with those who are experts in their fields. It is looking for writers familiar with the Christian Service Brigade program.

# CHICAGO STUDIES

**Civitas Dei Foundation**
**P. O. Box 665**
**Mundelein, Illinois 60060**          **Established: 1962**
**(708) 566-1462**                              **Circulation: 7000**

**Contact Person:** Father George J. Dyer, Editor.

**Type of Publication:** Theological journal.

**Audience:** Roman Catholic adults interested in theological education.

**How Frequently Published:** Three times a year (April, August, November).

**Recently Published Articles:** Theme issues about moral theology, the Bible, comparative religions, catechism and ministry.

**Current Needs:** Articles dealing with theology, the Bible, canon law, and liturgy with a practical application to the grass roots church.

**Policy on Seasonal Pieces:** Twelve months in advance.

**Usual Length Desired:** 5000 words.

**Author Writes on Speculation or Assignment?** Can be either.

**Are Free Sample Copies Available?** No.

**Payment Information:**
    **Rate:** $75 to $100 per article depending on length.
    **Mode:** On acceptance.
    **Advance Possible?** No.

**Rights Policy:** Assumes all rights.

**How to Contact:** Request writer's guidelines. Then send manuscript. Photocopy OK. Enclose a self-addressed, stamped envelope.

**What Not to Do:** Phone, send query, or drop in without an appointment. In addition, do not send articles with footnotes; references must be incorporated into the text.

**Time Needed For Reply:** Three months.

**Does Author Supply Photos?** No.

**Advice For Authors:** Authors need not be members of the clergy, but they must be professionally qualified (i.e., possess an appropriate academic background) to present material in a nontechnical way.

# THE CHRISTIAN CENTURY

**The Christian Century Foundation**
**407 S. Dearborn Street, Suite 1405**
**Chicago, Illinois 60605**     **Established: 1884**
**(312) 427-5380**     **Circulation: 36,000**

**Contact Person:** Rev. James Wall, Editor.

**Type of Publication:** General circulation magazine presenting a Protestant ethical perspective.

**Audience:** Church people of liberal, progressive bent; clergy of various denominations, theologians, and university professors.

**How Frequently Published:** Weekly, except every other week during Christmas, Lent, and summer.

**Recently Published Articles:** "Clinton's Bully Pulpit: Spiritual Changes"; "New Uses of the Military: Legitimate Force"; "Mallway to Heaven? Religious Choice for Baby Boomers."

**Current Needs:** Theologically informed analysis of current issues, such as welfare reform, health care, Third World development, as well as reflections on spiritual life in contemporary society.

**Policy on Seasonal Pieces:** At least six weeks in advance.

**Usual Length Desired:** 3000 words maximum.

**Author Writes on Speculation or Assignment?** Can be either.

**Are Free Sample Copies Available?** Yes. Enclose a self-addressed, stamped envelope.

**Payment Information:**
    **Rate:** Up to $125 per article.
    **Mode:** On publication.
    **Advance Possible?** Rarely.

**Rights Policy:** Buys all rights but offers generous reprint policy.

**How to Contact:** Send query or manuscript. Photocopy OK. Enclose a self-addressed, stamped envelope.

**What Not to Do:** Phone or drop in without an appointment.

**Time Needed for Reply:** Four to six weeks.

**Does Author Supply Photos?** Desirable but not necessary.

**Advice for Authors:** Authors should be familiar with The Christian Century before submitting articles. Readers are theologically sophisticated, socially engaged. The magazine is not interested in simplistic pieties.

# CHRISTIANITY & THE ARTS

P. O. Box 118088
Chicago, Illinois 60611
(312) 642-8606

Established: 1994
Circulation: 5000

**Contact Person:** Marci Whitney-Schenck, Publisher and Editor.

**Type of Publication:** Magazine that deals with Christian expression in art, music, dance, theater, literature, and film in Chicago and the Midwest.

**Audience:** Christians and artists of all kinds.

**How Frequently Published:** Quarterly (February, May, August, November).

**Recently Published Articles:** "The Faces of Christ in Art"; "The Verse and Vision of Poet Elizabeth Vanek"; "Swinging from the Rafters"; "Site-Specific Dance in a Landmark Church"; "The Majesty of a Bach Cantata at Grace Lutheran Church."

**Current Needs:** Articles about the arts in the Midwest; also poetry.

**Policy on Seasonal Pieces:** Three months in advance.

**Usual Length Desired:** 1500 words maximum.

**Author Writes on Speculation or Assignment?** Can be either.

**Are Free Sample Copies Available?** Query.

**Payment Information:** Two copies of issue in which contributor's work appears.

**Advance Possible?** No.

**Rights Policy:** Author retains rights; please credit Christianity & the Arts in reprints.

**How to Contact:** Send query; enclose a self-addressed, stamped envelope. May also phone or send manuscript.

**What Not to Do:** Drop in without an appointment.

**Time Needed for Reply:** Three weeks.

**Does Author Supply Photos?** Depends on project.

**Advice for Authors:** Keep your audience in mind. Write tight—i.e., make every word count.

# CHRISTIANITY TODAY
CTI Publications, Inc.
465 Gundersen Drive
Carol Stream, Illinois 60188
(708) 427-5380                    Circulation: 200,000

**Contact Person:** Carol Thiessen, Administrative Editor.

**Type of Publication:** General circulation magazine emphasizing orthodox evangelical Christianity.

**Audience:** Primarily professional clergy and lay leaders.

**How Frequently Published:** 15 times per year.

**Recently Published Articles:** "And God Created Pain"; "Racial Healing in the Land of Lynching"; "Getting Serious about Lust in an Age of Smirks"; "Will There Be Baseball in Heaven?"

**Current Needs:** Nonfiction articles about ethical, theological Christianity; a wide range of subjects having to do with the church, theology, and Christianity.

**Policy on Seasonal Pieces:** Eight to ten months in advance.

**Usual Length Desired:** 3000 words.

**Author Writes on Speculation or Assignment?** Can be either, but mostly speculation.

**Are Free Sample Copies Available?** Yes, and so are writer's guidelines.

**Payment Information:**
　**Rate:** Negotiable; $100 minimum per article.
　**Mode:** On acceptance.
　**Advance Possible?** Rarely.

**Rights Policy:** Buys all rights; may reassign following publication.

**How to Contact:** Send query or manuscript. Enclose a self-addressed, stamped envelope.

**What Not to Do:** Phone or drop in without an appointment.

**Time Needed for Reply:** Ten days for rejection; six weeks if holding for evaluation.

**Does Author Supply Photos?** Desirable, but not necessary.

**Advice for Authors:** Authors should be familiar with the evangelical community in order to write with relevancy.

# THE CHRISTIAN MINISTRY

**The Christian Century Foundation**
**407 S. Dearborn Street**
**Chicago, Illinois 60605**          **Established: 1969**
**(312) 427-5380**          **Circulation: 12,000**

**Contact Person:** Victoria Rebeck, Editor.

**Type of Publication:** Internationally distributed professional journal.

**Audience:** Interdenominational clergy.

**How Frequently Published:** Bimonthly.

**Recently Published Articles:** "Rediscovering Grace in an Impossible Calling"; "Using Illustrations in Sermons"; "High Commitment Leads to Renewal."

**Current Needs:** Articles about practical parish problems; personal experiences with parish situations.

**Policy on Seasonal Pieces:** Three months in advance.

**Usual Length Desired:** 1800 to 2000 words.

**Author Writes on Speculation or Assignment?** Can be either.

**Are Free Sample Copies Available?** Yes.

**Payment Information:**
    **Rate:** Negotiable; $25 to $75 per article.
    **Mode:** On publication.
    **Advance Possible?** No.

**Rights Policy:** Buys all rights, but will consider reassigning rights.

**How to Contact:** Phone, send query, or send manuscript. Photocopy OK. Enclose a self-addressed, stamped envelope.

**What Not to Do:** Drop in without an appointment.

**Time Needed for Reply:** Three to four weeks.

**Does Author Supply Photos?** Desirable, but not necessary.

**Advice for Authors:** A completely ecumenical magazine, The Christian Ministry reaches—and accepts material from—all denominations. Authors need not be members of the clergy, but the content of their articles must be relevant to the professional parish minister or priest.

# CHURCH HISTORY

**American Society of Church History**
**1025 E. 58th Street**
**Chicago, Illinois 60637**          **Established: 1936**
**(312) 702-8215**                   **Circulation: 3400**

**Contact Person:** Martin Marty, Editor.

**Type of Publication:** Journal reflecting the history of the Christian Church (through many denominations).

**Audience:** Academics, historians, ministers, religious personnel.

**How Frequently Published:** Quarterly.

**Recently Published Articles:** Articles about St. Augustine, 19th century African theologian Orishatukeh Faduma, and early missionary movements in America.

**Current Needs:** Articles about the ancient and medieval church.

**Policy on Seasonal Pieces:** Seven to nine months in advance.

**Usual Length Desired:** 25 typed (double-spaced) pages, including footnotes.

**Author Writes on Speculation or Assignment?** Speculation.

**Are Free Sample Copies Available?** Yes; enclose a self-addressed, stamped envelope with request.

**Payment Information:** 20 copies of issue in which contributor's work appears.

**Rights Policy:** Holds copyright.

**How to Contact:** Send manuscript.

**What Not to Do:** Phone.

**Time Needed for Reply:** Immediate acknowledgment; seven to nine months for final decision.

**Does Author Supply Photos?** Yes, if appropriate.

**Advice for Authors:** Church History examines events in the Christian Church and features other religions only as they relate to Christianity. The magazine does not want manuscripts dealing with ministerial studies or material dealing directly with the Bible.

# THE COVENANT COMPANION

**Covenant Publications**
**5101 N. Francisco Avenue**
**Chicago, Illinois 60625**    **Established: 1922**
**(312) 784-3000**    **Circulation: 21,000**

**Contact Person:** Rev. James R. Hawkinson, Editor; Jane Swanson-Nystrom, Managing Editor.

**Type of Publication:** Official organ of the Evangelical Covenant Church.

**Audience:** Families and friends of the Evangelical Covenant Church.

**How Frequently Published:** Monthly.

**Recently Published Articles:** Articles about Bible study, youth ministry, worship, church music, the devotional life, and contemporary social issues.

**Current Needs:** More of the same.

**Policy on Seasonal Pieces:** Three months in advance.

**Usual Length Desired:** 1000 words.

**Author Writes on Speculation or Assignment?** Speculation.

**Are Free Sample Copies Available?** No.

**Payment Information:**
　　**Rate:** $15 to $30 per article.
　　**Mode:** On publication.
　　**Advance Possible?** No.

**Rights Policy:** Buys all rights; generous reprint policy with credit given to The Covenant Companion.

**How to Contact:** Send query or manuscript. Photocopy OK. Enclose a self-addressed, stamped envelope.

**What Not to Do:** Phone or drop in without an appointment.

**Time Needed for Reply:** Three to six months.

**Does Author Supply Photos?** Sometimes, but not required.

**Advice for Authors:** As an official organ, The Covenant Companion seeks to inform and interest the church by putting its members in touch with each other and with the wider Christian world.

# DAUGHTERS OF SARAH

2121 Sheridan Road
Evanston, Illinois 60201          **Established: 1974**
(708) 866-3882                    **Circulation: 5000**

**Contact Person:** Reta Finger, Editor.

**Type of Publication:** Christian feminist magazine.

**Audience:** 95 percent women, 95 percent of whom are Christians.

**How Frequently Published:** Quarterly.

**Recently Published Articles:** Themed issues: e.g., women and food, womanist theology, racism, women in the ministry, women and family.

**Current Needs:** Articles about women and AIDS; articles about contemplative life and worship.

**Policy on Seasonal Pieces:** Seven months in advance.

**Usual Length Desired:** 750 to 2000 words.

**Author Writes on Speculation or Assignment?** Usually on speculation.

**Are Free Sample Copies Available?** No, but writer's guidelines are. Enclose a self-addressed, stamped envelope with request.

**Payment Information:**
    **Rate:** $15 per printed page.
    **Mode:** On publication.
    **Advance Possible?** No.

**Rights Policy:** Buys first rights; rights then revert back to author.

**How to Contact:** Request writer's guidelines. Then query.

**What Not to Do:** Phone or drop in without an appointment.

**Time Needed for Reply:** Four weeks to acknowledge; at least three months for a decision.

**Does Author Supply Photos?** Depends on the article.

**Advice for Authors:** Pay close attention to the magazine's content. Daughters of Sarah receives a great deal of material about women but often not from a feminist point of view or else from a feminist point of view but not a Christian one.

# EXTENSION

**Catholic Church Extension Society**
**35 E. Wacker Drive, Suite 400**
**Chicago, Illinois 60601**            **Established: 1906**
**(312) 784-3000**                     **Circulation: 90,000**

**Contact Person:** Marianna Bartholomew, Managing Editor.

**Type of Publication:** Magazine reporting on activities and issues of the U. S. home missions.

**Audience:** Donors to and friends of the Catholic Church Extension Society.

**How Frequently Published:** Nine times per year (combined issues: January/February, May/June, September/October).

**Recently Published Articles:** "Of Fire and Ice" (about Alaska missions); "A Minnesota Mission's Undying Faith"; "Mission America's New Priests Give Their All."

**Current Needs:** Articles about mission work within the United States and its territories, about religious education, evangelism, and campus ministry.

**Policy on Seasonal Pieces:** Three months.

**Usual Length Desired:** 800 to 1500 words.

**Author Writes on Speculation or Assignment?** Assignment.

**Are Free Sample Copies Available?** Yes.

**Payment Information:**
> **Rate:** Varies.
> **Mode:** On acceptance.
> **Advance Possible?** No.

**Rights Policy:** Buys first North American serial rights.

**How to Contact:** Send query and clips.

**What Not to Do:** Send complete manuscript.

**Time Needed for Reply:** One to three months.

**Does Author Supply Photos?** Depends on the project.

**Advice for Authors:** Please do not suggest story ideas about foreign missions.

# INTERLIT

**David C. Cook Foundation**
**850 N. Grove Avenue**
**Elgin, Illinois 60120**
**(708) 741-2400**

**Established: 1964**
**Circulation: 4000**

**Contact Person:** Ronda Oosterhoff, Editor.

**Type of Publication:** Christian communication magazine.

**Audience:** Those in the Christian communication field worldwide—particularly in developing nations.

**How Frequently Published:** Quarterly.

**Recently Published Articles:** Articles about training, literacy, and editor-writer relationships.

**Current Needs:** More of the same.

**Policy on Seasonal Pieces:** Three to six months in advance.

**Usual Length Desired:** 1500 to 1800 words.

**Author Writes on Speculation or Assignment?** Assignment.

**Are Free Sample Copies Available?** Yes.

**Payment Information:**
    **Rate:** $80 to $100 per article.
    **Mode:** On publication.
    **Advance Possible?** No.

**Rights Policy:** Buys first-time rights.

**How to Contact:** Send query.

**What Not to Do:** Phone.

**Time Needed for Reply:** Two weeks to two months.

**Does Author Supply Photos?** Yes, if possible.

**Advice for Authors:** Please study the publication, and then send a query before submitting a manuscript.

# JUF News

**Jewish Federation of Metropolitan Chicago**
**1 S. Franklin Street, Room 706**
**Chicago, Illinois 60606**          **Established: 1969**
**(312) 444-2853**          **Circulation: 55,000**

**Contact Person:** Joseph Aaron, Editor.

**Type of Publication:** Periodical covering topics of interest to Jewish readers.

**Audience:** Jewish adults in the Chicago area.

**How Frequently Published:** Monthly.

**Recently Published Articles:** "Spielberg's Latest"; "Visiting the Sick"; "Choosing to be Chosen"; "Teaching Children about God"; "Music Man."

**Current Needs:** Feature articles about Chicago Jewish history, Jewish holidays, spirituality, and anecdotal pieces.

**Policy on Seasonal Pieces:** Six weeks in advance.

**Usual Length Desired:** Five to eight typed (double-spaced) pages.

**Author Writes on Speculation or Assignment?** Speculation only.

**Are Free Sample Copies Available?** Yes.

**Payment Information:**
    **Rate:** $100 to $200 per article.
    **Mode:** On publication.
    **Advance Possible?** No.

**Rights Policy:** Buys first North American serial rights.

**How to Contact:** Send query and clips.

**What Not to Do:** Phone or drop in without an appointment.

**Time Needed for Reply:** One to six months.

**Does Author Supply Photos?** Depends on article.

**Advice for Authors:** Please don't send stories about a visit to Israel or the significance of the Holocaust. In addition, do not include JUF News as part of a multiple submission.

# THE LUTHERAN
**Evangelical Lutheran Church in America**
**8765 W. Higgins Road**
**Chicago, Illinois 60631**          **Established: 1988**
**(312) 380-2540**                   **Circulation: 950,000**

**Contact Person:** David Miller, Senior Features Editor; Kathy Kastilahn, Features Editor.

**Type of Publication:** Magazine with news and features about the world's religions, particularly the Evangelical Lutheran Church in America.

**Audience:** Lay people and clergy.

**How Frequently Published:** Monthly.

**Recently Published Articles:** Feature about a local congregation's efforts to minister to the homeless; news from war-ravaged Bosnia.

**Current Needs:** Articles about contemporary social/ethical issues, profiles about personalities, stories about ministries and programs of the denomination's congregations and social service agencies.

**Policy on Seasonal Pieces:** Features—five months in advance; news—ten days in advance.

**Usual Length Desired:** Features—2200 words; news—300 words.

**Author Writes on Speculation or Assignment?** Can be either.

**Are Free Sample Copies Available?** Yes.

**Payment Information:**
Rate: $100 to $600.
Mode: On acceptance.
Advance Possible? Yes.

**Rights Policy:** Buys first North American serial rights.

**How to Contact:** Queries with writing samples are preferred; may phone with a news story idea.

**What Not to Do:** Send unsolicited manuscript for features.

**Time Needed for Reply:** Two months.

**Does Author Supply Photos?** Depends on story.

**Advice for Authors:** The Lutheran is looking for writers with a strong, colorful, descriptive, highly readable style.

# PIONEER CLUBS' PERSPECTIVE
**Pioneer Clubs**
**P. O. Box 788**
**Wheaton, Illinois 60189**
**(708) 293-1600**                    **Established: 1967**

**Contact Person:** Rebecca Powell Parat, Editor.

**Type of Publication:** Magazine for lay leaders of Pioneer Clubs in churches.

**Audience:** Lay leaders of Pioneer Clubs and church leaders.

**How Frequently Published:** Three times a year (December, March, and August).

**Recently Published Articles:** "Tackling Problem Behavior"; "Planning with Pizzazz"; "Respecting Children: What Is It All About?"

**Current Needs:** Articles about club discipline, leadership skills, and relationship skills.

**Policy on Seasonal Pieces:** Nine months in advance.

**Usual Length Desired:** 1200 to 1800 words.

**Author Writes on Speculation or Assignment?** Almost exclusively assignment.

**Are Free Sample Copies Available?** No, but writer's guidelines are; enclose a self-addressed, stamped envelope with request.

**Payment Information:**
    **Rate:** $60 to $90 per article for first-time contributors.
    **Mode:** On acceptance.
    **Advance Possible?** No.

**Rights Policy:** Buys full rights to an assigned piece and first time rights to a piece received on speculation.

**How to Contact:** Send query or original manuscript.

**What Not to Do:** Phone or drop in without an appointment.

**Time Needed for Reply:** Up to six weeks.

**Does Author Supply Photos?** If possible, especially for an article about an actual club project.

**Advice for Authors:** It is most important that authors be familiar with Pioneer Clubs (for boys and girls ages 2 to 17).

# PROBE

**National Assembly of Religious Women**
**529 S. Wabash Avenue**
**Chicago, Illinois 60605**          **Established: 1970**
**(312) 663-1980**                   **Circulation: 3000**

**Contact Person:** Dihya Al Kahina, Administrative Coordinator.

**Type of Publication:** Magazine that seeks to raise consciousness and encourage theological reflection.

**Audience:** Members of the National Assembly of Religious Women.

**How Frequently Published:** Quarterly.

**Recently Published Articles:** Themed issues: e.g., "Understanding the Issues: Homophobia and Heterosexism"; "Crimes Against Humanity: Violence Against Women"; "Where Do Good People Stand?"

**Current Needs:** Articles about social justice.

**Policy on Seasonal Pieces:** Four months in advance.

**Usual Length Desired:** 500 to 3000 words.

**Author Writes on Speculation or Assignment?** Can be either.

**Are Free Sample Copies Available?** Yes.

**Payment Information:** Ten copies of the magazine in which the contributor's work appears and a year's membership in the organization.

**Rights Policy:** Author retains rights.

**How to Contact:** Send query or manuscript.

**What Not to Do:** Phone.

**Time Needed for Reply:** Within two weeks.

**Does Author Supply Photos?** Yes.

**Advice for Authors:** Although the National Assembly of Religious Women is Catholic-based, Probe includes information about and is of interest to women of many faiths.

# THE SENTINEL

**Sentinel Publishing Company**
**150 N. Michigan Avenue, Suite 2025**
**Chicago, Illinois 60604**          **Established: 1912**
**(312) 407-0060**                    **Circulation: 50,000**

**Contact Person:** Ruth Marcus, Managing Editor.

**Type of Publication:** Magazine covering news and issues of interest to Jewish people.

**Audience:** Jewish adults.

**How Frequently Published:** Weekly.

**Recently Published Articles:** News stories, features, and profiles of Jews in the U. S. and other parts of the world.

**Current Needs:** More of the same type of articles.

**Policy on Seasonal Pieces:** One to three weeks in advance.

**Usual Length Desired:** 1000 words.

**Author Writes on Speculation or Assignment?** Speculation.

**Are Free Sample Copies Available?** No.

**Payment Information:**
    **Rate:** $25 maximum per article.
    **Mode:** On acceptance.
    **Advance Possible?** No.

**Rights Policy:** Author retains copyright.

**How to Contact:** Phone with story ideas.

**What Not to Do:** Drop in without an appointment.

**Does Author Supply Photos?** Yes.

# TODAY'S CHRISTIAN WOMAN
CTi Publications
465 Gundersen Drive
Carol Stream, Illinois 60188     **Established:** 1979
(708) 260-6200     **Circulation:** 362,000

**Contact Person:** Jan Senn, Senior Editor.

**Type of Publication:** Magazine covering issues of interest to people trying to live according to biblical values.

**Audience:** Christian women of all ages, single or married.

**How Frequently Published:** Six times per year.

**Recently Published Articles:** "Being Grateful—Even When It Doesn't Make Sense"; "Five Dangerous Prayers"; "Everyday Idols"; "How to Pray for Enemies and Strangers."

**Current Needs:** Articles about relationships, including those with adult siblings, parents, co-workers, children, and self. Also articles emphasizing practical spiritual values.

**Policy on Seasonal Pieces:** Three to six months.

**Usual Length Desired:** 50 to 1800 words.

**Author Writes on Speculation or Assignment?** Speculation.

**Are Free Sample Copies Available?** Yes; for a sample copy and writer's guidelines, send request to Today's Christian Woman, P. O. Box 11618, Des Moines, Iowa 50397.

**Payment Information:**
    **Rate:** 15 cents per word.
    **Mode:** On publication.
    **Advance Possible?** No.

**Rights Policy:** Buys first rights.

**How to Contact:** Send query; enclose self-addressed, stamped envelope.

**What Not to Do:** Send unsolicited manuscripts or include Today's Christian Woman as part of a multiple submission.

**Time Needed for Reply:** Four to six weeks.

**Does Author Supply Photos?** No.

**Advice for Authors:** Read six issues of the magazine before sending a query. Articles should be personal in tone and full of real-life anecdotes as well as quotes/advice from noted Christian professionals. Articles should be practical and maintain a distinct Christian perspective throughout.

# URBAN MINISTRIES, INC.

**1350 W. 103rd Street**
**Chicago, Illinois 60643**
**(312) 233-4499**                                    **Established: 1970**

**Contact Person:** Shawan Brand, Production Manager.

**Type of Publication:** Religious magazines published in six different editions, one edition for each of six age groups ranging from four years old to adult.

**Audience:** Primarily urban African-Americans of all ages and many denominations.

**How Frequently Published:** Quarterly.

**Recently Published Articles:** Each issue of each magazine contains a series of Bible studies for the number of Sundays in that quarter. In addition, the adult magazine contains articles with a religious outlook.

**Current Needs:** Bible study guides for any one of six age levels.

**Policy on Seasonal Pieces:** Six months in advance.

**Usual Length Desired:** Ten typed (double-spaced) pages.

**Author Writes on Speculation or Assignment?** Assignment.

**Are Free Sample Copies Available?** Yes; enclose a self-addressed, stamped envelope with request.

**Payment Information:**
    **Rate:** Negotiable on a per article basis.
    **Mode:** On publication.
    **Advance Possible?** No.

**Rights Policy:** Buys all rights.

**How to Contact:** Send query and resume detailing qualifications for this type of writing.

**What Not to Do:** Send manuscript.

**Time Needed for Reply:** Four weeks.

**Does Author Supply Photos?** Yes, usually.

**Advice for Authors:** Know the African-American community and the Bible.

# VENTURE

**Christian Service Brigade**
**P. O. Box 150**
**Wheaton, Illinois 60189**   **Established: 1959**
**(708) 665-0630**   **Circulation: 18,000**

**Contact Person:** Deborah Christensen, Editor.

**Type of Publication:** Evangelical religious publication for young men.

**Audience:** Young men 10 to 15 years of age.

**How Frequently Published:** Bimonthly.

**Recently Published Articles:** Interviews with well-known Christians, nature stories, fiction.

**Current Needs:** Humor.

**Policy on Seasonal Pieces:** Two months in advance.

**Usual Length Desired:** 500 to 1500 words.

**Author Writes on Speculation or Assignment?** Mostly on speculation.

**Are Free Sample Copies Available?** No, but writer's guidelines are. Enclose a self-addressed, stamped envelope with request.

**Payment Information:**
   **Rate:** 5 to 10 cents per word.
   **Mode:** On publication.
   **Advance Possible?** No.

**Rights Policy:** Buys first rights or second reprint rights.

**How to Contact:** Send complete manuscript.

**What Not to Do:** Send query or phone.

**Time Needed for Reply:** One week.

**Does Author Supply Photos?** Depends on the project.

**Advice for Authors:** Keep the audience in mind, and write in a simple, down-to-earth style.

# WORLD ORDER

**The National Spiritual Assembly of the Baha'i's of the United States**
415 Linden Avenue
Wilmette, Illinois 60091          Established: 1966
(708) 251-1854          Circulation: 2000

**Contact Person:** Dr. Betty Fisher, Associate Editor.

**Type of Publication:** Magazine covering aspects of contemporary religious teachings and philosophies.

**Audience:** Educated laypeople.

**How Frequently Published:** Quarterly.

**Recently Published Articles:** Articles about World Order, eradication of racism, religious history, architecture, science, and the equality of men and women.

**Current Needs:** Articles about any aspect of the inevitable coming of the World Order.

**Policy on Seasonal Pieces:** At least nine months in advance.

**Usual Length Desired:** 20 to 25 typed (double-spaced) pages.

**Author Writes on Speculation or Assignment?** Can be either.

**Are Free Sample Copies Available?** Yes, after a discussion of a feasible article.

**Payment Information:** Ten copies of the issue in which contributor's work appears

**Rights Policy:** Some authors deed their work to the National Spiritual Assembly; others retain rights.

**How to Contact:** Send query with outline and synopsis.

**What Not to Do:** Phone or send complete manuscript.

**Time Needed for Reply:** One week for acknowledgment; up to three months for final decision on acceptance.

**Does Author Supply Photos?** Depends on project.

**Advice for Authors:** Request copy of writer's guidelines. Know about the Baha'i's before sending material.

# THE YOUNG CRUSADER

**National Women's Christian Temperance Union**
**1730 Chicago Avenue**
**Evanston, Illinois 60201**
**(708) 864-1396**

**Established: 1887**
**Circulation: 2500**

**Contact Person:** Rachel Kelly, Editor-in-Chief; Michael Vitucci, Managing Editor.

**Type of Publication:** Children's magazine concerned with moral issues.

**Audience:** Children between the ages of 6 and 12.

**How Frequently Published:** Monthly, September through June.

**Recently Published Articles:** "The Christmas Cat"; "Mark and Mr. Baxter"; "Puzzle Playground"; "Gary's Talent"; poems by and for children.

**Current Needs:** Uplifting stories with high morals; stories about nature.

**Policy on Seasonal Pieces:** At least one month in advance.

**Usual Length Desired:** 600 words.

**Author Writes on Speculation or Assignment?** Can be either.

**Are Free Sample Copies Available?** Yes.

**Payment Information:**
   **Rate:** 5 cents per word.
   **Mode:** On publication.
   **Advance Possible?** No.

**Rights Policy:** Author retains rights.

**How to Contact:** Send query.

**What Not to Do:** Drop in without an appointment.

**Time Needed for Reply:** Six months.

**Does Author Supply Photos?** No.

**Advice for Authors:** Articles should be informational but not preachy.

# ADVERTISING AGE

**Crain Communications, Inc.**
**740 N. Rush Street, Second Floor**
**Chicago, Illinois 60611**          **Established: 1963**
**(312) 280-3157**          **Circulation: 81,000**

**Contact Person:** Melanie Rigney, Managing Editor/News.

**Type of Publication:** Business newsmagazine specializing in advertising and related businesses.

**Audience:** Businesspeople in advertising and related fields.

**How Frequently Published:** Weekly.

**Recently Published Articles:** Articles that show where brands and trends are going, which accounts are moving.

**Current Needs:** News stories that inform agencies as to what the competition is doing.

**Usual Length Desired:** 750 to 1000 words.

**Author Writes on Speculation or Assignment?** Mostly assignment.

**Are Free Sample Copies Available?** No.

**Payment Information:**
   **Rate:** Varies.
   **Mode:** On publication.
   **Advance Possible?** Generally not.

**Rights Policy:** Reserves all rights.

**How to Contact:** Send query or manuscript. Photocopy OK. Enclose a self-addressed, stamped envelope.

**What Not to Do:** Phone on a Thursday or Friday or drop in without an appointment.

**Time Needed for Reply:** One week.

**Does Author Supply Photos?** Yes.

**Advice for Authors:** Authors should familiarize themselves with Advertising Age and its style. As a news publication, it looks for news value in the articles it publishes. Authors should have demonstrable expertise in advertising and related fields.

# AMERICAN LIBRARIES

**American Library Association**
**50 E. Huron Street**
**Chicago, Illinois 60611**  **Established: 1907**
**(312) 280-4216**  **Circulation: 56,000**

**Contact Person:** Thomas Gaughan, Editor.

**Type of Publication:** Magazine offering library news and features.

**Audience:** Library personnel, individuals in the publishing industry, members of the American Library Association.

**How Frequently Published:** Eleven times per year (combined July/August issue).

**Recently Published Articles:** "A Modest Proposal: No More Main Entry" (about cataloging); "Lawmakers, Lawbreakers: The Problem of Library Record Distribution"; "Zen and the Art of Troubleshooting."

**Current Needs:** Human interest stories that avoid cliches; nonsentimental profiles; library news stories.

**Policy on Seasonal Pieces:** Three months in advance.

**Usual Length Desired:** 1000 to 2000 words.

**Author Writes on Speculation or Assignment?** Can be either.

**Are Free Sample Copies Available?** Yes.

**Payment Information:**
    **Rate:** Up to $300 per article.
    **Mode:** On acceptance.
    **Advance Possible?** No.

**Rights Policy:** Buys first-time rights.

**How to Contact:** Send query or manuscript. Photocopy OK.

**What Not to Do:** Phone or drop in without an appointment.

**Time Needed for Reply:** Four to ten weeks.

**Does Author Supply Photos?** Preferably. Good graphics, including four-color illustrations, are important.

**Advice for Authors:** American Libraries wants articles that cover developments new to the library industry and that give new slants to traditional subjects. Chicago-area stories must be of national interest. Authors need not be librarians themselves, but they must be familiar with the system.

# BANK MANAGEMENT
**Bank Administration Institute**
**1 N. Franklin Street**
**Chicago, Illinois 60606**
**(312) 553-4600**                    **Circulation: 40,000**

**Contact Person:** Joan Ritter, Associate Publisher.

**Type of Publication:** Business magazine covering risk management.

**Audience:** Top-level banking executives.

**How Frequently Published:** Bimonthly.

**Recently Published Articles:** Articles about corporate finance and compliance laws.

**Current Needs:** More of the same.

**Policy on Seasonal Pieces:** Two months in advance.

**Usual Length Desired:** 2000 words.

**Author Writes on Speculation or Assignment?** Can be either.

**Are Free Sample Copies Available?** Yes.

**Payment Information:**
    **Rate:** Negotiable.
    **Mode:** On publication.
    **Advance Possible?** No.

**Rights Policy:** Negotiable.

**How to Contact:** Send query and clips. May also phone.

**What Not to Do:** Drop in without an appointment.

**Time Needed for Reply:** Two weeks.

**Does Author Supply Photos?** No.

**Advice for Authors:** Bank Management is interested only in strategic-level articles; this is not a magazine about general banking. A companion publication, Bank Fraud, covers fraud prevention in the banking industry; contact information is the same as for Bank Management.

# THE BAR EXAMINER

**National Conference of Bar Examiners**
**333 N. Michigan Avenue, Suite 1025**
**Chicago, Illinois 60601**      **Established: 1928**
**(312) 641-0963**      **Circulation: 3000**

**Contact Person:** Ann Fisher, Editor.

**Type of Publication:** Magazine dealing with legal issues.

**Audience:** Members of the National Conference of Bar Examiners, bar admissions authorities: judges, lawyers, law school deans and professors.

**How Frequently Published:** Quarterly.

**Recently Published Articles:** Articles about ethics, chemical dependency, technical issues, litigation reports, and the Americans with Disabilities Act (ADA).

**Current Needs:** New perspectives on relevant issues (e.g., ADA).

**Policy on Seasonal Pieces:** Six to nine months in advance.

**Usual Length Desired:** 20 typed (double-spaced) pages.

**Author Writes on Speculation or Assignment?** Can be either.

**Are Free Sample Copies Available?** Yes.

**Payment Information:** Ten free copies of the issue in which the contributor's work appears.

**Rights Policy:** Retains all rights.

**How to Contact:** Send query.

**What Not to Do:** Phone.

**Time Needed for Reply:** One month.

**Does Author Supply Photos?** Only a photo of self to accompany article.

**Advice for Authors:** One need not be a lawyer to write for The Bar Examiner, but it helps.

# BARRISTER

**The American Bar Association**
**750 N. Lake Shore Drive**
**Chicago, Illinois 60611**          **Established: 1973**
**(312) 988-6068**                    **Circulation: 160,000**

**Contact Person:** Cie Brown-Armstead, Editor.

**Type of Publication:** Professional journal for the Young Lawyers Division of the American Bar Association.

**Audience:** Lawyers between the ages of 25 and 36.

**How Frequently Published:** Five times per year (quarterly, plus a special profile issue each summer).

**Recently Published Articles:** "Life, Law, and the Pursuit of Balance"; "How to Make the Media Work for You"; "Computers Made Easy"; "Small-Town Lawyers."

**Current Needs:** Articles about practice management, career issues, and social policy.

**Policy on Seasonal Pieces:** Six months to one year in advance.

**Usual Length Desired:** Six to eight typed (double-spaced) pages.

**Author Writes on Speculation or Assignment?** Assignment.

**Are Free Sample Copies Available?** Yes.

**Payment Information:**
    **Rate:** Negotiable.
    **Mode:** On acceptance.
    **Advance Possible?** No.

**Rights Policy:** Buys first-time rights.

**How to Contact:** Send query and writing samples.

**What Not to Do:** Phone, send complete manuscript, or submit poetry, fiction, or puzzle-type features.

**Time Needed for Reply:** One to two months.

**Does Author Supply Photos?** Only if requested to do so.

**Advice for Authors:** Authors should request a sample copy of Barrister before submitting a query. Barrister prefers a clear, direct writing style with examples and anecdotes worked into the text. It is interested mainly in stories that involve practical tips and their application.

# BUSINESS INSURANCE

**Crain Communications, Inc.**
740 N. Rush Street
Chicago, Illinois 60611          **Established: 1967**
(312) 649-5398                   **Circulation: 52,800**

**Contact Person:** James Burcke, Editor.

**Type of Publication:** Business magazine for buyers of commercial insurance, both employee benefit plans and property casualty insurance (no personal insurance lines).

**Audience:** Risk managers, benefit managers, and financial executives. Also insurance company executives and insurance agents and brokers.

**How Frequently Published:** Weekly.

**Recently Published Articles:** Articles covering earthquake loss insurance, health care reform, Superfund reform, insurance company profits, and workers compensation fraud.

**Current Needs:** Any news of interest to buyers of commercial insurance—e.g., regulatory developments.

**Policy on Seasonal Pieces:** Two to four weeks in advance.

**Usual Length Desired:** 700 to 1000 words.

**Author Writes on Speculation or Assignment?** Assignment.

**Are Free Sample Copies Available?** No.

**Payment Information:**
    **Rate:** $10 per column inch or a negotiated fee based on time required to produce a good story.
    **Mode:** On publication.
    **Advance Possible?** Only to cover expenses.

**Rights Policy:** Buys all rights.

**How to Contact:** Send query.

**What Not to Do:** Phone, send manuscript, or drop in without an appointment.

**Time Needed for Reply:** Two or three weeks.

**Does Author Supply Photos?** Yes, if possible.

**Advice for Authors:** Due to the complexity of the subject, Business Insurance authors must possess knowledge in three areas: business, economics, and insurance.

# BUSINESS MARKETING

Crain Communications, Inc.
740 N. Rush Street
Chicago, Illinois 60611          Established: 1916
(312) 649-5260                   Circulation: 30,000

**Contact Person:** Jan Jaben, Editor; Chuck Paustian, Managing Editor.

**Type of Publication:** Tabloid covering business-to-business marketing.

**Audience:** Marketing executives.

**How Frequently Published:** Monthly.

**Recently Published Articles:** Articles about marketing on the information superhighway; business products; marketing strategies (advertising campaigns, direct marketing, marketplace positioning).

**Current Needs:** How-to pieces are OK, but news stories are preferred; even features should have a news-like quality.

**Policy on Seasonal Pieces:** One month in advance.

**Usual Length Desired:** 400 to 1200 words.

**Author Writes on Speculation or Assignment?** Mostly assignment.

**Are Free Sample Copies Available?** Yes.

**Payment Information:**
    **Rate:** Varies, depending on quality and length of the piece.
    **Mode:** On publication.
    **Advance Possible?** No.

**Rights Policy:** Buys all rights.

**How to Contact:** Send query, resume, and writing samples.

**What Not to Do:** Phone or send complete manuscript.

**Time Needed for Reply:** Four weeks.

**Does Author Supply Photos?** Appreciated, but not necessary.

**Advice for Authors:** A marketing background is helpful but not mandatory for writing for Business Marketing. The editors look primarily for solid reporting skills and a lively writing style.

# CHICAGO ADVERTISING AND MEDIA

**JB Communications**
**2249 W. 23rd Place**
**Chicago, Illinois 60608**          **Established: 1988**
**(312) 847-4444**                    **Circulation: 6000**

**Contact Person:** Joe Brar, Editor and Publisher.

**Type of Publication:** Magazine reporting current ideas affecting media and advertisers in the Chicago area.

**Audience:** Professionals in the fields of advertising and media.

**How Frequently Published:** Two times per month.

**Recently Published Articles:** Articles about Chicago advertising agencies; some pieces about Chicago media.

**Current Needs:** More of the same.

**Policy on Seasonal Pieces:** One week to one month in advance.

**Usual Length Desired:** 500 to 2000 words.

**Author Writes on Speculation or Assignment?** Assignment.

**Are Free Sample Copies Available?** Yes.

**Payment Information:**
   **Rate:** Negotiable.
   **Mode:** On publication.
   **Advance Possible?** No.

**Rights Policy:** Negotiable.

**How to Contact:** Send query and clips or phone.

**What Not to Do:** Send manuscript or drop in without an appointment.

**Time Needed for Reply:** Up to three weeks.

**Does Author Supply Photos?** Not usually.

**Advice for Authors:** Please don't include Chicago Advertising and Media as part of a multiple submission or share information with other reporters after agreeing to do a story for this magazine.

# CHICAGO DAILY LAW BULLETIN
**Law Bulletin Publishing Company**
**415 N. State Street**
**Chicago, Illinois 60610**          **Established: 1854**
**(312) 644-7800**                    **Circulation: 7000**

**Contact Person:** Steve Brown, Managing Editor.

**Type of Publication:** Professional newspaper journal.

**Audience:** People involved in the legal profession.

**How Frequently Published:** Daily, Monday through Friday.

**Recently Published Articles:** Summaries of state and federal appellate and Supreme Court decisions; articles about law firm management; stories about finance; columns about practice issues.

**Current Needs:** How-to articles based on interviews with legal experts; general news articles that play up unique aspects of the legal profession.

**Usual Length Desired:** 300 to 3000 words.

**Author Writes on Speculation or Assignment?** Usually assignment.

**Are Free Sample Copies Available?** Yes.

**Payment Information:**
> **Rate:** Minimum of $50 per article of five typed (double-spaced) pages.
> **Mode:** On acceptance.
> **Advance Possible?** No.

**Rights Policy:** Buys all rights.

**How to Contact:** Send query or manuscript. Photocopy and disk OK. Enclose a self-addressed, stamped envelope.

**What Not to Do:** Phone or drop in without an appointment.

**Time Needed for Reply:** One week.

**Does Author Supply Photos?** Yes, black-and-white glossies.

**Advice for Authors:** Authors should remember that they are writing for the legal profession. Most articles—though not the more general subjects—demand legal expertise or contact with a legal expert.

# CHICAGO FILM & VIDEO NEWS

**Real Estate News Corporation**
**3525 W. Peterson Avenue, Suite 103**
**Chicago, Illinois 60659**
**(312) 866-9900**

**Established: 1985**
**Circulation: 10,000**

**Contact Person:** Steven Polydoris, Managing Editor.

**Type of Publication:** Magazine aimed at promoting communication between corporate and independent producers and film and video professionals and advertising agencies.

**Audience:** Professionals involved in corporate communications, film and video, and advertising.

**How Frequently Published:** Twenty times per year.

**Recently Published Articles:** Industry news and trends; also features and profiles of personalities and companies.

**Current Needs:** More of the same type of articles.

**Policy on Seasonal Pieces:** At least two weeks in advance.

**Usual Length Desired:** No length restrictions.

**Author Writes on Speculation or Assignment?** Assignment.

**Are Free Sample Copies Available?** Yes.

**Payment Information:**
    **Rate:** Negotiable.
    **Mode:** Negotiable.
    **Advance Possible?** Yes.

**Rights Policy:** Negotiable.

**How to Contact:** Phone with story ideas.

**What Not to Do:** Drop in without an appointment.

**Time Needed for Reply:** Two or three days.

**Does Author Supply Photos?** Depends on article.

**Advice for Authors:** Writers for Chicago Film & Video News must have extensive knowledge of the film and video industry.

# CHICAGO LAWYER
**Law Bulletin Publishing Company**
**415 N. State Street**
**Chicago, Illinois 60610**
**(312) 644-7800**                    **Circulation: 12,000**

**Contact Person:** Donna Gill, Managing Editor.

**Type of Publication:** Magazine for people in the legal profession.

**Audience:** People involved in the legal profession.

**How Frequently Published:** Monthly.

**Recently Published Articles:** Articles about law firm management and about the business and financial aspects of the legal profession.

**Current Needs:** How-to articles based on interviews with legal experts; general news articles that play up unique aspects of the legal profession.

**Policy on Seasonal Pieces:** One month in advance.

**Usual Length Desired:** 300 to 3000 words.

**Author Writes on Speculation or Assignment?** Usually assignment.

**Are Free Sample Copies Available?** Yes.

**Payment Information:**
    **Rate:** $50 per article of five typed (double-spaced) pages.
    **Mode:** On acceptance.
    **Advance Possible?** No.

**Rights Policy:** Buys all rights.

**How to Contact:** Send query or manuscript. Photocopy and disk OK. Enclose a self-addressed, stamped envelope.

**What Not to Do:** Phone or drop in without an appointment.

**Time Needed for Reply:** One week.

**Does Author Supply Photos?** Yes, black-and-white glossies.

**Advice for Authors:** Authors should remember that they are writing for the legal profession. Most articles—though not the more general subjects—demand legal expertise or contact with a legal expert.

# CHICAGO PURCHASOR

**Purchasing Management Association of Chicago**
**201 N. Wells Street, Suite 618**
**Chicago, Illinois 60606**          **Established: 1923**
**(312) 782-1940**                    **Circulation: 5200**

**Contact Person:** John Pressley, Editor; Jackie Stinson, Sales Coordinator.

**Type of Publication:** Trade magazine for purchasing professionals.

**Audience:** Purchasing executives.

**How Frequently Published:** Bimonthly.

**Recently Published Articles:** "How to Plan a Winning Negotiation Series"; "JIT."

**Current Needs:** Stories about credit card purchasing and other popular topics.

**Usual Length Desired:** 1000 to 2000 words.

**Author Writes on Speculation or Assignment?** Assignment, mostly.

**Are Free Sample Copies Available?** Yes.

**Payment Information:**
    **Rate:** Negotiable.
    **Mode:** On publication.
    **Advance Possible?** No.

**Rights Policy:** Buys first serial rights.

**How to Contact:** Send query.

**What Not to Do:** Phone or send unsolicited manuscript.

**Time Needed for Reply:** One month.

**Does Author Supply Photos?** Usually not.

**Advice for Authors:** Authors who write for Chicago Purchasor should be familiar with the purchasing profession in general, and expertise in a particular technical field would be very helpful.

# COMMERCIAL INVESTMENT REAL ESTATE (CIRE) JOURNAL

**Commercial Investment Real Estate Institute (CIREI)**
**430 N. Michigan Avenue, Suite 600**
**Chicago, Illinois 60611**
**(312) 321-4464**

**Established: 1981**
**Circulation: 9000**

**Contact Person:** Lorene Norton Palm, Editor.

**Type of Publication:** Magazine that covers the commercial investment real estate industry in the United States and Canada.

**Audience:** Commercial real estate professionals.

**How Frequently Published:** Five times per year.

**Recently Published Articles:** "NAFTA and Commercial Real Estate"; "Senior Housing Comes of Age"; "What Corporate Clients Really Need from Service Providers."

**Current Needs:** Freelance editors with in-depth knowledge of commercial real estate to edit articles.

**Policy on Seasonal Pieces:** Four months in advance.

**Usual Length Desired:** Nine to twelve typed (double-spaced) pages.

**Author Writes on Speculation or Assignment?** Mostly assignment.

**Are Free Sample Copies Available?** Yes.

**Payment Information:**
    **Rate:** Negotiable.
    **Mode:** On acceptance.
    **Advance Possible?** No.

**Rights Policy:** Buys all rights.

**How to Contact:** Send query and writing samples.

**What Not to Do:** Propose articles that do not fit our style or focus.

**Time Needed for Reply:** One month.

**Does Author Supply Photos?** Yes.

**Advice for Authors:** Writers and editors should have a firm grasp of the commercial real estate business and be able to produce and edit technical copy.

# COMPUTERIZED INVESTING

**American Association of Individual Investors**
**625 N. Michigan Avenue, Suite 1900**
**Chicago, Illinois 60611**
**(312) 280-0170**

**Established: 1982**
**Circulation: 46,000**

**Contact Person:** John Bajkowski, Managing Editor.

**Type of Publication:** Magazine covering the use of computers for investment analysis.

**Audience:** Individual investors.

**How Frequently Published:** Bimonthly.

**Recently Published Articles:** Review of online services; examination of neural networks; technical analysis.

**Current Needs:** Articles pertaining to the development of the information superhighway.

**Policy on Seasonal Pieces:** Two months in advance.

**Usual Length Desired:** 4500 words.

**Author Writes on Speculation or Assignment?** Assignment.

**Are Free Sample Copies Available?** Yes.

**Payment Information:**
    **Rate:** Negotiable.
    **Mode:** On acceptance.
    **Advance Possible?** Yes.

**Rights Policy:** Buys first-time rights.

**How to Contact:** Send query, resume, and writing samples.

**What Not to Do:** Phone or send complete manuscript.

**Time Needed for Reply:** One month.

**Does Author Supply Photos?** No, but the author is responsible for supplying tables and graphs and other illustrative materials.

**Advice for Authors:** Writers for Computerized Investing must have solid knowledge of both computers and investment analysis.

# CONFETTI

**Randall Publishing Company, Inc.**
**1401 Lunt Avenue**
**P. O. Box 1426**
**Elk Grove Village, Illinois 60007**
**(708) 437-6604**

**Established: 1989**
**Circulation: 15,000**

**Contact Person:** Peg Short, Publisher/Editor-in-Chief.

**Type of Publication:** Magazine for professionals involved in the communications arts.

**Audience:** Designers, illustrators, photographers, art directors, creative individuals in advertising agencies and corporate communications departments.

**How Frequently Published:** Bimonthly.

**Recently Published Articles:** "Paper Marbling"; "The Illustration of Joel Nakamura"; "Portrait of the Artist as an Emerging Illustrator"; "Photo-Impressionism Enters the '90s"; "Electronic Studio Guide."

**Policy on Seasonal Pieces:** Three months in advance.

**Usual Length Desired:** 1000 to 1200 words.

**Author Writes on Speculation or Assignment?** Usually assignment, but can be either.

**Are Free Sample Copies Available?** Yes.

**Payment Information:**
   **Rate:** Negotiable.
   **Mode:** Negotiable.
   **Advance Possible?** No.

**Rights Policy:** Buys one-time rights.

**How to Contact:** Send query and/or request a copy of the writer's guidelines and copy of the magazine; may also phone.

**What Not to Do:** Send how-to articles.

**Time Needed for Reply:** Three months.

**Does Author Supply Photos?** Usually not.

**Advice for Authors:** Confetti is very visually oriented. Suggestions for profiles must be accompanied by copies of the artist's work. Strong writing with weak art is not usable.

---

# CORPORATE LEGAL TIMES

**Corporate Legal Times Corporation**
**222 Merchandise Mart Plaza, Suite 1513**
**Chicago, Illinois 60654**
**(312) 644-4378**

**Established: 1991**
**Circulation: 40,000**

**Contact Person:** Zan Hale, Managing Editor.

**Type of Publication:** National business publication for in-house corporate legal departments.

**Audience:** General counsel and other in-house attorneys; some government attorneys.

**How Frequently Published:** Monthly.

**Recently Published Articles:** Articles about managing in-house legal departments; relationships with outside counsel; the latest technology; litigation management; environmental and intellectual property law.

**Current Needs:** Articles about the latest technology; feature-oriented stories.

**Policy on Seasonal Pieces:** Four months in advance.

**Usual Length Desired:** Seven to ten typed (double-spaced) pages.

**Author Writes on Speculation or Assignment?** Assignment only.

**Are Free Sample Copies Available?** Yes.

**Payment Information:**
 **Rate:** Varies.
 **Mode:** On publication.
 **Advance Possible?** No.

**Rights Policy:** Buys all rights.

**How to Contact:** Send query and clips; may also phone.

**What Not to Do:** Send unsolicited manuscript.

**Time Needed for Reply:** One month.

**Does Author Supply Photos?** Preferably, but not mandatory.

**Advice for Authors:** Business writing expertise is a must—more important than legal writing experience. Corporate Legal Times is available through the LEXIS/NEXIS computer system.

# CURRICULUM REVIEW

**Lawrence Ragan Communications, Inc.**
**212 W. Superior Street, Suite 200**
**Chicago, Illinois 60610**
**(312) 335-0037**                    **Circulation: 5000**

**Contact Person:** Janine Wood, Editor.

**Type of Publication:** Reviews all K-12 print and software materials in language arts/reading, mathematics, social studies, and science. Articles cover all aspects of education but especially curriculum and its application.

**Audience:** Professional educators at all levels, textbook selection committees, librarians.

**How Frequently Published:** Nine times per year (September to May).

**Recently Published Articles:** Articles about debates in education, the value of grading, and the development of gifted behavior.

**Current Needs:** Fresh, informative articles about the evaluation of curriculum.

**Policy on Seasonal Pieces:** Two to three months in advance.

**Usual Length Desired:** 1000 to 2000 words.

**Author Writes on Speculation or Assignment?** Can be either.

**Are Free Sample Copies Available?** Yes; enclose a self-addressed, stamped envelope with request.

**Payment Information:**
    **Rate:** $25 to $100 per article.
    **Mode:** On publication.
    **Advance Possible?** No.

**Rights Policy:** Buys all rights, but has a generous reprint policy.

**How to Contact:** Send manuscript (photocopy OK); enclose a self-addressed, stamped envelope. May also phone.

**What Not to Do:** Drop in without an appointment.

**Time Needed for Reply:** Four to six weeks.

**Does Author Supply Photos?** No.

**Advice for Authors:** The only publication in its field that does in-depth K-12 textbook reviews, Curriculum Review is prepared by subject-matter specialists as a service to professionals in education.

# EDITOR & PUBLISHER

**8 S. Michigan Avenue, Suite 1601**
**Chicago, Illinois 60603**      **Established: 1884**
**(312) 641-0041**      **Circulation: 24,000**

**Contact Person:** Mark Fitzgerald, Midwest Editor.

**Type of Publication:** Magazine covering the newspaper industry.

**Audience:** Newspaper personnel on all levels.

**How Frequently Published:** Weekly.

**Recently Published Articles:** "Editorial Cartoon's Political Backfire in California"; "Tribal Council Shuts Hopi Newspaper"; "Campaigning for the Release of Hong Kong Journalist."

**Current Needs:** Articles about spot news that will interest the newspaper industry; also articles about trends and technological developments (especially interactive multimedia communications) in the industry.

**Policy on Seasonal Pieces:** Approximately two weeks in advance, but flexible.

**Usual Length Desired:** 1250 words.

**Author Writes on Speculation or Assignment?** Can be either.

**Are Free Sample Copies Available?** Yes.

**Payment Information:**
    **Rate:** $50 to $500 per article, depending on length and importance.
    **Mode:** On publication.
    **Advance Possible?** No.

**Rights Policy:** Buys all rights.

**How to Contact:** Phone, send query, or send manuscript. Photocopy OK. Enclose a self-addressed, stamped envelope.

**What Not to Do:** Any method of contact is acceptable.

**Time Needed for Reply:** Two weeks, minimum.

**Does Author Supply Photos?** Yes, if possible.

**Advice for Authors:** If articles are well written and pertinent, they stand an excellent chance of acceptance.

# EMPLOYEE BENEFIT PLAN REVIEW

**Charles D. Spencer & Associates, Inc.**
**250 S. Wacker Drive, Suite 600**       **Established: 1945**
**Chicago, Illinois 60606**              **Circulation: 23,000**

**Contact Person:** Sue Burzawa, Associate Editor/Product Manager; Margaret Keefe, Associate Editor.

**Type of Publication:** Magazine for people in the employee benefits field.

**Audience:** Corporate and public-sector employee benefits managers, executives, and administrators; human resources executives; service providers in the employee benefits field (e.g., health-care providers and insurance brokers).

**How Frequently Published:** Monthly.

**Recently Published Articles:** Articles about 401-K plans, benefits software and technology, prescription drug benefits, pension investments.

**Current Needs:** Depends on topics in editorial calendar.

**Policy on Seasonal Pieces:** At least six weeks in advance.

**Usual Length Desired:** 1500 words maximum.

**Author Writes on Speculation or Assignment?** Speculation.

**Payment Information:** Copies of the issue in which the contributor's work appears.

**Rights Policy:** Reserves all rights; reprints can be arranged.

**How to Contact:** Phone to find out editorial calendar topics; then send outline or complete manuscript.

**What Not to Do:** Send unsolicited manuscript.

**Time Needed for Reply:** Immediate acknowledgment if story is accepted.

**Does Author Supply Photos?** No.

**Advice for Authors:** Articles which conform to the scheduled topics on the editorial calendar are those most likely to receive consideration. Authors should assume that readers of Employee Benefit Plan Review have a working understanding of the field.

# FACETS

**American Medical Association Alliance**
**515 N. State Street**
**Chicago, Illinois 60610**          **Established: 1922**
**(312) 464-4470**                    **Circulation: 60,000**

**Contact Person:** Kathleen Jordan, Editor.

**Type of Publication:** Magazine for members of the AMA Alliance.

**Audience:** Physicians' spouses dedicated to the health of America.

**How Frequently Published:** Bimonthly.

**Recently Published Articles:** Articles about health reform and the family; teen stress; adolescent-on-adolescent violence.

**Current Needs:** Articles about timely health topics; health reform; social issues.

**Usual Length Desired:** 1500 to 2000 words.

**Author Writes on Speculation or Assignment?** Primarily assignment, but can be either.

**Are Free Sample Copies Available?** Yes.

**Payment Information:**
    **Rate:** Negotiable.
    **Mode:** On acceptance.
    **Advance Possible?** No.

**Rights Policy:** Reserves all rights, with generous reprint policy.

**How to Contact:** Send article outline or summary; may also phone.

**What Not to Do:** Send complete manuscript.

**Time Needed for Reply:** One month.

**Does Author Supply Photos?** Not necessary.

**Advice for Authors:** Familiarity with health issues is essential; knowledge of the AMA Alliance and its goals, membership, and readership is quite helpful.

# FIRE CHIEF

**Argus Business**
**35 E. Wacker Drive, Suite 700**
**Chicago, Illinois 60601**              **Established: 1956**
**(312) 726-7277**                          **Circulation: 44,000**

**Contact Person:** Scott Baltic, Editor.

**Type of Publication:** Management magazine for the fire service.

**Audience:** Paid or volunteer department and battalion chiefs, fire marshals, and others in management positions.

**How Frequently Published:** Monthly.

**Recently Published Articles:** Articles about financial management, computers in the fire service, productivity measurements, fire apparatus, sexual harassment in the fire service, gays in the fire service.

**Current Needs:** Articles about handling firefighting operations or about administration/management responsibilities.

**Policy on Seasonal Pieces:** Two months in advance.

**Usual Length Desired:** 1500 to 4000 words.

**Author Writes on Speculation or Assignment?** Usually assignment, but can be either.

**Are Free Sample Copies Available?** Yes.

**Payment Information:**
    **Rate:** $40 to $50 per printed page.
    **Mode:** On publication.
    **Advance Possible?** No.

**Rights Policy:** Usually reserves all rights, but policy can be negotiated.

**How to Contact:** Send query or manuscript. Photocopy OK.

**What Not to Do:** Phone or drop in without an appointment. Do not include Fire Chief as part of a simultaneous submission.

**Time Needed for Reply:** Two months.

**Does Author Supply Photos?** Yes.

**Advice for Authors:** Most of the material in Fire Chief is written either by staff members or by people in the fire service, but occasionally freelance work is used.

# FUTURES MAGAZINE
**Oster Communications**
**250 S. Wacker Drive, Suite 1150**
**Chicago, Illinois 60606**             **Established: 1972**
**(312) 977-0999**                      **Circulation: 60,000**

**Contact Person:** David Nusbaum, Senior Associate Editor.

**Type of Publication:** Business/financial magazine.

**Audience:** Professional futures, options, and derivatives traders; financial market users; portfolio managers.

**How Frequently Published:** Monthly.

**Recently Published Articles:** Think-piece on problems at the Chicago Board of Trade; articles about various trading strategies.

**Current Needs:** Software reviews and trading strategy analyses.

**Policy on Seasonal Pieces:** Three months in advance.

**Usual Length Desired:** Features—2000 words; departments—700 words.

**Author Writes on Speculation or Assignment?** Initially speculation; usually assignment thereafter.

**Are Free Sample Copies Available?** Yes.

**Payment Information:**
    **Rate:** 50 cents to $1 per word.
    **Mode:** On publication.
    **Advance Possible?** No.

**Rights Policy:** Reserves all rights.

**How to Contact:** Send query.

**What Not to Do:** Phone.

**Time Needed for Reply:** Two weeks.

**Does Author Supply Photos?** No.

**Advice for Authors:** Futures is always looking for fresh ideas. It prefers to receive articles on disk—Word Perfect 5.1 (Mac or PC); can also receive articles via modem.

# HEALTHCARE FINANCIAL MANAGEMENT

**Healthcare Financial Management Association**
**2 West Brook Corporate Center, Suite 700**
**Westchester, Illinois 60154**          **Established: 1947**
**(708) 531-9600**                        **Circulation: 32,000**

**Contact Person:** Cheryl T. Stachura, Editor and Publisher.

**Type of Publication:** Association magazine covering healthcare-finance topics.

**Audience:** Healthcare administrators, chief financial officers, controllers, accountants, and related personnel responsible for the administrative and financial procedures of hospitals and other healthcare providers.

**How Frequently Published:** Monthly.

**Recently Published Articles:** "Costs and Benefits of Integrated Healthcare Systems"; "Provider Alliances: Key to Healthcare Reform"; "Methods of Optimizing Revenue in Rural Healthcare Systems."

**Current Needs:** Articles about healthcare reform, provider networks, physician relations, mergers and acquisitions, information systems, cost and productivity management, marketing and competition in health care.

**Policy on Seasonal Pieces:** Six months in advance.

**Usual Length Desired:** Ten to twelve typed (doubled-spaced) pages.

**Author Writes on Speculation or Assignment?** Speculation.

**Are Free Sample Copies Available?** Yes, and so are writer's guidelines. Send requests to the attention of Sharon Malik.

**Payment Information:** Pays in copies in which contributor's work appears.

**Rights Policy:** Holds copyright.

**How to Contact:** Send query or complete manuscript; may also phone with a specific story idea.

**What Not to Do:** Phone without a specific story idea in mind.

**Time Needed for Reply:** Acknowledgment within one week; at least four months for acceptance/rejection notification.

**Does Author Supply Photos?** Yes, if possible.

**Advice for Authors:** Authors should familiarize themselves with the magazine before querying. All material is peer reviewed by healthcare practitioners before publication.

# HUMAN RIGHTS

**American Bar Association**
**750 N. Lake Shore Drive**
**Chicago, Illinois 60611**          **Established: 1973**
**(312) 988-5990**                   **Circulation: 6000**

**Contact Person:** Vicki Quade, Editor.

**Type of Publication:** Magazine covering human rights issues.

**Audience:** Lawyers handling cases covering the rights of minorities, women, gays, and others.

**How Frequently Published:** Quarterly.

**Recently Published Articles:** Articles about the rights of the homeless, war crimes in Bosnia, feminist jurisprudence, Native American tribal rights.

**Current Needs:** Articles about civil and constitutional rights.

**Policy on Seasonal Pieces:** Four months in advance.

**Usual Length Desired:** 2000 words.

**Author Writes on Speculation or Assignment?** Mostly on assignment, but can be either.

**Are Free Sample Copies Available?** Yes.

**Payment Information:**
   **Rate:** $100 to $250 per article.
   **Mode:** On acceptance.
   **Advance Possible?** No.

**Rights Policy:** Buys first North American serial rights.

**How to Contact:** Send query and clips; may also phone.

**What Not to Do:** Drop in without an appointment.

**Time Needed for Reply:** One month.

**Does Author Supply Photos?** No.

**Advice for Authors:** Get to know Human Rights and the kind of material it publishes before sending a query.

# ILLINOIS LEGAL TIMES
**Giant Steps Publishing Corporation**
**222 Merchandise Mart Plaza, Suite 1513**
**Chicago, Illinois 60654**          **Established: 1991**
**(312) 644-4378**                   **Circulation: 13,500**

**Contact Person:** Kelly Fox, Managing Editor.

**Type of Publication:** Magazine about the business of law.

**Audience:** Attorneys (primarily those who work in law firms) in Illinois.

**How Frequently Published:** Monthly.

**Recently Published Articles:** Articles about management, marketing, business development, litigation, attorney-client relationships, environmental law, and technology.

**Current Needs:** Feature articles about similar topics.

**Policy on Seasonal Pieces:** Four months in advance.

**Usual Length Desired:** Seven typed (double-spaced) pages.

**Author Writes on Speculation or Assignment?** Assignment.

**Are Free Sample Copies Available?** Yes.

**Payment Information:**
    **Rate:** Varies.
    **Mode:** On publication.
    **Advance Possible?** No.

**Rights Policy:** Buys all rights.

**How to Contact:** Send query and clips; may also phone.

**What Not to Do:** Send unsolicited manuscript.

**Time Needed for Reply:** One month.

**Does Author Supply Photos?** Preferably, but not mandatory.

**Advice for Authors:** Business writing expertise is a must—more important than legal writing experience. Illinois Legal Times is available through the LEXIS/NEXIS computer system.

# INDUSTRIAL FIRE CHIEF

**Argus Business**
**35 E. Wacker Drive, Suite 700**
**Chicago, Illinois 60601**          **Established: 1992**
**(312) 726-7277**                    **Circulation: 20,000**

**Contact Person:** Barry Hochfelder, Editor.

**Type of Publication:** Business magazine covering industrial fire protection and emergency response.

**Audience:** Managers in industrial fire brigades.

**How Frequently Published:** Bimonthly.

**Recently Published Articles:** "Cold Weather Firefighting"; "Training with Self-Contained Breathing Apparatus"; "Mutual Aid in Chemical Emergencies."

**Current Needs:** Articles about topics of a similar nature.

**Policy on Seasonal Pieces:** Two months in advance.

**Usual Length Desired:** 2000 words maximum.

**Author Writes on Speculation or Assignment?** Usually assignment, but can be either.

**Are Free Sample Copies Available?** Yes.

**Payment Information:**
    **Rate:** $60 per printed page.
    **Mode:** On publication.
    **Advance Possible?** No.

**Rights Policy:** Usually reserves all rights, but policy can be negotiated.

**How to Contact:** Send query or manuscript. Photocopy OK. Enclose a self-addressed, stamped envelope.

**What Not to Do:** Phone or drop in without an appointment.

**Time Needed for Reply:** Three weeks.

**Does Author Supply Photos?** Yes, if possible.

**Advice for Authors:** Most of the material in Industrial Fire Chief is written either by staff members or by people in the fire service, but occasionally freelance work is used.

# INLAND ARCHITECT
**Real Estate News Corporation**
**3525 W. Peterson Avenue**
**Chicago, Illinois 60659**
**(312) 866-9900**

**Established: 1883**
**Circulation: 3500**

**Contact Person:** Steven Klebba, Editor.

**Type of Publication:** Professional journal covering architecture, design, and urban and environmental issues.

**Audience:** Architects, builders, planners, and policymakers.

**How Frequently Published:** Bimonthly.

**Recently Published Articles:** Articles about various architectural styles, profiles of personalities and companies, features about affordable housing.

**Current Needs:** Articles about urban issues—e.g., design, critical analyses of buildings, architectural preservation and renovation; also interviews with leading architects and policymakers.

**Policy on Seasonal Pieces:** At least two months prior to issue date.

**Usual Length Desired:** 500 to 2500 words.

**Author Writes on Speculation or Assignment?** Can be either.

**Are Free Sample Copies Available?** No.

**Payment Information:**
    **Rate:** Negotiable.
    **Mode:** On publication.
    **Advance Possible?** No.

**Rights Policy:** Negotiable.

**How to Contact:** Send query and samples of previous work; may also send complete manuscript or phone.

**What Not to Do:** Drop in without an appointment.

**Time Needed for Reply:** One month.

**Does Author Supply Photos?** Yes, usually.

**Advice for Authors:** Keep in mind that Inland Architect looks at all angles of architecture—as a subject and as an industry.

# JOURNAL OF PROPERTY MANAGEMENT

**Institute of Real Estate Management**
430 N. Michigan Avenue
Chicago, Illinois 60611          **Established: 1934**
(312) 329-6058                   **Circulation: 20,300**

**Contact Person:** Mariwyn Evans, Editor.

**Type of Publication:** Journal covering property management and related real estate topics.

**Audience:** Property managers and managers in fields related to real estate.

**How Frequently Published:** Bimonthly.

**Recently Published Articles:** Articles about tenant retention; case studies of renovation to enhance resale value; stories about marketing and training programs; pieces about business operations applicable to property management.

**Current Needs:** More articles on similar topics.

**Policy on Seasonal Pieces:** Four months in advance.

**Usual Length Desired:** 1500 to 2000 words.

**Author Writes on Speculation or Assignment?** Mostly on assignment, but can be either.

**Are Free Sample Copies Available?** Yes.

**Payment Information:**
    **Rate:** Varies.
    **Mode:** On acceptance.
    **Advance Possible?** Only to cover expenses.

**Rights Policy:** Buys all rights.

**How to Contact:** Send query.

**What Not to Do:** Phone or drop in without an appointment.

**Time Needed for Reply:** Six weeks.

**Does Author Supply Photos?** Preferably, but not mandatory.

**Advice for Authors:** Journal of Property Management is interested in articles that are practically oriented and written for a sophisticated real estate audience. The tone should be neither too jovial nor too academic. The journal does not cover residential property brokerage.

# LUTHERAN EDUCATION

**Concordia University**
**7400 Augusta Street**
**River Forest, Illinois 60305**          **Established: 1865**
**(708) 771-8300**                        **Circulation: 5000**

**Contact Person:** Dr. Wayne Lucht, Editor.

**Type of Publication:** Educational journal.

**Audience:** Lutheran schoolteachers (mostly elementary, some secondary).

**How Frequently Published:** Five times per year, September through June.

**Recently Published Articles:** "The Future of the Lutheran Teaching Ministry"; "Math Education"; "Mainstreaming."

**Current Needs:** Articles about the philosophical aspects of education and new methodologies.

**Policy on Seasonal Pieces:** Four months in advance.

**Usual Length Desired:** Twelve typed (double-spaced) pages.

**Author Writes on Speculation or Assignment?** Speculation.

**Are Free Sample Copies Available?** Yes; enclose a self-addressed, stamped envelope with request.

**Payment Information:** Five or six copies of the issue in which contributor's work appears.

**Rights Policy:** Author retains rights.

**How to Contact:** Send query or complete manuscript.

**What Not to Do:** Phone or drop in without an appointment.

**Time Needed for Reply:** Immediate acknowledgment of receipt; two to three weeks for notification regarding decision to publish.

**Does Author Supply Photos?** Yes; submit 4x6 or larger black-and-white photos (journal measures 6x9).

**Advice for Authors:** Articles that appear in Lutheran Education are written, for the most part, by teachers for teachers.

# MARKETING RESEARCH

**American Marketing Association**
**250 S. Wacker Drive, Suite 200**
**Chicago, Illinois 60606**      **Established: 1989**
**(312) 648-0536**      **Circulation: 4000**

**Contact Person:** Lynn Coleman, Editor.

**Type of Publication:** Association magazine about the application and management of marketing research.

**Audience:** Marketing research practitioners.

**How Frequently Published:** Quarterly.

**Recently Published Articles:** Articles about brand equity and general functioning at research firms; also software reviews.

**Current Needs:** Feature articles relevant to magazine's focus.

**Policy on Seasonal Pieces:** Three months in advance.

**Usual Length Desired:** Seven to ten typed (double-spaced) pages.

**Author Writes on Speculation or Assignment?** Can be either.

**Are Free Sample Copies Available?** Yes.

**Payment Information:** Pays in copies in which contributor's work appears.

**Rights Policy:** Assumes all rights.

**How to Contact:** Send query; may also phone.

**What Not to Do:** Drop in without an appointment.

**Time Needed for Reply:** Within two weeks.

**Does Author Supply Photos?** Not necessary.

**Advice for Authors:** Authors whose work appears in this magazine possess demonstrable expertise in the field of marketing research.

# THE NEIGHBORHOOD WORKS

Center for Neighborhood Technology
2125 W. North Avenue
Chicago, Illinois 60647                    Established: 1978
(312) 278-4800, ext. 113                   Circulation: 2000

**Contact Person:** Patti Wolter, Editor.

**Type of Publication:** Nonprofit magazine covering neighborhood development, community organizing, and the environmental movement.

**Audience:** Community development organizers, city planners, academics, interested citizens.

**How Frequently Published:** Bimonthly.

**Recently Published Articles:** Articles about food systems in low-income communities, community development planning, community development financial institutions, and affordable housing.

**Current Needs:** Articles that distill to the local and personal level the essence of issues having national or international scope; news and features about energy efficiency, housing, transportation, economic development, and the environment.

**Policy on Seasonal Pieces:** Two to four months in advance.

**Usual Length Desired:** 1500 to 2500 words.

**Author Writes on Speculation or Assignment?** Can be either.

**Are Free Sample Copies Available?** Yes; enclose a self-addressed, stamped envelope with request.

**Payment Information:**
   **Rate:** Negotiable.
   **Mode:** On publication.
   **Advance Possible?** No.

**Rights Policy:** Reserves all rights.

**How to Contact:** Send a well-targeted query with resume and three writing samples.

**What Not to Do:** Phone.

**Time Needed for Reply:** Two to four months.

**Does Author Supply Photos?** Yes, if possible.

**Advice for Authors:** Writers must read and know The Neighborhood Works before submitting a query; they must also thoroughly understand the community organizing angle of a potential story.

# PENSIONS & INVESTMENTS

**Crain Communications, Inc.**
**740 N. Rush Street**
**Chicago, Illinois 60611**
**(312) 649-5200**

**Established: 1973**
**Circulation: 52,000**

**Contact Person:** Nancy Webman, Executive Editor.

**Type of Publication:** Institutional financial news magazine.

**Audience:** Professionals in the institutional investment industry.

**How Frequently Published:** Biweekly.

**Recently Published Articles:** "The Thousand Largest Pension Funds"; "The Nation's Leading Investment Advisors."

**Current Needs:** Opinion pieces about issues in the institutional investing field; articles about portfolio management theory.

**Policy on Seasonal Pieces:** At least three weeks in advance.

**Usual Length Desired:** 1500 words.

**Author Writes on Speculation or Assignment?** Can be either.

**Are Free Sample Copies Available?** Yes.

**Payment Information:**
**Rate:** Varies.
**Mode:** On publication.
**Advance Possible?** No.

**Rights Policy:** Reserves all rights.

**How to Contact:** Send query or article; may also phone.

**What Not to Do:** Drop in without an appointment.

**Time Needed for Reply:** At least ten days.

**Does Author Supply Photos?** Yes, if possible.

**Advice for Authors:** Take the time to contact Pensions & Investments to find out what the editors need and how to approach the topic.

# PLANNING
**American Planning Association**
**1313 E. 60th Street**
**Chicago, Illinois 60637**              **Established: 1972**
**(312) 955-9100**                       **Circulation: 31,500**

**Contact Person:** Sylvia Lewis, Editor.

**Type of Publication:** Magazine about urban planning and related issues.

**Audience:** City planners.

**How Frequently Published:** Monthly.

**Recently Published Articles:** Articles about transportation planning, geographic information systems, and social and environmental issues.

**Current Needs:** Solidly researched, factual articles about city and regional planning; major pieces about trends in cities; think pieces about planning trends; first-person accounts by planners; news articles and book reviews.

**Usual Length Desired:** Features—3000 words; news articles and book reviews—500 words maximum.

**Author Writes on Speculation or Assignment?** Can be either; book reviews, however, are always assigned.

**Are Free Sample Copies Available?** Yes, and so are writer's guidelines; enclose a self-addressed, stamped envelope with request.

**Payment Information:**
    **Rate:** Minimum of 20 cents per word for news and feature articles.
    **Mode:** On publication.
    **Advance Possible?** No.

**Rights Policy:** Buys first rights; other rights negotiable.

**How to Contact:** Send query.

**What Not to Do:** Phone, send complete manuscript, or drop in without an appointment.

**Time Needed for Reply:** Five weeks.

**Does Author Supply Photos?** Yes, with caption material; pays $25 to $100 for each 8x10 black-and-white glossy, $200 for color transparency used on front cover.

**Advice for Authors:** Send for and study Planning and the writer's guidelines. The editors are open to story ideas.

# PRINTING NEWS MIDWEST

Quoin Publishing, Inc.
800 W. Huron Street, Third Floor
Chicago, Illinois 60622
(312) 226-5600                    Circulation: 18,000

**Contact Person:** Vicki Cessna, Editor.

**Type of Publication:** Magazine covering the graphic communications field.

**Audience:** Graphic arts executives.

**How Frequently Published:** Monthly.

**Recently Published Articles:** News and feature articles about industry concerns, technical information, and company profiles.

**Current Needs:** More of the same type of articles.

**Policy on Seasonal Pieces:** Three months in advance.

**Usual Length Desired:** Features—2000 words; news—800 words.

**Author Writes on Speculation or Assignment?** Assignment.

**Are Free Sample Copies Available?** No.

**Payment Information:**
    **Rate:** $300 to $500 per article.
    **Mode:** On publication.
    **Advance Possible?** No.

**Rights Policy:** Buys all rights.

**How to Contact:** Send query and writing samples; may also phone.

**What Not to Do:** Send complete manuscript.

**Time Needed for Reply:** Three weeks.

**Does Author Supply Photos?** Yes, if possible.

**Advice for Authors:** Writers for Printing News Midwest must know the industry well.

# REAL ESTATE BUSINESS
The Hollingsworth Group
213 W. Wesley Street, Suite 202
Wheaton, Illinois 60187      Established: 1981
(708) 752-0500      Circulation: 30,000

**Contact Person:** Pierce Hollingsworth, Publisher.

**Type of Publication:** Official magazine of the Residential Sales Council and the Real Estate Brokerage Managers Council of the National Association of Realtors.

**Audience:** Residential real estate agents and brokers.

**How Frequently Published:** Quarterly.

**Recently Published Articles:** Articles about technology, personal productivity management, marketing, personal promotion, and selling.

**Current Needs:** Story abstracts relating to topics of interest to residential real estate sales professionals.

**Policy on Seasonal Pieces:** At least three months in advance.

**Usual Length Desired:** 2500 words.

**Author Writes on Speculation or Assignment?** Assignment.

**Are Free Sample Copies Available?** No.

**Payment Information:**
> **Rate:** $500 to $850 per article.
> **Mode:** On acceptance.
> **Advance Possible?** Usually not.

**Rights Policy:** Retains all rights, but is willing to negotiate reprint rights.

**How to Contact:** First send a written request for writer's guidelines and editorial calendar; enclose a self-addressed, stamped envelope. Then submit an abstract of story idea.

**What Not to Do:** Phone.

**Time Needed for Reply:** At least two weeks.

**Does Author Supply Photos?** Yes, if possible.

**Advice for Authors:** Authors should submit their ideas in abstract form first. They must be specific about story ideas and be well versed in the subject matter. Editors will make the assignment if a story concept is sound.

# RESTAURANTS & INSTITUTIONS
**Cahners Publishing Company**
**1350 E. Touhy Avenue**
**Des Plaines, Illinois 60017**
**(708) 390-2028**

**Established: 1938**
**Circulation: 162,000**

**Contact Person:** Michael Bartlett, Editor-in-Chief.

**Type of Publication:** Business magazine about the foodservice industry.

**Audience:** Professionals in the foodservice industry.

**How Frequently Published:** 24 times per year.

**Recently Published Articles:** Articles about food and menu trends; how-to articles about restaurants.

**Current Needs:** Contact the magazine for information about current needs.

**Policy on Seasonal Pieces:** Two months in advance.

**Usual Length Desired:** 300 to 3000 words.

**Author Writes on Speculation or Assignment?** Assignment.

**Are Free Sample Copies Available?** Yes.

**Payment Information:**
    **Rate:** Negotiable.
    **Mode:** On publication.
    **Advance Possible?** No.

**Rights Policy:** Negotiable, though the magazine usually buys all rights.

**How to Contact:** Send short query.

**What Not to Do:** Send unsolicited manuscript, phone, or drop in without an appointment.

**Time Needed for Reply:** Ten to fifteen days.

**Does Author Supply Photos?** Depends on story.

# SCREEN MAGAZINE

**Screen Enterprises, Inc.**
**720 N. Wabash Avenue**
**Chicago, Illinois 60611**          **Established: 1979**
**(312) 664-5236**                   **Circulation: 10,000**

**Contact Person:** Maureen Canny, Assistant Publisher.

**Type of Publication:** Publication covering the motion-picture production industry in Chicago.

**Audience:** Professional film/video makers and advertising agencies.

**How Frequently Published:** Weekly.

**Recently Published Articles:** Articles about new faces in the business, major technology changes, companies starting up and closing down.

**Current Needs:** More of the same and news-oriented articles.

**Usual Length Desired:** 600 to 800 words.

**Author Writes on Speculation or Assignment?** Assignment.

**Are Free Sample Copies Available?** Yes, and so are writer's guidelines; enclose a self-addressed, stamped envelope with request.

**Payment Information:**
    **Rate:** $75 to $150 per article.
    **Mode:** On publication.
    **Advance Possible?** No.

**Rights Policy:** Varies.

**How to Contact:** Send resume and clips of recent stories.

**What Not to Do:** Phone or submit ideas oriented to consumer film magazines.

**Time Needed for Reply:** Two weeks.

**Does Author Supply Photos?** Yes, if appropriate.

**Advice for Authors:** A background in the production of film, video, audio visuals, or advertising is essential for anyone who wants to write for Screen's sophisticated, knowledgeable audience. Stylish writing is always valued.

# STUDENT LAWYER

**American Bar Association**
**750 N. Lake Shore Drive**
**Chicago, Illinois 60611**          **Established: 1972**
**(312) 988-6048**                    **Circulation: 31,000**

**Contact Person:** Sarah Hoban, Editor; Miriam Krasno, Managing Editor.

**Type of Publication:** Legal-affairs magazine.

**Audience:** Law students who are members of the ABA's Law Student Division.

**How Frequently Published:** Nine times per year (monthly September through May).

**Recently Published Articles:** "Legal Aspects of the American Family"; "Where is the Best Place to Practice Law?"; "How I Got My First Job"; "Taking Lives in Their Hands."

**Current Needs:** Feature stories and news items about the law and legal education.

**Policy on Seasonal Pieces:** Three to six months in advance.

**Usual Length Desired:** Features—3000 to 4000 words; departments—1200 to 1800 words.

**Author Writes on Speculation or Assignment?** Mostly on assignment.

**Are Free Sample Copies Available?** No, but free writer's guidelines are.

**Payment Information:**
    **Rate:** Features—$600 to $900; departments—$250 to $350.
    **Mode:** On acceptance.
    **Advance Possible?** No.

**Rights Policy:** Buys first rights.

**How to Contact:** Send query and outline with writing samples; may also send manuscript.

**What Not to Do:** Phone or drop in without an appointment.

**Time Needed for Reply:** Four to six weeks.

**Does Author Supply Photos?** Sometimes.

**Advice for Authors:** Student Lawyer is not a legal research or technical publication. Writers need not have a legal background; good reporting and writing skills are more important.

# AMERICAN CLEAN CAR

**American Trade Magazines**
**500 N. Dearborn Street, Suite 1100**
**Chicago, Illinois 60610**
**(312) 337-7700**                              **Circulation: 13,400**

**Contact Person:** Larry Ebert, Editor.

**Type of Publication:** Trade magazine for the car-wash and detailing industries.

**Audience:** Owners and operators of car washes.

**How Frequently Published:** Bimonthly.

**Recently Published Articles:** Case studies of full-service and self-service washes; interviews with car-wash owners; articles about merchandising car washes.

**Current Needs:** More of the same type of articles.

**Policy on Seasonal Pieces:** At least two months in advance.

**Usual Length Desired:** 1000 to 1500 words.

**Author Writes on Speculation or Assignment?** Assignment.

**Are Free Sample Copies Available?** Yes.

**Payment Information:**
  **Rate:** Minimum of 7 cents per word; $8 to $10 per published photo.
  **Mode:** On publication.
  **Advance Possible?** No.

**Rights Policy:** Buys all rights.

**How to Contact:** Send query; may also phone.

**What Not to Do:** Send manuscript or drop in without an appointment.

**Time Needed for Reply:** One week.

**Does Author Supply Photos?** Yes, five or six photos per article.

**Advice for Authors:** Case studies should be management—not technique—oriented.

# AMERICAN COIN-OP

**American Trade Magazines**
**500 N. Dearborn Street, Suite 1100**
**Chicago, Illinois 60610**
**(312) 337-7700**

**Established: 1972**
**Circulation: 18,900**

**Contact Person:** Laurance Cohen, Editor.

**Type of Publication:** Trade magazine for the coin-op laundry and drycleaning industries.

**Audience:** Owners of coin-operated laundry and drycleaning stores.

**How Frequently Published:** Monthly.

**Recently Published Articles:** Case studies that profile simple success stories of businesses rebuilt and made profitable. Also stories about special advertising or promotional programs.

**Current Needs:** More of the same type of articles.

**Policy on Seasonal Pieces:** Three to four months.

**Usual Length Desired:** 1000 to 2000 words.

**Author Writes on Speculation or Assignment?** Assignment.

**Are Free Sample Copies Available?** Yes.

**Payment Information:**
    **Rate:** 6 cents per word; $6 minimum per published photo.
    **Mode:** Two weeks prior to publication.
    **Advance Possible?** No.

**Rights Policy:** Buys all rights.

**How to Contact:** Send query; may also phone.

**What Not to Do:** Send manuscript or drop in without an appointment.

**Time Needed for Reply:** Two weeks.

**Does Author Supply Photos?** Yes; black-and-white photos only.

**Advice for Authors:** Stories for American Coin-Op should be written in simple, straightforward language.

# AMERICAN DRYCLEANER

**American Trade Magazines**
**500 N. Dearborn Street, Suite 1100**
**Chicago, Illinois 60610**          **Established: 1934**
**(312) 337-7700**          **Circulation: 30,000**

**Contact Person:** Earl Fischer, Editor.

**Type of Publication:** Trade magazine for the drycleaning industry.

**Audience:** Owners of drycleaning establishments.

**How Frequently Published:** Monthly.

**Recently Published Articles:** "Good News, Bad News from the BBB" (news summary); "Neglected No Longer" (case study of successful plant).

**Current Needs:** Articles about environmental regulations and how drycleaners can and do adapt.

**Policy on Seasonal Pieces:** At least two months in advance.

**Usual Length Desired:** 500 to 4000 words

**Author Writes on Speculation or Assignment?** Can be either.

**Are Free Sample Copies Available?** Yes.

**Payment Information:**
  **Rate:** Minimum of 8 cents per word.
  **Mode:** Negotiable.
  **Advance Possible?** Yes.

**Rights Policy:** Usually buys all rights.

**How to Contact:** Query first; may also phone or send manuscript.

**What Not to Do:** Drop in without an appointment.

**Time Needed for Reply:** Varies.

**Does Author Supply Photos?** Yes, if appropriate.

**Advice for Authors:** American Drycleaner tries to provide the maximum amount of helpful information in a minimum of space. It prefers to publish case studies about drycleaners away from Chicago—especially in out-of-the-way areas.

# AMERICAN LAUNDRY DIGEST

**American Trade Magazines**
**500 N. Dearborn Street, Suite 1100**
**Chicago, Illinois 60610**          **Established: 1936**
**(312) 337-7700**                    **Circulation: 11,500**

**Contact Person:** Larry Ebert, Editor.

**Type of Publication:** Trade magazine for the laundry industry.

**Audience:** Owners and managers of laundries and laundry facilities.

**How Frequently Published:** Monthly.

**Recently Published Articles:** Case studies and how-to articles about institutional, commercial, and rental laundries.

**Current Needs:** Practical features about laundry ownership; stories about improving management techniques; articles about cost-saving methods.

**Policy on Seasonal Pieces:** Two months in advance.

**Usual Length Desired:** 1000 to 1500 words.

**Author Writes on Speculation or Assignment?** Can be either.

**Are Free Sample Copies Available?** Yes, and so are free writer's guidelines; enclose a self-addressed, stamped envelope with request.

**Payment Information:**
   **Rate:** Minimum 7 cents per word; $10 per published photo.
   **Mode:** On publication.
   **Advance Possible?** No.

**Rights Policy:** Buys all rights.

**How to Contact:** Send query; may also phone.

**What Not to Do:** Send manuscript or drop in without an appointment.

**Time Needed for Reply:** Two to three weeks.

**Does Author Supply Photos?** Preferably.

**Advice for Authors:** Writers should keep in mind that American Laundry Digest does not cover the coin-operated laundry business.

# AMERICAN NURSERYMAN

**American Nurseryman Publishing Company**
**77 W. Washington Street, Suite 2100**
**Chicago, Illinois 60602**          **Established: 1904**
**(312) 782-5505**                    **Circulation: 16,000**

**Contact Person:** Julie Higginbotham, Editor.

**Type of Publication:** Magazine about horticulture, nursery, and garden center management.

**Audience:** Owners of garden centers, retailers, growers, and landscapers.

**How Frequently Published:** Semimonthly.

**Recently Published Articles:** Articles about plant recommendations, employee and financial management, and issues confronting the industry; news and trends; profiles of successful companies.

**Current Needs:** Sophisticated marketing and financial stories; also articles about employee and resource management.

**Policy on Seasonal Pieces:** Two months in advance.

**Usual Length Desired:** Ten to fifteen typed (double-spaced) pages.

**Author Writes on Speculation or Assignment?** Can be either.

**Are Free Sample Copies Available?** Yes, and so are writer's guidelines.

**Payment Information:**
    **Rate:** Varies with length and quality of article.
    **Mode:** On acceptance.
    **Advance Possible?** Rarely.

**Rights Policy:** Buys first-time rights.

**How to Contact:** Send query and writing samples; may phone to request free writer's guidelines.

**What Not to Do:** Send complete manuscript.

**Time Needed for Reply:** Indefinite; will contact only if interested.

**Does Author Supply Photos?** Yes, preferably 35mm color slides.

**Advice for Authors:** American Nurseryman does not want consumer-oriented gardening articles. Prospective writers should be familiar with horticulture, business, and/or management.

# AMERICAN PRINTER

**Maclean Hunter Publishing Company**
**29 N. Wacker Drive**
**Chicago, Illinois 60606**
**(312) 726-2802**

**Established: 1883**
**Circulation: 97,000**

**Contact Person:** Jill Roth, Editorial Director.

**Type of Publication:** Magazine covering the printing and publishing markets.

**Audience:** Professionals in the graphic arts.

**How Frequently Published:** Monthly.

**Recently Published Articles:** "Unsettled Forecast"; "The Digital Print Shop"; "Pioneering Efforts"; "The Bindery-Finishing Services Directory."

**Current Needs:** Technical articles about prepress, press, or finishing processes; also articles about management and marketing.

**Policy on Seasonal Pieces:** At least two months in advance.

**Usual Length Desired:** Four to twelve typed (double-spaced) pages.

**Author Writes on Speculation or Assignment?** Speculation.

**Are Free Sample Copies Available?** Yes.

**Payment Information:**
    **Rate:** $200 to $650 per article.
    **Mode:** On publication.
    **Advance Possible?** Yes.

**Rights Policy:** Buys first North American serial rights.

**How to Contact:** Send query or manuscript (photocopy OK); may also phone.

**What Not to Do:** Drop in without an appointment.

**Time Needed for Reply:** One month.

**Does Author Supply Photos?** Yes.

**Advice for Authors:** Request a sample issue of American Printer and read it. Writers should possess technical knowledge of the printing industry.

# AMERICA'S NETWORK
**Advanstar Communications**
**233 N. Michigan Avenue, Suite 2423**
**Chicago, Illinois 60601**          **Established: 1909**
**(312) 938-2300**                    **Circulation: 40,000**

**Contact Person:** Bob Stoffels, Editor.

**Type of Publication:** Magazine for the professionals in the telecommunications industry.

**Audience:** Primarily people at the middle levels of management and up in the telecommunications industry.

**How Frequently Published:** Semimonthly.

**Recently Published Articles:** Articles about transmissions, switching, wireless, and cable television.

**Current Needs:** Technology-based articles.

**Policy on Seasonal Pieces:** Two months in advance.

**Usual Length Desired:** 1500 words.

**Author Writes on Speculation or Assignment?** Speculation, mostly.

**Are Free Sample Copies Available?** Yes.

**Payment Information:**
> **Rate:** $175 to $300 per article.
> **Mode:** On acceptance.
> **Advance Possible?** No.

**Rights Policy:** Buys all rights.

**How to Contact:** Phone with story ideas.

**What Not to Do:** Drop in without an appointment.

**Does Author Supply Photos?** No.

**Advice for Authors:** A technology background is important when writing for America's Network. The magazine accepts articles on disk as well as hard copy.

# APPLIANCE SERVICE NEWS

Gamit Enterprises, Inc.
110 W. Saint Charles Road
Lombard, Illinois 60148          **Established: 1950**
(708) 932-9550                   **Circulation: 42,000**

**Contact Person:** William Wingstedt, Editor and Publisher.

**Type of Publication:** Tabloid for people who repair major appliances and electrical housewares.

**Audience:** Appliance service technicians.

**How Frequently Published:** Monthly.

**Recently Published Articles:** Articles containing technical information about ozone-safe refrigerants and explaining the difference between U. S. schematic symbols and those used in European appliances.

**Current Needs:** Any news of interest to the appliance service industry and business features about appliance shop management.

**Policy on Seasonal Pieces:** Three months in advance.

**Usual Length Desired:** 2000 to 4500 words for features.

**Author Writes on Speculation or Assignment?** Can be either.

**Are Free Sample Copies Available?** Yes.

**Payment Information:**
    **Rate:** $200 to $300 per article.
    **Mode:** On publication.
    **Advance Possible?** No.

**Rights Policy:** Buys first North American serial rights.

**How to Contact:** Send query. Photocopied manuscripts also OK.

**What Not to Do:** Phone or drop in without an appointment.

**Time Needed for Reply:** Ten days to two weeks.

**Does Author Supply Photos?** Sometimes.

**Advice for Authors:** Readers of Appliance Service News are expert technicians, but they are not necessarily experts in business matters. Therefore, general business features are of particular interest.

# ASSEMBLY

**Hitchcock Publishing Company**
**191 S. Gary Avenue**
**Carol Stream, Illinois 60188**
**(708) 665-1000**                     **Circulation: 60,000**

**Contact Person:** Donald Hegland, Editor.

**Type of Publication:** Magazine about the assembly of hard goods, including mechanical and electrical products.

**Audience:** Manufacturing, design, and industrial engineers; managers of companies that make assembled products.

**How Frequently Published:** Ten times per year (combined issues in July/August and November/December).

**Recently Published Articles:** Articles about parts positions, assembly automation, quality assurance, management issues, power tools, adhesives, computers, and computer software.

**Current Needs:** Articles about plant management and how to reduce costs, increase productivity and profits.

**Usual Length Desired:** 1500 to 2000 words.

**Author Writes on Speculation or Assignment?** Speculation.

**Are Free Sample Copies Available?** Yes.

**Payment Information:**
    **Rate:** Varies.
    **Mode:** On publication.
    **Advance Possible?** No.

**Rights Policy:** Varies.

**How to Contact:** Send query; then follow up with an outline. May also phone or send complete manuscript. Photocopy OK, but do not include Assembly as part of a simultaneous submission.

**What Not to Do:** Drop in without an appointment.

**Time Needed for Reply:** At least one month.

**Does Author Supply Photos?** Yes, whenever possible.

**Advice for Authors:** The best topics for freelance contributors to Assembly are those dealing with managerial subjects.

# BILLIARDS DIGEST

**Luby Publishing**
**200 S. Michigan Avenue, Suite 1430**
**Chicago, Illinois 60604**
**(312) 341-1110**

**Established: 1978**
**Circulation: 18,000**

**Contact Person:** Michael Panozzo, Editor/Advertising Manager.

**Type of Publication:** Trade magazine serving the billiards industry.

**Audience:** Adults interested in billiards as an industry and a sport.

**How Frequently Published:** Bimonthly.

**Recently Published Articles:** Tournament coverage; instructional information; profiles of businesses and individuals.

**Current Needs:** Business-oriented articles; stories of top players; tournament information; interviews.

**Policy on Seasonal Pieces:** Three months in advance.

**Usual Length Desired:** 1200 to 2400 words.

**Author Writes on Speculation or Assignment?** Can be either.

**Are Free Sample Copies Available?** Yes.

**Payment Information:**
  **Rate:** $150 to $300 per article.
  **Mode:** On publication.
  **Advance Possible?** No.

**Rights Policy:** Buys first North American serial rights.

**How to Contact:** Send query and clips.

**What Not to Do:** Drop in without an appointment.

**Time Needed for Reply:** One to three months.

**Does Author Supply Photos?** Yes, when possible.

**Advice for Authors:** Billiards Digest favors features that provide an overview of events and personalities. The approach is similar to that of Sports Illustrated.

# BOWLERS JOURNAL

**Luby Publishing**
**200 S. Michigan Avenue, Suite 1430**
**Chicago, Illinois 60604**          **Established: 1913**
**(312) 341-1110**                    **Circulation: 24,000**

**Contact Person:** Jim Dressel, Editor.

**Type of Publication:** Trade magazine covering all aspects of the bowling industry.

**Audience:** Adults interested in bowling as an industry and a sport.

**How Frequently Published:** Monthly.

**Recently Published Articles:** Articles about business aspects of the bowling industry; coverage of tournaments; profiles of well-known bowlers.

**Current Needs:** More of the same.

**Policy on Seasonal Pieces:** Three months in advance.

**Usual Length Desired:** 1200 to 2000 words.

**Author Writes on Speculation or Assignment?** Can be either.

**Are Free Sample Copies Available?** Yes.

**Payment Information:**
    **Rate:** $150 to $300 per article.
    **Mode:** On acceptance.
    **Advance Possible?** No.

**Rights Policy:** Buys first North American serial rights.

**How to Contact:** Send query and clips.

**What Not to Do:** Drop in without an appointment.

**Time Needed for Reply:** One to three months.

**Does Author Supply Photos?** Yes, whenever possible.

**Advice for Authors:** Bowlers Journal prefers features that provide an overview of events and personalities. The approach is similar to that of Sports Illustrated.

# BOXBOARD CONTAINERS

**Maclean Hunter Publishing Company**
**29 N. Wacker Drive**
**Chicago, Illinois 60606**          **Established: 1882**
**(312) 726-2802**                   **Circulation: 15,000**

**Contact Person:** Greg Kishbaugh, Editor.

**Type of Publication:** Magazine about the manufacture of corrugated boxes and folding cartons.

**Audience:** Manufacturers, especially plant management personnel.

**How Frequently Published:** Monthly.

**Recently Published Articles:** Articles about management issues—e.g., training and employer-employee relations; also articles about end users and the latest technology.

**Current Needs:** More of the same type of articles.

**Usual Length Desired:** 1000 to 2000 words.

**Author Writes on Speculation or Assignment?** Can be either.

**Are Free Sample Copies Available?** Yes, on a limited basis to qualified individuals who submit queries.

**Payment Information:**
　　**Rate:** Generally $75 per printed page, but negotiable.
　　**Mode:** On publication.
　　**Advance Possible?** No.

**Rights Policy:** Negotiable.

**How to Contact:** Send query or complete manuscript; may also phone.

**What Not to Do:** Drop in without an appointment.

**Time Needed for Reply:** One month.

**Does Author Supply Photos?** Yes, if at all possible.

**Advice for Authors:** Writers who submit publishable photos definitely improve their chances of selling stories to Boxboard Containers.

# BREWERS DIGEST

**Ammark Publishing Company**
**4049 W. Peterson Avenue**
**Chicago, Illinois 60646**          **Established: 1926**
**(312) 463-3400**                   **Circulation: 3000**

**Contact Person:** Dori Whitney, Editor.

**Type of Publication:** Trade magazine serving the brewing industry.

**Audience:** Purchasers, exporters, importers, wholesalers, suppliers, and others in the brewing industry.

**How Frequently Published:** Monthly.

**Recently Published Articles:** Articles about the science and technology of brewing; general news and product information; research paper abstracts; brewery case histories; stories about sales and marketing.

**Current Needs:** More of the same.

**Policy on Seasonal Pieces:** Two months in advance.

**Usual Length Desired:** No limit.

**Author Writes on Speculation or Assignment?** Can be either.

**Are Free Sample Copies Available?** Yes.

**Payment Information:**
    **Rate:** Varies.
    **Mode:** On publication.
    **Advance Possible?** No.

**Rights Policy:** Buys all rights.

**How to Contact:** Send query or phone.

**What Not to Do:** Drop in without an appointment.

**Time Needed for Reply:** Two weeks.

**Does Author Supply Photos?** Yes.

**Advice for Authors:** The window of opportunity for freelancers is open just a crack here—but it is open.

# BUSINESS COMMUNICATIONS REVIEW

**BCR Enterprises, Inc.**
**950 York Road**
**Hinsdale, Illinois 60521**          **Established: 1971**
**(708) 986-1432**                    **Circulation: 15,000**

**Contact Person:** Fred Knight, Editor.

**Type of Publication:** Journal covering technology, management, and regulations within the telecommunications industry.

**Audience:** Managers of telecomunications facilities for large companies.

**How Frequently Published:** Monthly.

**Recently Published Articles:** Articles about the information superhighway and about voice, video, and data networking.

**Current Needs:** Articles relevant to telecommunications—i.e., issue analysis and management oriented topics.

**Policy on Seasonal Pieces:** Three months in advance.

**Usual Length Desired:** 2500 to 3000 words.

**Author Writes on Speculation or Assignment?** Assignment.

**Are Free Sample Copies Available?** Yes.

**Payment Information:**
    **Rate:** Varies, ranging up to $1500 per article.
    **Mode:** On publication.
    **Advance Possible?** No.

**Rights Policy:** Reserves all rights.

**How to Contact:** Send query and/or manuscript. Photocopy OK. May also phone.

**What Not to Do:** Send material without enclosing a self-addressed, stamped envelope.

**Time Needed for Reply:** One month.

**Does Author Supply Photos?** Preferably, but not mandatory.

**Advice for Authors:** Authors should avoid highly technical information, keeping in mind that they are writing for managers and not for engineers. Some familiarity with the telecommunications field is helpful.

# C & D DEBRIS RECYCLING
**Maclean Hunter Publishing Company**
**29 N. Wacker Drive**
**Chicago, Illinois 60606**    **Established: 1993**
**(312) 726-2802**    **Circulation: 13,000**

**Contact Person:** William Turley, Editor.

**Type of Publication:** Magazine for the construction and demolition waste-recycling industry.

**Audience:** Recyclers, government officials.

**How Frequently Published:** Quarterly.

**Recently Published Articles:** Article about recycling debris left from natural disasters; operating cost survey of companies in the industry.

**Current Needs:** Case histories; application articles.

**Policy on Seasonal Pieces:** Three months in advance.

**Usual Length Desired:** 2000 words.

**Author Writes on Speculation or Assignment?** Speculation.

**Are Free Sample Copies Available?** Yes, usually.

**Payment Information:**
    **Rate:** Negotiable.
    **Mode:** On publication.
    **Advance Possible?** No.

**Rights Policy:** Buys all rights.

**How to Contact:** Send query and clips; may also phone.

**What Not to Do:** Drop in without an appointment.

**Time Needed for Reply:** Two months.

**Does Author Supply Photos?** Yes, if at all possible.

**Advice for Authors:** Writers who do not know the meaning of "C & D" had best not consider writing for this magazine. C & D Debris Recycling is not interested in stories that read like promotional pieces for manufacturers.

# CHEF MAGAZINE

**Talcott Communications Corporation**
**20 N. Wacker Drive, Suite 3230**
**Chicago, Illinois 60606**          **Established: 1991**
**(312) 849-2220**                    **Circulation: 40,000**

**Contact Person:** Paul Clarke, Editor.

**Type of Publication:** Foodservice magazine.

**Audience:** Chefs.

**How Frequently Published:** Nine times per year.

**Recently Published Articles:** Articles about management and marketing strategies within the industry.

**Current Needs:** Profiles of chefs; more articles about management and marketing strategies.

**Policy on Seasonal Pieces:** Six weeks to two months in advance.

**Usual Length Desired:** 2000 words.

**Author Writes on Speculation or Assignment?** Assignment only.

**Are Free Sample Copies Available?** No.

**Payment Information:**
    **Rate:** $250 per article.
    **Mode:** On publication.
    **Advance Possible?** No.

**Rights Policy:** Buys all rights.

**How to Contact:** Send query.

**What Not to Do:** Phone.

**Does Author Supply Photos?** No.

**Advice for Authors:** Writers for Chef Magazine must have food-industry experience.

# CONCRETE PRODUCTS

**Maclean Hunter Publishing Company**
**29 N. Wacker Drive**
**Chicago, Illinois 60606**     **Established: 1947**
**(312) 726-2802**     **Circulation: 20,000**

**Contact Person:** Don Marsh, Editor.

**Type of Publication:** Magazine about concrete products and ready-mix concrete.

**Audience:** Producers of ready-mix and precast concrete.

**How Frequently Published:** Monthly.

**Recently Published Articles:** Articles about construction topics and developments.

**Current Needs:** News-based articles.

**Policy on Seasonal Pieces:** One month.

**Usual Length Desired:** 1500 words.

**Author Writes on Speculation or Assignment?** Assignment.

**Are Free Sample Copies Available?** Yes.

**Payment Information:**
    **Rate:** Negotiable.
    **Mode:** On acceptance.
    **Advance Possible?** No.

**Rights Policy:** Negotiable.

**How to Contact:** Send query; may also phone.

**What Not to Do:** Send complete manuscript.

**Time Needed for Reply:** Two to three weeks.

**Does Author Supply Photos?** Yes.

**Advice for Authors:** Writers who want to be published in Concrete Products should be knowledgeable about the concrete production industry.

# CONTROL

**Putman Publishing Company, Inc.**
**301 E. Erie Street**
**Chicago, Illinois 60611**          **Established: 1988**
**(312) 644-2020**                    **Circulation: 75,000**

**Contact Person:** Keith Larson, Executive Editor; Peggy Smedley, Editor-in-Chief.

**Type of Publication:** Magazine for instrumentation- and control-systems professionals in the process industries.

**Audience:** Engineering, operations, and management in process manufacturing plants.

**How Frequently Published:** Monthly.

**Recently Published Articles:** Articles about controllers and control systems, software, field instruments.

**Current Needs:** More of the same kind of articles.

**Policy on Seasonal Pieces:** Three months in advance.

**Usual Length Desired:** 1500 to 2500 words.

**Author Writes on Speculation or Assignment?** Assignment, usually.

**Are Free Sample Copies Available?** Yes, on a limited basis to qualified individuals who submit queries.

**Payment Information:**
    **Rate:** Negotiable per assignment.
    **Mode:** On acceptance.
    **Advance Possible?** No.

**Rights Policy:** Buys all rights.

**How to Contact:** Send query.

**What Not to Do:** Phone or send complete manuscript.

**Time Needed for Reply:** Two to three weeks.

**Does Author Supply Photos?** Yes, if possible.

**Advice for Authors:** Writers who want to be published in Control should possess at least a working knowledge of the technical nature of the industry.

# DISTRIBUTOR
**Palmer Publishing Company**
**651 W. Washington Street, Suite 300**
**Chicago, Illinois 60661**          **Established: 1983**
**(312) 993-0929**          **Circulation: 16,500**

**Contact Person:** Edwin Schwenn, Executive Editor.

**Type of Publication:** Trade magazine covering aspects of heating, ventilation, air conditioning/refrigeration (HVAC/R) distribution.

**Audience:** HVAC/R wholesalers and distributors.

**How Frequently Published:** Bimonthly.

**Recently Published Articles:** "How to Compete with Home Depot"; "Critical First Days of Training for the New Employee"; "Screening Credit Applicants."

**Current Needs:** Relevant how-to articles.

**Policy on Seasonal Pieces:** Two to three months in advance.

**Usual Length Desired:** 1000 to 2500 words.

**Author Writes on Speculation or Assignment?** Assignment.

**Are Free Sample Copies Available?** No.

**Payment Information:**
    **Rate:** 10 cents per word.
    **Mode:** On publication.
    **Advance Possible?** No.

**Rights Policy:** Buys first North American serial rights.

**How to Contact:** Send query.

**What Not to Do:** Phone.

**Time Needed for Reply:** Three weeks.

**Does Author Supply Photos?** Yes.

**Advice for Authors:** Writers must be familiar with wholesale operations specifically and the HVAC/R industry generally.

# ELECTRONIC PACKAGING & PRODUCTION

**Cahners Publishing Company**
**1350 E. Touhy Avenue**
**Des Plaines, Illinois 60018**          **Established: 1961**
**(708) 635-8800**                              **Circulation: 44,000**

**Contact Person:** Donald Swanson, Editor.

**Type of Publication:** Magazine that deals with electronic engineering for packaging fabrication and assembly.

**Audience:** Electronic engineers and equipment designers.

**How Frequently Published:** Monthly.

**Recently Published Articles:** Articles about computer and circuit board packaging and about fabrication, assembly, and testing of products.

**Current Needs:** Short, down-to-earth articles describing current activities in the industry; also technical articles.

**Policy on Seasonal Pieces:** Four months in advance.

**Usual Length Desired:** 1200 words.

**Author Writes on Speculation or Assignment?** Can be either.

**Are Free Sample Copies Available?** Yes, and so are writer's guidelines.

**Payment Information:**
    **Rate:** Negotiable.
    **Mode:** Negotiable.
    **Advance Possible?** No.

**Rights Policy:** Retains all rights.

**How to Contact:** Phone, send query, or send manuscript. Photocopy OK. Enclose a self-addressed, stamped envelope.

**What Not to Do:** Drop in without an appointment.

**Time Needed for Reply:** Two to six months.

**Does Author Supply Photos?** Yes; also charts and tables where appropriate.

**Advice for Authors:** Electronic Packaging & Production wants freelance contributions, but it is difficult to write in this field unless you are involved in the industry. Articles should be very specific rather than an overview.

# ENERGY FOCUS
**Palmer Publishing Company**
**651 W. Washington Street, Suite 300**
**Chicago, Illinois 60661**          **Established: 1991**
**(312) 993-0929**                    **Circulation: 20,000**

**Contact Person:** Jeff Ferenc, Editor.

**Type of Publication:** Business-to-business magazine covering aspects of energy efficiency in the operation of commercial and industrial buildings.

**Audience:** Commercial building managers, owners, and facility operators.

**How Frequently Published:** Bimonthly.

**Recently Published Articles:** "How the Local Utility Company Can Cut Costs"; "How to Deal with CFC Phase Out"; "Planning for Affordable Efficiency Upgrade."

**Current Needs:** How-to articles written in a semi-technical to technical manner.

**Policy on Seasonal Pieces:** Two months in advance.

**Usual Length Desired:** 1500 words.

**Author Writes on Speculation or Assignment?** Assignment, usually.

**Are Free Sample Copies Available?** Yes.

**Payment Information:**
   **Rate:** Negotiable.
   **Mode:** 30 days after publication.
   **Advance Possible?** No.

**Rights Policy:** Negotiable.

**How to Contact:** Send query and writing samples. May also send complete manuscript or phone.

**What Not to Do:** Drop in without an appointment.

**Time Needed for Reply:** Three weeks.

**Does Author Supply Photos?** Yes, usually.

**Advice for Authors:** Writers should have at least some familiarity with the industry.

# FANCY FOOD

**Talcott Communications Corporation**
**20 N. Wacker Drive**
**Chicago, Illinois 60606**   **Established: 1983**
**(312) 849-2220**   **Circulation: 25,500**

**Contact Person:** Alfreda Vaughn, Executive Editor.

**Type of Publication:** Magazine for retailers of gourmet foods.

**Audience:** Food buyers and store owners.

**How Frequently Published:** Monthly.

**Recently Published Articles:** Articles about special coffees, chocolates, snacks, mustards, regional cuisines, and the gift-basket industry; also an issue devoted to Italian food.

**Current Needs:** Articles about food marketing.

**Policy on Seasonal Pieces:** Three months in advance.

**Usual Length Desired:** 2000 to 2500 words.

**Author Writes on Speculation or Assignment?** Assignment.

**Are Free Sample Copies Available?** Yes.

**Payment Information:**
    **Rate:** 10 cents per word.
    **Mode:** On publication.
    **Advance Possible?** No.

**Rights Policy:** Buys all rights.

**How to Contact:** Send query and writing samples (preferably about some aspect of the food industry).

**What Not to Do:** Phone or send complete manuscript.

**Time Needed for Reply:** Ten days.

**Does Author Supply Photos?** Depends on the story.

**Advice for Authors:** Fancy Food prefers writers who have knowledge of the food industry in general and of marketing in particular.

# FLEET EQUIPMENT

**Maple Publishing**
**134 W. Slade Street**
**Palatine, Illinois 60067**          **Established: 1974**
**(708) 359-6100**          **Circulation: 63,000**

**Contact Person:** Tom Gelinas, Editor.

**Type of Publication:** Magazine covering various aspects of the trucking fleet industry.

**Audience:** Equipment managers of trucking fleets.

**How Frequently Published:** Monthly.

**Recently Published Articles:** Articles about shop environments, electrical engine control, tire management, and technician training.

**Current Needs:** Technical articles of interest to trucking fleet managers.

**Policy on Seasonal Pieces:** At least two months in advance.

**Usual Length Desired:** Six to nine typed (double-spaced) pages.

**Author Writes on Speculation or Assignment?** Assignment, mostly.

**Are Free Sample Copies Available?** Yes.

**Payment Information:**
    **Rate:** $350 to $400 per article.
    **Mode:** On acceptance.
    **Advance Possible?** No.

**Rights Policy:** Buys all rights.

**How to Contact:** Phone or send query.

**What Not to Do:** Send complete manuscript or drop in without an appointment.

**Time Needed for Reply:** Two weeks, maximum.

**Does Author Supply Photos?** Yes, if possible.

**Advice for Authors:** A relatively technical magazine, Fleet Equipment prides itself on its in-depth and specific approach. Its goal is to help trucking managers do their jobs more efficiently and economically. It is not interested in product-oriented articles.

# FOOD BUSINESS

**Putman Publishing Company, Inc.**
**301 E. Erie Street**
**Chicago, Illinois 60601**            **Established: 1988**
**(312) 644-2020**                     **Circulation: 50,000**

**Contact Person:** Charles Maurer, Editor.

**Type of Publication:** Magazine covering the latest food business and marketing developments.

**Audience:** Senior-level marketing and general managers.

**How Frequently Published:** Monthly.

**Recently Published Articles:** New product information; coverage of marketplace trends.

**Current Needs:** More of the same type of news-oriented articles.

**Policy on Seasonal Pieces:** Three or four months in advance.

**Usual Length Desired:** 800 words.

**Author Writes on Speculation or Assignment?** Assignment only.

**Are Free Sample Copies Available?** Yes.

**Payment Information:**
   **Rate:** Negotiable.
   **Mode:** On acceptance.
   **Advance Possible?** No.

**Rights Policy:** Buys all rights.

**How to Contact:** Send query and clips.

**What Not to Do:** Phone or send complete manuscript.

**Time Needed for Reply:** One month.

**Does Author Supply Photos?** Yes.

**Advice for Authors:** Writers for Food Business should be familiar with the food industry and have strong reporting skills.

# FOOD INDUSTRY NEWS

**Foodservice Publishing Company**
**3166 N. River Road, Suite 40/44**
**Des Plaines, Illinois 60018**       **Established: 1973**
**(708) 699-3300**              **Circulation: 20,000**

**Contact Person:** Jim Contis, Editor.

**Type of Publication:** Magazine about the restaurant, hotel, and grocery industries.

**Audience:** Managers of restaurants and fast-food outlets; hotel and corporate headquarters executives.

**How Frequently Published:** Monthly.

**Recently Published Articles:** Articles about Pepsi-Cola's control of 24 percent of the pizza industry; profiles of chefs; how-to stories; column presenting new products.

**Current Needs:** Stories detailing trends in the industry.

**Policy on Seasonal Pieces:** Six weeks in advance.

**Usual Length Desired:** 100 to 1200 words.

**Author Writes on Speculation or Assignment?** Assignment.

**Are Free Sample Copies Available?** Yes.

**Payment Information:**
    **Rate:** Varies.
    **Mode:** On acceptance.
    **Advance Possible?** No.

**Rights Policy:** Buys all rights.

**How to Contact:** Send query and clips.

**What Not to Do:** Phone or send complete manuscript.

**Time Needed for Reply:** Two weeks.

**Does Author Supply Photos?** Yes.

**Advice for Authors:** Prospective contributors to Food Industry News should keep in mind that they are writing for a publication that occupies a premier niche in the industry.

# FOOD PROCESSING

**Putman Publishing Company**
**301 E. Erie Street**
**Chicago, Illinois 60601**
**(312) 644-2020**

**Established: 1954**
**Circulation: 65,000**

**Contact Person:** Charles Maurer, Editor.

**Type of Publication:** Magazine covering the food-processing industry.

**Audience:** Product developers, plant-operations managers and engineers.

**How Frequently Published:** Monthly.

**Recently Published Articles:** Articles about the technology of different kinds of foods and their ingredients; articles about food warehousing, distribution, and processing.

**Current Needs:** More of the same type of articles.

**Policy on Seasonal Pieces:** Three or four months in advance.

**Usual Length Desired:** 2000 words.

**Author Writes on Speculation or Assignment?** Assignment only.

**Are Free Sample Copies Available?** Yes.

**Payment Information:**
    **Rate:** Negotiable.
    **Mode:** On acceptance.
    **Advance Possible?** No.

**Rights Policy:** Buys all rights.

**How to Contact:** Send query and clips.

**What Not to Do:** Phone or send complete manuscript.

**Time Needed for Reply:** One month.

**Does Author Supply Photos?** Yes.

**Advice for Authors:** Writers for Food Processing must have a strong understanding of the technical side (in contrast to the business side) of the food industry.

# FOODSERVICE EQUIPMENT & SUPPLIES SPECIALIST

**Cahners Publishing Company**
**1350 E. Touhy Avenue**
**Des Plaines, Illinois 60018**          **Established: 1948**
**(708) 635-8800**                       **Circulation: 22,100**

**Contact Person:** Greg Richards, Editor.

**Type of Publication:** Magazine covering the specifying and distributing of foodservice equipment and supplies.

**Audience:** Facilities designers and distributors, manufacturers' representatives, and chain specifiers.

**How Frequently Published:** Thirteen times per year.

**Recently Published Articles:** "The Giants: The Top One Hundred Equipment Dealers"; "1994 Industry Forecast"; "Food Safety: Whose Job Is It?"; "Tabletop Design Awards."

**Current Needs:** Stories about distribution activities of foodservice equipment manufacturers and dealers to any away-from-home eating markets; also articles about kitchen design as well as any news relating to the industry.

**Policy on Seasonal Pieces:** Three months in advance.

**Usual Length Desired:** 1000 to 1200 words.

**Author Writes on Speculation or Assignment?** Assignment.

**Are Free Sample Copies Available?** Yes.

**Payment Information:**
    **Rate:** Varies
    **Mode:** On acceptance.
    **Advance Possible?** Yes, for expenses only.

**Rights Policy:** Buys all rights.

**How to Contact:** Send query and clips.

**What Not to Do:** Phone or send complete manuscript.

**Time Needed for Reply:** One month.

**Does Author Supply Photos?** Yes; pays extra for photos.

**Advice for Authors:** Most articles in Foodservice Equipment & Supplies Specialist are staff written. Freelancers who want to see their work published in the magazine must know the industry well.

# GAS INDUSTRIES

P. O. Box 558
Park Ridge, Illinois 60068
(708) 693-3682                    Established: 1956

**Contact Person:** William Dannhausen, Publisher.

**Type of Publication:** Magazine covering the natural gas pipeline and utility distribution market in North America.

**Audience:** Executives in the natural gas utility industry.

**How Frequently Published:** Monthly.

**Recently Published Articles:** Articles about leak-detection technology, corrosion prevention, safety and liability, and natural gas research and development.

**Current Needs:** Articles about NGV and Ferc 636; other topics relating to the gas pipeline and utility market.

**Policy on Seasonal Pieces:** Three months in advance.

**Usual Length Desired:** 1000 words.

**Author Writes on Speculation or Assignment?** Can be either.

**Are Free Sample Copies Available?** Yes.

**Payment Information:**
  **Rate:** Varies.
  **Mode:** On publication.
  **Advance Possible?** Only if on assignment.

**Rights Policy:** Buys first publication rights.

**How to Contact:** Send query or manuscript; photocopy OK.

**What Not to Do:** Phone or drop in without an appointment.

**Time Needed for Reply:** Varies.

**Does Author Supply Photos?** Yes.

**Advice for Authors:** Gas Industries wants articles that emphasize new technology, faster/easier work methods, costs savings, and dealing with regulation.

# GLOBAL TELEPHONY

**Intertec Publishing Corporation**
**55 E. Jackson Boulevard**
**Chicago, Illinois 60604**
**(312) 922-2435**

**Established: 1993**
**Circulation: 17,500**

**Contact Person:** Steve Titch, Editor.

**Type of Publication:** Magazine for telecommunications providers and large end-users throughout the world.

**Audience:** PTT ministries, private network operators, wireless network operators, international telecommunications carriers, and Fortune 500 companies that operate their own international networks.

**How Frequently Published:** Ten times per year (no issues in August or December).

**Recently Published Articles:** "ISDN: A Final Drink at the Last Chance Saloon"; "Australia Jumps to Broadband"; "Hong Kong's Telecommunications Free-for-All"; "The Eleven Steps in the Outsourcing Pyramid."

**Current Needs:** Case histories and articles about the application of new technology.

**Policy on Seasonal Pieces:** Four or five months in advance.

**Usual Length Desired:** Department pieces—800 to 1200 words; features—2000 to 3000 words.

**Author Writes on Speculation or Assignment?** Assignment, mostly.

**Are Free Sample Copies Available?** Yes.

**Payment Information:**
    **Rate:** Department pieces—$300; features—varies.
    **Mode:** On acceptance.
    **Advance Possible?** No.

**Rights Policy:** Buys all rights.

**How to Contact:** Send query with resume and writing samples (preferably by electronic mail: Telephony on MCI Mail).

**What Not to Do:** Phone or send unsolicited manuscripts.

**Time Needed for Reply:** One week.

**Does Author Supply Photos?** Yes, if possible.

**Advice for Authors:** Authors must be knowledgeable about the telecommunications industry in general and the approach of Global Telephony in particular.

# GOOD CENTS

**Palmer Publishing Company**
**651 W. Washington Street, Suite 300**
**Chicago, Illinois 60661**  **Established: 1990**
**(312) 993-0929**  **Circulation: 25,000**

**Contact Person:** Jeff Ferenc, Editor.

**Type of Publication:** Magazine covering energy efficiency in residential building construction.

**Audience:** Builders and contractors.

**How Frequently Published:** Bimonthly.

**Recently Published Articles:** "Window Rating System"; "Energy Solutions for Multi-Family Housing"; "Green Construction."

**Current Needs:** How-to articles written in a semi-technical to technical manner.

**Policy on Seasonal Pieces:** Two months in advance.

**Usual Length Desired:** 1500 words.

**Author Writes on Speculation or Assignment?** Can be either.

**Are Free Sample Copies Available?** Yes.

**Payment Information:**
**Rate:** Negotiable.
**Mode:** 30 days after publication.
**Advance Possible?** No.

**Rights Policy:** Negotiable.

**How to Contact:** Send query and writing samples. May also send complete manuscript or phone.

**What Not to Do:** Drop in without an appointment.

**Time Needed for Reply:** Three weeks.

**Does Author Supply Photos?** Yes, usually.

**Advice for Authors:** Writers should have at least some familiarity with the industry.

# GROCERY DISTRIBUTION
Grocery Market Publications
455 Frontage Road, Suite 116
Burr Ridge, Illinois 60521          Established: 1974
(708) 986-8767                       Circulation: 15,000

**Contact Person:** Thomas Smith, Managing Editor.

**Type of Publication:** Magazine covering supermarket chains and food manufacturers and wholesalers.

**Audience:** Executives in the food distribution industry: manufacturers, wholesalers, and supermarket operators.

**How Frequently Published:** Bimonthly.

**Recently Published Articles:** "Complete Distribution Center Sets Base for Chain's Growth"; "Solving Dock Gridlock in a General Merchandise Center."

**Current Needs:** Technical articles about distribution; case histories; features; interviews; surveys.

**Policy on Seasonal Pieces:** Two to three weeks in advance.

**Usual Length Desired:** 1000 to 3000 words.

**Author Writes on Speculation or Assignment?** Assignment.

**Are Free Sample Copies Available?** Yes; enclose a self-addressed, stamped envelope with request.

**Payment Information:**
  **Rate:** $125 to $300 per article; $400 for photo/story package.
  **Mode:** On publication.
  **Advance Possible?** Only for authorized travel expenses.

**Rights Policy:** Buys all rights.

**How to Contact:** Send query, story lead, and samples of previously published work.

**What Not to Do:** Send complete manuscript or drop in without an appointment.

**Time Needed for Reply:** One to two weeks.

**Does Author Supply Photos?** Yes; submit captions with pictures.

**Advice for Authors:** Grocery Distribution needs writers who can write good case history features and use a camera at a fairly professional level.

# GROOM & BOARD

**H. H. Backer Associates, Inc.**
**20 E. Jackson Boulevard**
**Chicago, Illinois 60604**          **Established: 1980**
**(312) 222-2000**                    **Circulation: 18,300**

**Contact Person:** Karen Long MacLeod, Editor.

**Type of Publication:** Trade magazine serving pet-care professionals.

**Audience:** Groomers, kennel operators, some veterinarians, pet-care auxiliary servers.

**How Frequently Published:** Monthly, with combined issues in January/February, September/October, and November/December.

**Recently Published Articles:** Articles offering technical grooming advice, dealing with the importance of complying with OSHA rules, and showing how Midwest pet-care professionals coped during the Great Flood of 1993.

**Current Needs:** More of the same.

**Policy on Seasonal Pieces:** Six months in advance.

**Usual Length Desired:** 1000 to 3000 words.

**Author Writes on Speculation or Assignment?** Can be either.

**Are Free Sample Copies Available?** No.

**Payment Information:**
    **Rate:** Varies.
    **Mode:** On acceptance.
    **Advance Possible?** No.

**Rights Policy:** Buys first North American serial rights.

**How to Contact:** Send query and clips.

**What Not to Do:** Phone.

**Time Needed for Reply:** Six to eight weeks.

**Does Author Supply Photos?** Yes, if possible. Pays for photos used.

**Advice for Authors:** Most articles in Groom & Board involve dog care. News or feature ideas should have an unusual slant. Familiarity with the pet-care field is, of course, helpful.

# HEALTH FACILITIES MANAGEMENT

**American Hospital Publishing, Inc.**
**737 N. Michigan Avenue, Suite 700**
**Chicago, Illinois 60611**          **Established: 1988**
**(312) 440-6800**                    **Circulation: 45,000**

**Contact Person:** Michael Hemmes, Editor.

**Type of Publication:** Nonclinical magazine covering the design, construction, and maintenance of healthcare facilities.

**Audience:** Facilities managers, plant engineers, environmental services managers (housekeeping, laundry/linen), safety and security professionals, etc.

**How Frequently Published:** Monthly.

**Recently Published Articles:** Articles about building codes and standards, physical plant products and systems, safety and security, interior design, housekeeping, etc.; also case histories of individual construction projects.

**Current Needs:** Technical articles written in a readable, how-to fashion; checklists.

**Policy on Seasonal Pieces:** Three to four months in advance.

**Usual Length Desired:** Four to eight typed (double-spaced) pages.

**Author Writes on Speculation or Assignment?** Can be either.

**Are Free Sample Copies Available?** Yes, on a limited basis, and so are writer's guidelines.

**Payment Information:**
    **Rate:** Varies, depending on research required.
    **Mode:** On acceptance.
    **Advance Possible?** No.

**Rights Policy:** Buys all rights.

**How to Contact:** Send for and review the writer's guidelines; then send a query and no more than two writing samples.

**What Not to Do:** Phone or send complete manuscript.

**Time Needed for Reply:** Six to eight weeks.

**Does Author Supply Photos?** Depends on project.

**Advice for Authors:** Health Facilities Management is the only facilities-management magazine with a healthcare focus. As a consequence, writers must make certain that their article ideas are specific to the generally stricter requirements of the healthcare industry.

# INTERIOR LANDSCAPE
**American Nurseryman Publishing Company**
**77 W. Washington Street, Suite 2100**
**Chicago, Illinois 60602**          **Established: 1984**
**(312) 782-5505**                    **Circulation: 4400**

**Contact Person:** Julie Higginbotham, Managing Editor.

**Type of Publication:** Trade magazine covering business and technical aspects of interior landscaping.

**Audience:** Interior landscapers.

**How Frequently Published:** Quarterly.

**Recently Published Articles:** Articles about new trends in the industry; business how-to pieces; stories dealing with the technical aspects of interior landscaping.

**Current Needs:** More of the same.

**Policy on Seasonal Pieces:** Six months in advance.

**Usual Length Desired:** Ten to fifteen typed (double-spaced) pages.

**Author Writes on Speculation or Assignment?** Can be either.

**Are Free Sample Copies Available?** Yes.

**Payment Information:**
　　**Rate:** Varies with length and quality of article.
　　**Mode:** On acceptance
　　**Advance Possible?** Rarely.

**Rights Policy:** Buys first-time rights.

**How to Contact:** Send query and writing samples.

**What Not to Do:** Send complete manuscript.

**Time Needed for Reply:** Two months.

**Does Author Supply Photos?** Yes, preferably 35mm color slides.

**Advice for Authors:** Prospective writers should be familiar with horticulture and/or business. Articles that appear in Interior Landscape must be targeted to professional interior landscapers.

# LUXURY HOMES
**Cahners Publishing Company**
**1350 E. Touhy Avenue**
**Des Plaines, Illinois 60018**      **Established: 1992**
**(708) 635-8800**      **Circulation: 144,000**

**Contact Person:** Laura Hengstler, Managing Editor.

**Type of Publication:** Magazine covering the luxury home market.

**Audience:** Builders and buyers of luxury homes.

**How Frequently Published:** Bimonthly.

**Recently Published Articles:** Case histories of residential designs; articles about products used in the construction of luxury homes.

**Current Needs:** Features on aspects of design in the building of luxury homes.

**Policy on Seasonal Pieces:** Three months in advance.

**Usual Length Desired:** 1200 words.

**Author Writes on Speculation or Assignment?** Assignment.

**Are Free Sample Copies Available?** Yes, to qualified individuals who submit queries.

**Payment Information:**
    **Rate:** Varies.
    **Mode:** On acceptance.
    **Advance Possible?** No.

**Rights Policy:** Buys all rights.

**How to Contact:** Send query and two writing samples; may also phone.

**What Not to Do:** Send complete manuscript.

**Time Needed for Reply:** Two weeks.

**Does Author Supply Photos?** Depends on project.

**Advice for Authors:** Focusing as it does on the design of buildings rather than on the nuts-and-bolts of construction, Luxury Homes is not a particularly technical magazine in its approach and tone. Writers should have a background in residential design.

# MANUFACTURED HOME MERCHANDISERS

RLD Group, Inc.
203 N. Wabash Avenue, Suite 800
Chicago, Illinois 60601
(312) 236-3528

**Established:** 1952
**Circulation:** 15,000

**Contact Person:** Robert Overend, Editor.

**Type of Publication:** Magazine covering the manufactured housing industry.

**Audience:** Retailers of manufactured houses, the manufacturers themselves, and their suppliers.

**How Frequently Published:** Monthly.

**Recently Published Articles:** "Develop Your Own Mini-Marketing Plan"; "Industry Innovation Is Badly Needed."

**Current Needs:** General business articles geared to small retail operations (i.e., those with a dozen or fewer employees).

**Policy on Seasonal Pieces:** At least two months in advance.

**Usual Length Desired:** 1500 words

**Author Writes on Speculation or Assignment?** Assignment, mostly.

**Are Free Sample Copies Available?** No.

**Payment Information:**
    **Rate:** Varies.
    **Mode:** Varies.
    **Advance Possible?** No.

**Rights Policy:** Buys first rights.

**How to Contact:** Send query and writing samples; may also phone.

**What Not to Do:** Include Manufactured Home Merchandisers as part of a simultaneous submission.

**Time Needed for Reply:** Three weeks.

**Does Author Supply Photos?** Yes, two or three black-and-white photos.

**Advice for Authors:** Individuals who wish to write for Manufactured Home Merchandisers must have an understanding of the manufactured home industry. They must also not expect to see their articles published in a specific issue of the magazine. Freelance pieces are used on a space-available basis.

# MATERIALS MANAGEMENT IN HEALTH CARE

**American Hospital Publishing, Inc.**
**737 N. Michigan Avenue, Suite 700**
**Chicago, Illinois 60611**
**(312) 440-6800**

**Established: 1992**
**Circulation: 27,000**

**Contact Person:** Laura Souhrada, Editor.

**Type of Publication:** Magazine covering medical supplies and healthcare equipment.

**Audience:** Purchasors and users of medical supplies and healthcare equipment; also those responsible for infection control and for sterilizing medical devices for reuse in hospitals.

**How Frequently Published:** Monthly.

**Recently Published Articles:** Articles about regulations regarding the purchase and use of tuberculosis respirators; purchasing supplies for off-site care facilities; product evaluation and standardizing committees.

**Current Needs:** Feature stories focusing on actions of end users (i.e., hospitals).

**Policy on Seasonal Pieces:** Three months in advance.

**Usual Length Desired:** Nine to twelve typed (double-spaced) pages.

**Author Writes on Speculation or Assignment?** Can be either.

**Are Free Sample Copies Available?** Yes, to qualified individuals who submit queries.

**Payment Information:**
**Rate:** Varies.
**Mode:** On acceptance.
**Advance Possible?** No.

**Rights Policy:** Buys all rights.

**How to Contact:** Send query and three writing samples.

**What Not to Do:** Phone or submit product promotion pieces.

**Time Needed for Reply:** Eight weeks.

**Does Author Supply Photos?** Yes, if possible.

**Advice for Authors:** Writers for Materials Management in Health Care must be able to make technical subjects readable to a general audience. Knowledge of the healthcare industry is helpful.

# MAY TRENDS

**George S. May International Company**
**303 S. Northwest Highway**
**Park Ridge, Illinois 60068**       **Established: 1966**
**(708) 825-8806**                          **Circulation: 40,000**

**Contact Person:** John McArdle, Editor.

**Type of Publication:** Magazine addressing issues and concerns of small and medium-sized businesses and health-care facilities.

**Audience:** Manufacturers, retailers, wholesalers, distributors, service company owners and managers, owners and managers of health-care businesses.

**How Frequently Published:** Variable, usually one to three issues per year.

**Recently Published Articles:** "Myths About Quality"; "Small Business—Engine for Job Creation"; "The Global Marketplace"; "Health-Care Trends in the Decade Ahead."

**Current Needs:** Articles that address the problems of operating small and medium-sized businesses, especially ones that describe trends—business, marketing, or technological—that may impact those businesses.

**Usual Length Desired:** 2000 to 3000 words.

**Author Writes on Speculation or Assignment?** Speculation.

**Are Free Sample Copies Available?** Yes; enclose a self-addressed, stamped envelope with request.

**Payment Information:**
    **Rate:** $100 to $250 per article.
    **Mode:** On publication.
    **Advance Possible?** No.

**Rights Policy:** Buys all rights.

**How to Contact:** Send query or manuscript.

**What Not to Do:** Phone or drop in without an appointment.

**Time Needed for Reply:** Varies.

**Does Author Supply Photos?** No.

**Advice for Authors:** Study May Trends carefully before submitting an article or a query.

# MERCHANDISER/AMOCO JOBBER

**Amoco Oil Company**
**P. O. Box 6110A, MC3708**
**Chicago, Illinois 60680**          **Established: 1972**
**(312) 856-5373**                    **Circulation: 10,500**

**Contact Person:** Neil Geary, Managing Editor.

**Type of Publication:** Magazine for owners of Amoco service stations.

**Audience:** Amoco dealers and jobbers.

**How Frequently Published:** Quarterly.

**Recently Published Articles:** Articles about new station strategies, environmental initiatives, and dealer success stories.

**Current Needs:** How-to articles about marketing and increasing profitability.

**Policy on Seasonal Pieces:** Three months in advance.

**Usual Length Desired:** 1000 to 1500 words.

**Author Writes on Speculation or Assignment?** Assignment.

**Are Free Sample Copies Available?** Yes.

**Payment Information:**
    **Rate:** $350 per article (minimum if article does not need extensive editing or rewriting).
    **Mode:** On publication.
    **Advance Possible?** No.

**Rights Policy:** Buys first rights.

**How to Contact:** Send query and writing sample.

**What Not to Do:** Phone, send manuscript, or drop in without an appointment.

**Time Needed for Reply:** Two to three weeks.

**Does Author Supply Photos?** Yes; color photos for Merchandiser, black-and-white for Jobber.

**Advice for Authors:** Merchandiser and Amoco Jobber typically buy just one or two manuscripts per year from freelancers.

# MOTOR SERVICE

**Hunter Publishing Company**
**25 Northwest Point Boulevard, Suite 800**
**Elk Grove Village, Illinois 60007**
**(708) 427-9512**

**Established: 1921**
**Circulation: 175,000**

**Contact Person:** James Halloran, Editorial Director.

**Type of Publication:** Trade magazine covering management, technical, and news issues for the motor service industry.

**Audience:** Garage and repair-shop owners and operators.

**How Frequently Published:** Monthly.

**Recently Published Articles:** "Rack and Pinion Opinion"; "Clinton Ignites Alternate Fuels Drive."

**Current Needs:** Technical how-to articles about auto repair; management and merchandising articles about promotion, advertising, and employee training; profiles of successful operations.

**Policy on Seasonal Pieces:** One month in advance.

**Usual Length Desired:** 1000 to 2000 words.

**Author Writes on Speculation or Assignment?** Assignment.

**Are Free Sample Copies Available?** Yes.

**Payment Information:**
    **Rate:** $300 to $500 per article.
    **Mode:** On acceptance.
    **Advance Possible?** Only if special expenses are involved.

**Rights Policy:** Reserves all rights.

**How to Contact:** Send query or phone.

**What Not to Do:** Send complete manuscript or drop in without an appointment.

**Time Needed for Reply:** One month.

**Does Author Supply Photos?** Yes, usually.

**Advice for Authors:** Most articles are staff written, but freelancers able to show knowledge of how successful small businesses (not necessarily automotive) operate can receive assignments.

# MUSIC INC.

Maher Publications, Inc.
180 W. Park Avenue
Elmhurst, Illinois 60126
(708) 941-2030                    **Circulation: 8000**

**Contact Person:** Ed Enright, Editor; John Janowiak, Managing Editor.

**Type of Publication:** Magazine serving the music industry.

**Audience:** Manufacturers and retailers of musical instruments, audio components, and printed sheet music.

**How Frequently Published:** Eleven times per year (combined February/March issue).

**Recently Published Articles:** Product news; manufacturing and retailing news stories; how-to pieces detailing marketing, financial, and sales techniques.

**Current Needs:** Articles about the retail music business.

**Usual Length Desired:** 1500 to 2000 words.

**Author Writes on Speculation or Assignment?** Can be either.

**Are Free Sample Copies Available?** Yes.

**Payment Information:**
    **Rate:** Up to $100 per article.
    **Mode:** On publication.
    **Advance Possible?** Usually not.

**Rights Policy:** Buys first North American rights.

**How to Contact:** Send query and writing samples.

**What Not to Do:** Phone.

**Time Needed for Reply:** One month.

**Does Author Supply Photos?** Yes.

**Advice for Authors:** Writers for Music Inc. should remember that they are addressing the business issues of the music industry. Articles must be carefully researched.

# NATIONAL PROVISIONER

**Stagnito Publishing Company**
**1935 Shermer Road, Suite 100**
**Northbrook, Illinois 60062**          **Established: 1892**
**(708) 205-5660**          **Circulation: 17,500**

**Contact Person:** Barbara Young, Editor.

**Type of Publication:** Magazine covering the meat-, poultry-, and seafood provision industry.

**Audience:** Provision processors.

**How Frequently Published:** Monthly.

**Recently Published Articles:** Features covering market trends and new technology; also corporate profiles and industry news.

**Current Needs:** More of the same.

**Policy on Seasonal Pieces:** One month.

**Usual Length Desired:** 1200 to 1500 words.

**Author Writes on Speculation or Assignment?** Assignment.

**Are Free Sample Copies Available?** Yes.

**Payment Information:**
   **Rate:** $300 to $700 for features.
   **Mode:** On publication.
   **Advance Possible?** No.

**Rights Policy:** Buys all rights.

**How to Contact:** Send query.

**What Not to Do:** Send complete manuscript.

**Time Needed for Reply:** One month.

**Does Author Supply Photos?** Yes.

**Advice for Authors:** National Provisioner is interested only in writers with food-industry experience.

# NEW PRODUCT NEWS

**Trend Publishing, Inc.**
**625 N. Michigan Avenue, Suite 2500**
**Chicago, Illinois 60611**          **Established: 1964**
**(312) 654-2300**                   **Circulation: 1000**

**Contact Person:** Lynn Dornblaser, Publisher.

**Type of Publication:** Magazine covering new food and nonfood products.

**Audience:** Manufacturers and retailers of gourmet and health foods; also supermarkets.

**How Frequently Published:** Monthly.

**Recently Published Articles:** Shorter articles that track the introduction of new products; also pieces that present strategies to help new product marketers do their jobs better.

**Current Needs:** Articles about new product development.

**Policy on Seasonal Pieces:** Two months in advance.

**Usual Length Desired:** 800 to 1500 words.

**Author Writes on Speculation or Assignment?** Can be either.

**Are Free Sample Copies Available?** Yes, to qualified individuals who query.

**Payment Information:**
   **Rate:** Varies.
   **Mode:** On acceptance.
   **Advance Possible?** No.

**How to Contact:** Send query and writing samples; may also send complete manuscript. Enclose a self-addressed, stamped envelope.

**What Not to Do:** Phone.

**Time Needed for Reply:** One month.

**Does Author Supply Photos?** Usually not.

**Advice for Authors:** Most articles in New Product News are written by experts in their fields.

# PET AGE

**H. H. Backer Associates, Inc.**
**20 E. Jackson Boulevard**
**Chicago, Illinois 60604**
**(312) 222-2000**

**Established:** 1971
**Circulation:** 19,400

**Contact Person:** Karen Long MacLeod, Editor.

**Type of Publication:** Trade magazine serving the pet-supplies industry.

**Audience:** Pet-supplies retailers, wholesalers, and manufacturers.

**How Frequently Published:** Monthly.

**Recently Published Articles:** Articles covering the advent of superstores and the effect on owners of individual stores, store design, an overview of the industry from a demographic perspective.

**Current Needs:** Articles geared toward coverage of products and merchandising.

**Policy on Seasonal Pieces:** Six months in advance.

**Usual Length Desired:** 1000 to 3000 words.

**Author Writes on Speculation or Assignment?** Can be either.

**Are Free Sample Copies Available?** No.

**Payment Information:**
    **Rate:** Varies.
    **Mode:** On acceptance.
    **Advance Possible?** No.

**Rights Policy:** Buys first North American serial rights.

**How to Contact:** Send query and clips.

**What Not to Do:** Phone.

**Time Needed for Reply:** Six to eight weeks.

**Does Author Supply Photos?** Yes, if possible. Pays for photos used.

**Advice for Authors:** Writers should possess business-writing experience and/or familiarity with retail operations.

# PIMA MAGAZINE
**Paper Industry Management Association**
**2400 E. Oakton Street**
**Arlington Heights, Illinois 60005**
**(708) 956-0250**

**Established: 1919**
**Circulation: 20,000**

**Contact Person:** Alan Rooks, Editor-in-Chief.

**Type of Publication:** Magazine for paper and paperboard manufacturers.

**Audience:** Managers of paper mills.

**How Frequently Published:** Monthly.

**Recently Published Articles:** Articles about total quality management, machinery, automation, pulping and bleaching, and papermaking engineering.

**Current Needs:** News and feature articles about any aspect of the industry.

**Policy on Seasonal Pieces:** Three months in advance.

**Usual Length Desired:** 1000 to 3000 words.

**Author Writes on Speculation or Assignment?** Assignment.

**Are Free Sample Copies Available?** Yes, on a limited basis to qualified individuals who submit queries and enclose a self-addressed, stamped envelope.

**Payment Information:**
    **Rate:** Negotiable.
    **Mode:** On acceptance.
    **Advance Possible?** No.

**Rights Policy:** Buys all rights.

**How to Contact:** Send query; may also phone.

**What Not to Do:** Send complete manuscript.

**Time Needed for Reply:** One month.

**Does Author Supply Photos?** Yes.

**Advice for Authors:** Although PIMA Magazine has limited freelance opportunities, it welcomes ideas from writers who know the industry and can produce articles of interest that are free of technical jargon.

# PIZZA & PASTA

**Talcott Communications Corporation**
**20 N. Wacker Drive, Suite 3230**
**Chicago, Illinois 60606**          **Established: 1989**
**(312) 849-2220**          **Circulation: 50,000**

**Contact Person:** Joseph Declan Moran, Editor.

**Type of Publication:** Business magazine for the Italian-American food-service industry.

**Audience:** Owners and operators of U. S. pizzerias and Italian restaurants of all sizes.

**How Frequently Published:** Monthly.

**Recently Published Articles:** New-product showcase; cheese report; equipment update; profiles of people in the industry; article about restaurant seating.

**Current Needs:** More of the same type of news-oriented stories and features.

**Policy on Seasonal Pieces:** At least one month in advance.

**Usual Length Desired:** 1000 words (features).

**Author Writes on Speculation or Assignment?** Assignment.

**Are Free Sample Copies Available?** Yes.

**Payment Information:**
   **Rate:** Varies.
   **Mode:** On publication.
   **Advance Possible?** No.

**Rights Policy:** Buys all rights.

**How to Contact:** Send query and resume and clips; may also phone.

**What Not to Do:** Send unsolicited manuscript.

**Time Needed for Reply:** One week.

**Does Author Supply Photos?** Yes, if possible.

**Advice for Authors:** Writers need not be experts in this field. Pizza & Pasta regards general reporting skills as more important than industry expertise. If a reporter has foodservice-related experience, however, that is all the better.

# P-O-P TIMES

Hoyt Publishing
7400 Skokie Boulevard
Skokie, Illinois 60077
(708) 675-7400

Established: 1988
Circulation: 18,000

**Contact Person:** Rex Davenport, Editor.

**Type of Publication:** Magazine covering point-of-purchase advertising and display.

**Audience:** Consumer products marketers, display manufacturers and designers.

**How Frequently Published:** Ten times per year (combined issues July/August and November/December).

**Recently Published Articles:** Articles about display efforts; coverage of industry news and trends; salary surveys.

**Current Needs:** News-based articles about the industry.

**Policy on Seasonal Pieces:** Two months in advance.

**Usual Length Desired:** 500 to 1000 words.

**Author Writes on Speculation or Assignment?** Assignment.

**Are Free Sample Copies Available?** No.

**Payment Information:**
    **Rate:** Negotiable.
    **Mode:** On acceptance.
    **Advance Possible?** No.

**Rights Policy:** Buys all rights.

**How to Contact:** Send query and writing samples; may also phone.

**What Not to Do:** Send complete manuscript.

**Time Needed for Reply:** Within two weeks.

**Does Author Supply Photos?** Usually not.

**Advice for Authors:** Above all, freelancers for P-O-P Times must have very strong newswriting skills.

# PROGRESSIVE RAILROADING
**Murphy-Richter Publishing Company**
**230 W. Monroe Street, Suite 2210**
**Chicago, Illinois 60606**
**(312) 629-1200**

**Established: 1957**
**Circulation: 25,000**

**Contact Person:** Tom Judge, Editor.

**Type of Publication:** Magazine about the railroad industry.

**Audience:** Railroad executives and others who work with railroad equipment.

**How Frequently Published:** Monthly.

**Recently Published Articles:** Articles about the privatization of railroads in Argentina, the new turnout maintenance system used by Amtrak, and why subsidies to U. S. motorists are hurting the transit industry.

**Current Needs:** Articles about the technical aspects of the railroad industry, emphasizing freight rather than passenger trains.

**Policy on Seasonal Pieces:** At least two months in advance.

**Usual Length Desired:** 1000 to 5000 words.

**Author Writes on Speculation or Assignment?** Can be either.

**Are Free Sample Copies Available?** Not usually.

**Payment Information:**
    **Rate:** Varies.
    **Mode:** On publication.
    **Advance Possible?** No.

**Rights Policy:** Buys both first-time rights and exclusive rights to the railroad industry.

**How to Contact:** Send query and clips; may also phone.

**What Not to Do:** Drop in without an appointment.

**Time Needed for Reply:** Two or three weeks.

**Does Author Supply Photos?** Yes; color preferred.

**Advice for Authors:** Progressive Railroading is not interested in railroad buff stories—e.g., "The Glories of the Old Steam Days."

# REMODELED HOMES

**Cahners Publishing Company**
**1350 E. Touhy Avenue**
**Des Plaines, Illinois 60018**   **Established: 1991**
**(708) 635-8800**   **Circulation: 200,000**

**Contact Person:** Eric Benderoff, Managing Editor.

**Type of Publication:** Magazine covering the residential remodeling market.

**Audience:** Mainly general contractors; also consumers who wish to remodel their homes.

**How Frequently Published:** Bimonthly.

**Recently Published Articles:** Project case histories for whole-house and specialty-room remodeling; also articles about room additions and conversions.

**Current Needs:** Case histories about remodeling that adds value to houses.

**Policy on Seasonal Pieces:** Three months in advance.

**Usual Length Desired:** 500 to 1000 words.

**Author Writes on Speculation or Assignment?** Can be either.

**Are Free Sample Copies Available?** Yes, to qualified individuals who submit queries.

**Payment Information:**
   **Rate:** $200 to $500 per article.
   **Mode:** On publication.
   **Advance Possible?** No.

**Rights Policy:** Buys first North American serial rights.

**How to Contact:** Send query with two or three photos (nonreturnable slides or transparencies of good quality) depicting remodeling project.

**What Not to Do:** Send product promotion pieces.

**Time Needed for Reply:** One month.

**Does Author Supply Photos?** Depends on project.

**Advice for Authors:** Remodeled Homes is interested in hearing from writers who can deal with technical matters in a way that a general readership can understand.

# SUCCESSFUL DEALER

**Kona-Cal, Inc.**
**707 Lake Cook Road, Suite 300**
**Deerfield, Illinois 60015**    **Established: 1982**
**(708) 498-3180**    **Circulation: 17,000**

**Contact Person:** Denise Rondini, Editorial Director.

**Type of Publication:** Business magazine for truck and heavy-equipment dealers.

**Audience:** Truck and heavy-equipment dealers.

**How Frequently Published:** Bimonthly.

**Recently Published Articles:** "Selling Finance and Insurance"; "Service Department Incentives"; "Automating Your Sales Department"; "Selling High-Horsepower Engines"; "Preventing Employee Theft."

**Current Needs:** Features that provide suggestions on improving dealership profitability in terms of parts and service, leasing, telemarketing, and financial management.

**Policy on Seasonal Pieces:** Two months in advance.

**Usual Length Desired:** Eight typed (double-spaced) pages.

**Author Writes on Speculation or Assignment?** Can be either.

**Are Free Sample Copies Available?** Yes.

**Payment Information:**
    **Rate:** $125 per printed page.
    **Mode:** On publication.
    **Advance Possible?** No.

**Rights Policy:** Buys first rights.

**How to Contact:** Send query.

**What Not to Do:** Phone, send complete manuscript, or include Successful Dealer as part of a simultaneous submission.

**Time Needed for Reply:** Two weeks.

**Does Author Supply Photos?** Yes, if possible.

**Advice for Authors:** Writers for Successful Dealer must be very familiar with the truck and heavy-equipment industry.

# TELEPHONY
**Intertec Publishing Corporation**
**55 E. Jackson Boulevard**
**Chicago, Illinois 60604**       **Established: 1901**
**(312) 922-2435**              **Circulation: 45,000**

**Contact Person:** Karen Woodward, Managing Editor.

**Type of Publication:** Magazine for the telecommunications industry.

**Audience:** Telephone companies, carriers, major telephone service users, cable companies, cellular providers.

**How Frequently Published:** Weekly.

**Recently Published Articles:** Articles about communications testing, broadband deployment, convergence, video technology, and managing public networks.

**Current Needs:** Technology tutorials; also case histories of telecommunications companies solving technical and business problems.

**Policy on Seasonal Pieces:** At least three months in advance.

**Usual Length Desired:** 2000 words.

**Author Writes on Speculation or Assignment?** Assignment, mostly.

**Are Free Sample Copies Available?** Yes, to qualified individuals who submit queries.

**Payment Information:**
    **Rate:** Usually $75 per printed page but may vary.
    **Mode:** On publication.
    **Advance Possible?** No.

**Rights Policy:** Buys first-time rights to original material.

**How to Contact:** Send query; may also send manuscript (disk preferred). If material is to be returned, enclose a self-addressed, stamped envelope.

**What Not to Do:** Phone.

**Time Needed for Reply:** Two to four weeks.

**Does Author Supply Photos?** Photos and illustrations (no more than three diagrams) are appreciated.

**Advice for Authors:** Writers seeking to write for Telephony must have a thorough knowledge of the telecommunications industry.

# 3X/400 SYSTEMS MANAGEMENT

**Hunter Publishing Company**
**25 Northwest Point Boulevard, Suite 800**
**Elk Grove Village, Illinois 60007**     **Established: 1967**
**(708) 427-9512**        **Circulation: 55,000**

**Contact Person:** Ross Brown, Managing Editor.

**Type of Publication:** Trade magazine for DP/MIS managers with an IBM 34, 36, 38, or AS/400 on-site.

**Audience:** Data processors, managers, and controllers.

**How Frequently Published:** Monthly.

**Recently Published Articles:** "Are You Ready for Client/Server?"; "AS/400 to RS/6000 Integration"; "Managing Your Management."

**Current Needs:** Articles dealing with management topics by writers familiar with minicomputer technology.

**Policy on Seasonal Pieces:** Two months in advance.

**Usual Length Desired:** 1200 to 2500 words.

**Author Writes on Speculation or Assignment?** Can be either.

**Are Free Sample Copies Available?** Yes.

**Payment Information:**
    **Rate:** $500 to $1000 per article.
    **Mode:** On publication.
    **Advance Possible?** No.

**Rights Policy:** Reserves all rights.

**How to Contact:** Send query or manuscript. Photocopy OK, but diskette or modem transmission preferred. May also phone.

**What Not to Do:** Drop in without an appointment.

**Time Needed for Reply:** Two weeks.

**Does Author Supply Photos?** Not necessary.

**Advice for Authors:** Articles for 3X/400 Systems Management must be in-depth but also easy to read.

# TRANSPORT FLEET NEWS
**Transport Publishing Company**
**1962 N. Bissell Street**
**Chicago, Illinois 60614**        **Established: 1980**
**(312) 523-6669**              **Circulation: 10,500**

**Contact Person:** Phillip Scopelite, Editor and Publisher.

**Type of Publication:** Magazine covering the Midwest regional trucking industry.

**Audience:** Truck fleet supervisors.

**How Frequently Published:** Monthly.

**Recently Published Articles:** News coverage, new-product information, historical profiles of companies.

**Current Needs:** More of the same types of articles.

**Policy on Seasonal Pieces:** Two months in advance.

**Author Writes on Speculation or Assignment?** Assignment.

**Are Free Sample Copies Available?** Yes.

**Payment Information:**
    **Rate:** Varies.
    **Mode:** On publication.
    **Advance Possible?** No.

**Rights Policy:** Buys first-time rights.

**How to Contact:** Phone with story idea(s).

**What Not to Do:** Send complete manuscript.

**Time Needed for Reply:** Two weeks.

**Does Author Supply Photos?** Yes.

**Advice for Authors:** Most of the articles in Transport Fleet News are written by people in the industry, but queries from freelancers are welcome. The magazine is also interested in hearing from freelance photographers and graphic artists.

# NEWSPAPER PUBLISHERS

# BOLINGBROOK METROPOLITAN NEWSPAPERS, INC.

223 Main Street
Lamont, Illinois 60439
(708) 739-3900                    Circulation: 12,000

**Contact Person:** Peggy Drey, Editor.

**Type of Publication:** Four community newspapers.

**Audience:** Residents of Bolingbrook, Darien, Romeoville, and Lamont.

**How Frequently Published:** Weekly.

**Current Needs:** Local news coverage and features.

**Policy on Seasonal Pieces:** Two weeks in advance.

**Author Writes on Speculation or Assignment?** Assignment.

**Payment Information:**
  **Rate:** Varies.
  **Mode:** On acceptance.
  **Advance Possible?** No.

**Rights Policy:** Buys all rights.

**How to Contact:** Send query.

**What Not to Do:** Phone.

**Time Needed for Reply:** Three or four weeks.

**Does Author Supply Photos?** Yes, depending on the assignment; pays extra for photos used.

**Advice for Authors:** Individuals who want to write for Bolingbrook Metropolitan Newspapers must know the communities served by the papers very well.

# CHICAGO READER

Chicago Reader, Inc.
11 E. Illinois Street
Chicago, Illinois 60611
(312) 828-0350                     Circulation: 130,000

**Contact Person:** Tom Terranova, Editorial Assistant.

**Type of Publication:** General circulation newspaper in tabloid format.

**Audience:** Young adults in Chicago and Evanston lakefront areas.

**How Frequently Published:** Weekly.

**Current Needs:** Locally oriented magazine-type features of lengths varying from short to very long: short personality profiles of local people; reviews of pop music and of performing and visual arts.

**Policy on Seasonal Pieces:** One to six weeks in advance.

**Usual Length Desired:** Feature stories—rarely less than 2500 words; reviews—rarely more than 1200 words.

**Author Writes on Speculation or Assignment?** Speculation.

**Are Free Sample Copies Available?** Yes.

**Payment Information:**
   **Rate:** Varies.
   **Mode:** On publication (by the 15th of the following month).
   **Advance Possible?** No.

**Rights Policy:** Buys first rights unless other arrangements have been made prior to publication.

**How to Contact:** Send manuscript. Photocopy OK, but notify if part of a simultaneous submission. Enclose a self-addressed, stamped envelope.

**What Not to Do:** Phone; send query; send commentaries, hard news, poetry, or fiction; or drop in without an appointment.

**Time Needed for Reply:** Three to eight weeks.

**Does Author Supply Photos?** Not usually.

**Advice for Authors:** Chicago Reader obtains roughly 70 percent of its material from freelancers. It wants to maximize the number of contributors in order to create a fresh, unpredictable, interesting paper. The Reader values the quality of writing more than the nature of the topic; the way a writer treats a topic is of prime importance.

# CHICAGO SUN-TIMES

**401 N. Wabash Avenue**
**Chicago, Illinois 60611**
**(312) 321-3000**

**Contact Person:** Henry Kisor, Book Editor; Darel Jevens, Assistant Entertainment Editor; Laura Emerick, Arts and Show Editor; Tim Bannon, Weekend Plus Editor.

**Type of Publication:** Metropolitan newspaper.

**Audience:** Chicago-area residents.

**How Frequently Published:** Daily.

**Current Needs:** Book reviews; profiles of entertainers coming to Chicago; theater reviews; trends in entertainment stories.

**Usual Length Desired:** 300 to 2000 words.

**Author Writes on Speculation or Assignment?** Assignment.

**Payment Information:**
**Rate:** $50 to $250 per article, depending on length and placement.
**Mode:** On publication.
**Advance Possible?** No.

**Rights Policy:** Negotiable.

**How to Contact:** Send query with resume and writing samples. Enclose a self-addressed, stamped envelope.

**What Not to Do:** Phone or drop in without an appointment.

**Time Needed for Reply:** Two weeks.

**Does Author Supply Photos?** Sometimes; pays extra for good original photos.

**Advice for Authors:** The Weekend Plus section offers freelance writers the best chance at being published in the Chicago Sun-Times.

# CHICAGO TRIBUNE MAGAZINE
**Chicago Tribune**
**435 N. Michigan Avenue**
**Chicago, Illinois 60611**
**(312) 222-3232**

**Contact Person:** Denis Gosselin, Editor-in-Chief.

**Type of Publication:** Local general interest magazine included in the Sunday paper.

**Audience:** Chicago-area residents.

**How Frequently Published:** Weekly.

**Current Needs:** Magazine-style articles—not newspaper pieces—about contemporary subjects; personality pieces about high-profile people; stories of local issues, problems, tragedies, and achievements told through the lives of less well-known people.

**Policy on Seasonal Pieces:** Two to three months in advance.

**Usual Length Desired:** Up to 3000 words.

**Author Writes on Speculation or Assignment?** Initially on speculation; subsequent work can be done either on assignment or speculation.

**Payment Information:**
  **Rate:** $200 to $400 for short articles; $500 to $1000 for major articles.
  **Mode:** On publication.
  **Advance Possible?** No.

**Rights Policy:** Buys first North American serial rights.

**How to Contact:** Send query or manuscript; photocopy OK. Enclose a self-addressed, stamped envelope.

**What Not to Do:** Phone or drop in without an appointment.

**Time Needed for Reply:** Two weeks.

**Does Author Supply Photos?** Occasionally.

**Advice for Authors:** Although the articles that appear in the Chicago Tribune Magazine need not be strictly local in content, they must be of interest to a Chicago-area readership. Stories must well told, engaging, display a point of view, and involve substantial human contact.

# CRAIN'S CHICAGO BUSINESS

Crain Communications, Inc.
740 N. Rush Street
Chicago, Illinois 60611
(312) 649-1111                    Circulation: 50,000

**Contact Person:** David Snyder, Editor.

**Type of Publication:** Newspaper covering business and finance issues in the Chicago area.

**Audience:** People interested in Chicago business and local economic issues.

**How Frequently Published:** Weekly.

**Current Needs:** Inside company stories; articles about new products and new marketing programs; profiles of Chicago-area businesspeople.

**Usual Length Desired:** 800 to 1000 words.

**Author Writes on Speculation or Assignment?** Assignment.

**Payment Information:**
  **Rate:** $13.20 per column inch.
  **Mode:** Can be either on acceptance or publication.
  **Advance Possible?** No.

**Rights Policy:** Buys all rights.

**How to Contact:** Send query or manuscript (photocopy OK) with resume and references.

**What Not to Do:** Phone or drop in without an appointment.

**Time Needed for Reply:** One week.

**Does Author Supply Photos?** No.

**Advice for Authors:** Writers must read Crain's Chicago Business in order to understand its purpose. The paper will consider only those articles that deal with Chicago business (in the broadest sense).

# DAILY HERALD

**Paddock Publications, Inc.**
**P. O. Box 280**
**Arlington Heights, Illinois 60005**
**(708) 870-3600**                                    **Circulation: 130,000**

**Contact Person:** Renee Trappe, City Editor; Jean Rudolph, Features Editor; Marty Stengle, Prep Sports Editor.

**Type of Publication:** Suburban newspaper.

**Audience:** Residents in Chicago's western, northern, and northwestern suburbs.

**How Frequently Published:** Daily.

**Current Needs:** Coverage of meetings and high school sports; also simple features.

**Usual Length Desired:** 400 to 750 words.

**Author Writes on Speculation or Assignment?** Can be either.

**Payment Information:**
  **Rate:** Varies on a per-article basis.
  **Mode:** On acceptance.
  **Advance Possible?** No.

**Rights Policy:** Buys first-time rights; author retains copyright.

**How to Contact:** Send query, resume, and no more than three writing samples.

**What Not to Do:** Phone.

**Time Needed for Reply:** Varies from department to department.

**Does Author Supply Photos?** Depends on story.

**Advice for Authors:** When considering freelancers, the Daily Herald places a premium on reporting—rather than on writing—skills.

# DES PLAINES PUBLISHING COMPANY

**1000 Executive Way**
**Des Plaines, Illinois 60018**
**(708) 824-1111**                                    **Circulation: 52,000**

**Contact Person:** Joyce Diebel, Managing Editor.

**Type of Publication:** Eight community newspapers.

**Audience:** Residents in Des Plaines, Rosemont, Mount Prospect, Elk Grove Village, Niles, Edison Park, and Edgebrook.

**How Frequently Published:** Weekly.

**Current Needs:** Coverage of meetings and high school sports events.

**Author Writes on Speculation or Assignment?** Assignment only.

**Payment Information:**
    **Rate:** Varies.
    **Mode:** On publication.
    **Advance Possible?** No.

**Rights Policy:** Buys all rights.

**How to Contact:** Send query.

**What Not to Do:** Phone or send complete story.

**Time Needed for Reply:** Two weeks.

**Does Author Supply Photos?** Not usually.

**Advice for Authors:** Stringers for the Des Plaines Publishing Company must know the communities served by the newspapers, and they must have a good, clear writing style.

# DuPage Business Ledger

**Ledger Publications, Inc.**
**2200 S. Main Street, Suite 205**
**Lombard, Illinois 60148**
**(708) 268-1860**                    **Circulation: 12,000**

**Contact Person:** Don Kopriva, Editor.

**Type of Publication:** Business newspaper.

**Audience:** CEOs, managers, and executives who work in DuPage County.

**How Frequently Published:** Monthly.

**Current Needs:** Articles that examine national issues for local relevance; company profiles; business trend stories.

**Policy on Seasonal Pieces:** Two to three months in advance.

**Usual Length Desired:** 800 words.

**Author Writes on Speculation or Assignment?** Assignment, mostly.

**Payment Information:**
    **Rate:** Varies.
    **Mode:** On acceptance.
    **Advance Possible?** No.

**Rights Policy:** Buys all rights.

**How to Contact:** Send query and clips.

**What Not to Do:** Phone or send complete manuscript.

**Time Needed for Reply:** Within one month.

**Does Author Supply Photos?** Depends on assignment.

**Advice for Authors:** Almost all Ledger stories are written on a freelance basis. Writers must be experienced business reporters, and they must know the DuPage area very well.

# EXTRA BILINGUAL COMMUNITY NEWSPAPERS

HispaniMedia L. P.
3918 W. North Avenue
Chicago, Illinois 60647
(312) 252-3534                              Circulation: 56,200

**Contact Person:** Andrew Sharp, South Side Editor; Christine Nielsen, North Side Editor.

**Type of Publication:** Group of seven community newspapers.

**Audience:** Mostly residents of Chicago's Southwest Side and near west suburbs: Pilsen/Little Village, Bridgeport/Back of the Yards, West Town/Wicker Park, Logan Square/Bucktown, Northwest Side, Metro Chicago (Loop and Lakefront), and Cicero/Berwyn.

**How Frequently Published:** Weekly.

**Current Needs:** Features, especially profiles of community leaders; also news of grassroots community programs, events, and issues, especially from a Latino point of view.

**Policy on Seasonal Pieces:** At least three weeks in advance.

**Usual Length Desired:** 300 to 1000 words.

**Author Writes on Speculation or Assignment?** Assignment, usually.

**Payment Information:** Pays in copies in which contributor's work appears.

**Rights Policy:** Author retains rights.

**How to Contact:** Phone or send query and clips.

**What Not to Do:** Phone Tuesday afternoons (deadline).

**Time Needed for Reply:** One week.

**Does Author Supply Photos?** Yes.

**Advice for Authors:** Extra Newspapers trades publishing exposure and experience in exchange for unpaid work from reporters. Latino journalists are especially encouraged to submit story ideas. Although some pieces are in Spanish, most of the Extra Newspapers are published in English.

# HYDE PARK HERALD
**Herald Newspapers, Inc.**
**5240 S. Harper Avenue**
**Chicago, Illinois 60615**
**(312) 643-8533**                    **Circulation: 7000**

**Contact Person:** Florence Goold, Editor.

**Type of Publication:** Newspaper serving the Hyde Park area of Chicago.

**Audience:** Residents of Hyde Park and Kenwood.

**How Frequently Published:** Weekly.

**Current Needs:** Occasional need for news coverage, features, and reviews of art, theater, and music.

**Policy on Seasonal Pieces:** Two weeks in advance.

**Usual Length Desired:** 1000 words maximum.

**Author Writes on Speculation or Assignment?** Assignment, usually.

**Payment Information:**
    **Rate:** Negotiable.
    **Mode:** Negotiable.
    **Advance Possible?** No.

**Rights Policy:** Buys all rights.

**How to Contact:** Send complete manuscript for a review; send query for all other material.

**What Not to Do:** Phone.

**Time Needed for Reply:** Within one week.

**Does Author Supply Photos?** Yes; photos are greatly appreciated.

**Advice for Authors:** The focus of the Hyde Park Herald is very local, and it seldom accepts freelance work.

# INSIDE

**Inside Publications**
**4710 N. Lincoln Avenue**
**Chicago, Illinois 60625**
**(312) 643-8533**                    **Circulation: 45,000**

**Contact Person:** Rob Snarski, Managing Editor.

**Type of Publication:** Community newspaper for Chicago's Near North Side.

**Audience:** Residents of the Gold Coast, Lincoln Park, Lakeview, and Ravenswood areas.

**How Frequently Published:** Weekly.

**Current Needs:** News items about the areas covered; also feature stories about cultural aspects of the areas and profiles about the accomplishments of area residents.

**Policy on Seasonal Pieces:** At least two weeks in advance.

**Usual Length Desired:** 500 to 1000 words.

**Author Writes on Speculation or Assignment?** Assignment.

**Payment Information:**
    **Rate:** Varies.
    **Mode:** 30 days after publication.
    **Advance Possible?** No.

**Rights Policy:** Buys all rights.

**How to Contact:** Phone or send query and clips.

**What Not to Do:** Send complete manuscript.

**Time Needed for Reply:** Within a week.

**Does Author Supply Photos?** No.

**Advice for Authors:** Inside is looking for stories from writers who know the importance of details in news stories and who can gather more than the usual "talking heads" quotes.

# LAKELAND PUBLISHERS, INC.

**30 S. Whitney Street**
**Grayslake, Illinois 60030**
**(708) 223-8161**                    **Circulation: 40,000**

**Contact Person:** Rhonda Vinzant, Editor-in-Chief.

**Type of Publication:** Thirteen community newspapers.

**Audience:** Residents in most of Lake County and a portion of McHenry County.

**How Frequently Published:** Weekly.

**Current Needs:** Coverage of meetings and some high school sports events.

**Policy on Seasonal Pieces:** Two weeks in advance.

**Usual Length Desired:** 500 to 750 words.

**Author Writes on Speculation or Assignment?** Assignment, generally.

**Payment Information:**
    **Rate:** $21 per one-story meeting; $5 to $20 for each extra story based on same meeting.
    **Mode:** On publication.
    **Advance Possible?** No.

**Rights Policy:** Buys all rights.

**How to Contact:** Send query.

**What Not to Do:** Phone.

**Time Needed for Reply:** At least one week.

**Does Author Supply Photos?** Sometimes; pays extra for photos used.

**Advice for Authors:** The newspapers of Lakeland Publishers are especially interested in reporters who can make meeting stories not sound like meeting minutes.

# LEADER PAPERS, INC.

**6010 W. Belmont Avenue**
**Chicago, Illinois 60634**
**(312) 281-7500**                    **Circulation: 100,000**

**Contact Person:** Jackie Pledger-Skwerski, Executive Editor.

**Type of Publication:** Five community newspapers serving Chicago's Northwest Side and some near-west suburbs.

**Audience:** Residents of Elmwood Park, Franklin Park, Schiller Park, River Grove, Galewood.

**How Frequently Published:** Weekly.

**Current Needs:** Features and high school sports stories.

**Policy on Seasonal Pieces:** Two to four weeks in advance.

**Usual Length Desired:** 1250 to 2000 words.

**Author Writes on Speculation or Assignment?** Assignment, usually.

**Payment Information:**
   **Rate:** Varies.
   **Mode:** On publication.
   **Advance Possible?** No.

**Rights Policy:** Buys first-time rights.

**How to Contact:** Send query and clips.

**What Not to Do:** Phone or send complete story.

**Time Needed for Reply:** Four to six weeks.

**Does Author Supply Photos?** Yes, if possible; pays extra for photos.

**Advice for Authors:** Research the circulation area of the relevant Leader paper(s) before submitting story ideas.

# LERNER COMMUNICATIONS, INC.

1115 W. Belmont Avenue
Chicago, Illinois 60657          **Established: 1904**
(312) 281-7500          **Circulation: 150,000**

**Contact Person:** William Santamour, Executive Editor.

**Type of Publication:** Five community newspapers.

**Audience:** Residents from the Loop to Lake Forest; also northwest side of Chicago and adjacent suburbs.

**How Frequently Published:** Weekly.

**Current Needs:** Profiles of prominent citizens, places, and situations in the readership areas of Lerner newspapers.

**Policy on Seasonal Pieces:** Three weeks in advance.

**Usual Length Desired:** 900 words maximum.

**Author Writes on Speculation or Assignment?** Can be either.

**Payment Information:**
    **Rate:** Variable hourly wage; average of $40 per article.
    **Mode:** 30 days after publication.
    **Advance Possible?** No.

**Rights Policy:** Buys all rights.

**How to Contact:** Phone main office with story idea.

**What Not to Do:** Send complete manuscript.

**Time Needed for Reply:** One week.

**Does Author Supply Photos?** Yes, if appropriate; papers pay a nominal fee for photos.

**Advice for Authors:** Lerner newspapers want articles with a people-oriented slant—e.g., human interest stories, unusual hobbies or jobs.

# LIFE NEWSPAPERS
**2601 S. Harlem Avenue**
**Berwyn, Illinois 60402**  **Established: 1926**
**(708) 484-1234**  **Circulation: 100,000**

**Contact Person:** Bob Lifka, Managing Editor of the Cicero/Berwyn paper; Joseph DeRosier, Managing Editor of Suburban Life Citizen and Suburban Life Graphic newspapers (P. O. Box 3667, Oak Brook, Illinois 60522).

**Type of Publication:** Community suburban newspapers.

**Audience:** Residents of Chicago's western suburbs.

**How Frequently Published:** Cicero/Berwyn—three times per week; Suburban papers—two times per week.

**Current Needs:** Articles about topics of interest to residents of the western suburbs.

**Usual Length Desired:** 600 words.

**Author Writes on Speculation or Assignment?** Speculation.

**Payment Information:**
**Rate:** Varies.
**Mode:** On publication.
**Advance Possible?** No.

**Rights Policy:** Negotiable.

**How to Contact:** Phone first with article idea to find out whether or not to proceed.

**What Not to Do:** Send complete article.

**Time Needed for Reply:** Immediate reply to idea; two weeks after submission for response to article.

**Does Author Supply Photos?** Depends on author's photographic ability; papers pay extra for photos.

**Advice for Authors:** Be sure to contact appropriate editor with story idea.

# NEW CITY

New City Communications, Inc.
770 N. Halsted Street, Suite 208
Chicago, Illinois 60622
(312) 243-8786

Established: 1986
Circulation: 55,000

**Contact Person:** Dale Eastman, Senior Editor.

**Type of Publication:** General circulation newspaper in tabloid format.

**Audience:** Residents of Chicago and selected suburbs.

**How Frequently Published:** Weekly.

**Current Needs:** Profiles, short reviews, news stories, features.

**Policy on Seasonal Pieces:** One month in advance.

**Usual Length Desired:** 200 to 4000 words.

**Author Writes on Speculation or Assignment?** Initially on speculation; assignment thereafter.

**Are Free Sample Copies Available?** Yes; available throughout Chicago and suburbs.

**Payment Information:**
  **Rate:** Varies; minimum of 10 cents per word.
  **Mode:** On publication.
  **Advance Possible?** No.

**Rights Policy:** Buys all rights.

**How to Contact:** Send written request for writer's guidelines; then submit a detailed query and writing samples.

**What Not to Do:** Phone or use New City's name when writing on speculation.

**Time Needed for Reply:** Two to four weeks.

**Does Author Supply Photos?** No.

**Advice for Authors:** New City is always looking for new story topics and formats.

# PIONEER PRESS, INC.
1232 Central Avenue
Wilmette, Illinois 60091          Established: 1876
(708) 251-4300                    Circulation: 180,000

**Contact Person:** Executive Editors—Alan Henry, North Group (address above); Paul Sassone, West Group (1148 Westgate, Oak Park, IL 60001); Jo Hansen, Northwest Group (200 James Street, Barrington, IL 60010); Carol Goddard, Lake County Group (2201 Waukegan Road, Suite E-175, Bannockburn, IL 60015).

**Type of Publication:** 41 community newspapers.

**Audience:** Families living in Chicago's northern, western, and northwest/central suburbs.

**How Frequently Published:** Weekly, plus several annual specials (real estate, fashion, etc.)

**Current Needs:** Freelance photographers to cover prep sports.

**Policy on Seasonal Pieces:** Six to eight weeks in advance.

**Usual Length Desired:** No set limits, but generally no more than would fill a tabloid-size page.

**Author Writes on Speculation or Assignment?** Assignment.

**Payment Information:**
    **Rate:** Varies on a per-article basis.
    **Mode:** On publication.
    **Advance Possible?** No.

**Rights Policy:** Buys all rights.

**How to Contact:** Send query, resume, and clips to appropriate executive editor.

**What Not to Do:** Send manuscript or drop in without an appointment.

**Time Needed for Reply:** One week.

**Does Author Supply Photos?** No.

**Advice for Authors:** Pioneer Press seldom uses freelance writers.

# PRESS PUBLICATIONS

112 S. York Street
Elmhurst, Illinois 60126     **Established: 1889**
(708) 834-0900              **Circulation: 85,000**

**Contact Person:** Kathy Catrambone, Editor-in-Chief; Kevin Beese, Managing Editor.

**Type of Publication:** 21 community newspapers covering the news in DuPage County and western Cook County.

**Audience:** Residents in 26 communities of Chicago's far western suburbs.

**How Frequently Published:** Eight newspapers twice per week; 13 newspapers once per week.

**Current Needs:** Writers to cover meetings and prepare features.

**Policy on Seasonal Pieces:** Two to four weeks in advance.

**Usual Length Desired:** 750 to 1250 words.

**Author Writes on Speculation or Assignment?** Assignment.

**Payment Information:**
   **Rate:** Features—$45 to $70; news—$35 per story.
   **Mode:** On acceptance.
   **Advance Possible?** No.

**Rights Policy:** Buys all rights.

**How to Contact:** Send query and clips or complete manuscript; may also phone.

**What Not to Do:** Drop in without an appointment.

**Time Needed for Reply:** One week.

**Does Author Supply Photos?** No.

**Advice for Authors:** Press Publications needs writers who can cover meetings in such a way that their articles don't sound like a recounting of the gathering's minutes.

# REGIONAL NEWS

**Regional Publishing Corporation**
**12243 S. Harlem Avenue**
**Palos Heights, Illinois 60463**          **Established: 1942**
**(708) 448-4000**                         **Circulation: 18,000**

**Contact Person:** Richard Parmater, Managing Editor.

**Type of Publication:** Suburban newspaper.

**Audience:** Residents in a 108 square mile area of Chicago's southwest suburbs.

**How Frequently Published:** Weekly.

**Current Needs:** Coverage of governmental meetings; on rare occasions, a profile.

**Usual Length Desired:** 750 to 1000 words.

**Author Writes on Speculation or Assignment?** Assignment.

**Payment Information:**
    **Rate:** $25 per article for meeting coverage; negotiable fee for features.
    **Mode:** On publication.
    **Advance Possible?** No.

**Rights Policy:** Buys all rights.

**How to Contact:** Send query and published writing sample of meeting coverage or coverage of other governmental business.

**What Not to Do:** Phone or send stories on speculation.

**Time Needed for Reply:** Three weeks.

**Does Author Supply Photos?** Occasionally.

**Advice for Authors:** The Regional News has won 246 major awards during its 52 years, including selection by the Illinois Press Association as the best weekly newspaper in the state. Therefore, it accepts only the work of experienced, highly polished writers who know Chicago's southwest suburbs.

# REPORTER/PROGRESS NEWSPAPERS

922 Warren Avenue
Downers Grove, Illinois 60515     **Established: 1883**
(708) 969-0188     **Circulation: 72,000**

**Contact Person:** Jennifer Parello, Managing Editor.

**Type of Publication:** Six community newspapers.

**Audience:** Residents of Downers Grove, Westmont, Clarendon Hills, Woodridge, Lamont, and Darien.

**How Frequently Published:** Weekly except for Downers Grove Reporter (twice weekly).

**Current Needs:** Coverage of municipal meetings and some high school sports events.

**Policy on Seasonal Pieces:** One week in advance,

**Usual Length Desired:** 750 to 1000 words.

**Author Writes on Speculation or Assignment?** Assignment, usually.

**Payment Information:**
   **Rate:** Varies.
   **Mode:** On publication.
   **Advance Possible?** No.

**Rights Policy:** Buys all rights.

**How to Contact:** Send query with resume and sample clippings; may also phone.

**What Not to Do:** Drop in without an appointment.

**Time Needed for Reply:** Two weeks.

**Does Author Supply Photos?** Usually not, but occasionally the newspapers will use and pay extra for photos by the author.

**Advice for Authors:** Stringers for the Reporter/Progress Newspapers should know the communities very well. They must also write with the readers—not the municipal government officials—in mind.

# RUSSELL PUBLICATIONS, INC.

**120 W. North Street**
**Peotone, Illinois 60468**
**(708) 258-3473**                                    **Circulation: 10,000**

**Contact Person:** Paula Franke, Managing Editor.

**Type of Publication:** Seven community newspapers.

**Audience:** Residents of eastern Will County and far north Kankakee County.

**How Frequently Published:** Weekly.

**Current Needs:** Meeting coverage, primarily.

**Policy on Seasonal Pieces:** One week in advance.

**Usual Length Desired:** No length limitation.

**Author Writes on Speculation or Assignment?** Assignment, usually.

**Are Free Sample Copies Available?** Yes.

**Payment Information:**
> **Rate:** 20 cents per published column inch, plus $10 per meeting and 20 cents per mile to meeting.
> **Mode:** On publication.
> **Advance Possible?** No.

**Rights Policy:** Holds copyright, but will relinquish upon request.

**How to Contact:** Send clips and query; state clearly areas of interest and experience.

**What Not to Do:** Request coverage of sports events.

**Time Needed for Reply:** One week.

**Does Author Supply Photos?** Yes; papers provide film.

**Advice for Authors:** Only those writers who cover meetings may submit features. Russell newspapers need reporters who can turn out standard news stories—not just submit the minutes of meetings.

# STAR PUBLICATIONS
**1526 Otto Boulevard**
**Chicago Heights, Illinois 60411**
**(708) 755-6161**                    **Circulation: 80,000**

**Contact Person:** Lester Sons, Executive Editor; Franklin Shuftan, Managing Editor; Dennis Wheeler, Features Editor.

**Type of Publication:** 20 newspapers.

**Audience:** Residents in 55 communities in Chicago's south and southwest suburbs.

**How Frequently Published:** Twice a week.

**Current Needs:** Features stories and profiles.

**Policy on Seasonal Pieces:** Three weeks in advance.

**Usual Length Desired:** 1250 words for features.

**Author Writes on Speculation or Assignment?** Assignment, usually.

**Payment Information:**
    **Rate:** Varies.
    **Mode:** On publication.
    **Advance Possible?** No.

**Rights Policy:** Buys all rights.

**How to Contact:** Send query and clips.

**What Not to Do:** Phone or send complete manuscript.

**Time Needed for Reply:** One week.

**Does Author Supply Photos?** Sometimes; pays extra for photos.

**Advice for Authors:** Star Publications newspapers serve specific needs of targeted communities and don't try to compete with the large metropolitan daily newspapers. Writers must know the south and southwest suburbs.

# WEDNESDAY JOURNAL

**141 S. Oak Park Avenue**
**Oak Park, Illinois 60302**
**(708) 524-8300**                    **Circulation: 21,000**

**Contact Person:** Thom Wilder, Managing Editor (both newspapers); Ken Trainor, Features Editor, The Wednesday Journal.

**Type of Publication:** Two newspapers: The Wednesday Journal of Oak Park and River Forest and The Forest Park Review.

**Audience:** Residents of Oak Park, River Forest, and Forest Park.

**How Frequently Published:** Weekly.

**Current Needs:** Targeted feature stories; occasional need for profiles.

**Policy on Seasonal Pieces:** Two weeks in advance.

**Usual Length Desired:** 800 to 1000 words (Wednesday Journal); 500 to 1000 words (Forest Park Review).

**Author Writes on Speculation or Assignment?** Can be either.

**Are Free Sample Copies Available?** Yes.

**Payment Information:**
    **Rate:** Varies from $25 to $60 per article.
    **Mode:** On publication.
    **Advance Possible?** No.

**Rights Policy:** Buys first-time rights; rights then revert to author.

**How to Contact:** Send query and writing samples; may also phone or send complete manuscript. Enclose a self-addressed, stamped envelope.

**What Not to Do:** Drop in without an appointment.

**Time Needed for Reply:** One week.

**Does Author Supply Photos?** Yes, if possible; pays extra for photos.

**Advice for Authors:** Writers should keep in mind that these are strictly local newspapers that do not compete with the area's major metropolitan dailies for news.

# AUDIO-VISUAL PRODUCERS

# AGS & R COMMUNICATIONS

**314 W. Superior Street**
**Chicago, Illinois 60610**
**(312) 649-4500**                          **Established: 1947**

**Contact Person:** Walt Marquardt, Vice President—Creative Services.

**Types of Material Purchased:** Scripts for video productions, slide shows, 16mm films, cassettes, multi-image and multimedia productions; also print support.

**Audience:** Business and industry.

**Recent Titles Produced:** AV and multimedia productions for numerous business meetings, trade shows, and training.

**Current Needs:** To be discussed with appropriate writer.

**Author Writes on Speculation or Assignment?** Assignment.

**Payment Information:** Varies according to project and medium.

**Rights Policy:** Buys all rights; author writes on a work-for-hire basis.

**How to Contact:** Send query with resume and samples.

**What Not to Do:** Phone.

**Time Needed for Reply:** One to two weeks.

**Advice for Authors:** Writers for AGS & R Communications should be clear, concise, and accurate. They should also be good researchers. Experience in audio-visual writing would be helpful.

# CLEARVUE/EAV, INC.

**6465 N. Avondale Avenue**
**Chicago, Illinois 60631**
**(312) 775-9433**                    **Established: 1970**

**Contact Person:** Mark Ventling, President; Mary Watanabe, Manager of Editorial Production.

**Types of Material Purchased:** Educational materials for students in kindergarten through 12th grade.

**Audience:** Teachers and students.

**Recent Titles Produced:** Videos and CD-ROMs for reading, math, science, language arts, music, art, and social studies.

**Current Needs:** Materials in subjects listed above for students in kindergarten through 12th grade.

**Author Writes on Speculation or Assignment?** Assignment only.

**Payment Information:** Fee paid upon completion of assignment.

**Rights Policy:** Buys all rights.

**How to Contact:** Send query, resume, and writing samples.

**What Not to Do:** Drop in without an appointment.

**Time Needed for Reply:** Indefinite; the company will contact only when a specific need arises.

**Advice for Authors:** Writers must understand—and write for—the audience that uses the company's educational materials. CLEARVUE also welcomes the opportunity to look at completed video projects for possible distribution.

# DARBY MEDIA GROUP
4015 N. Rockwell Avenue
Chicago, Illinois 60618
(312) 583-5090

**Contact Person:** Dennis Cyrier, Production Manager.

**Types of Material Purchased:** Primarily scripts for audio-visual programs, especially multi-image productions (slide shows), along with films and videotapes.

**Audience:** Primarily business and industry.

**Recent Titles Produced:** Sales meeting and sales training programs; sales support (slides) for large corporations.

**Current Needs:** Writers experienced in audio-visual for business and industry.

**Author Writes on Speculation or Assignment?** Varies depending on client. Proposals are usually written on speculation, scripts on assignment.

**Payment Information:** Varies according to project, client, and writer.

**Rights Policy:** Buys all rights; author writes on a work-for-hire basis.

**How to Contact:** Send resume and writing samples.

**What Not to Do:** Phone.

**Time Needed for Reply:** Indefinite; the company keeps materials on file and replies only when an appropriate assignment becomes available.

**Advice for Authors:** Writers who work for the Darby Media Group should have a sense of urgency—i.e., understand deadlines and pressure. They must also have the ability to compile a worthwhile script from incoherent and/or disorganized source materials. Darby Media Group is looking for three essential qualities in an author: cleverness, intelligence, and the ability to deliver grammatically correct writing.

# GENNERA, KNAB & COMPANY
**1415 N. Dayton Street**
**Chicago, Illinois 60622**
**(312) 337-2010**

**Contact Person:** Michael Knab, President.

**Types of Material Purchased:** Print and audio-visual (multimedia, films, and videotapes).

**Audience:** Business and consumer markets.

**Recent Titles Produced:** Print materials of all kinds and audio-visual scripts.

**Current Needs:** More of the same.

**Author Writes on Speculation or Assignment?** Assignment.

**Payment Information:** Negotiable.

**Rights Policy:** Usually buys all rights, but is willing to negotiate.

**How to Contact:** Submit material in any medium or media, audio-visual or print.

**What Not to Do:** Phone or drop in without an appointment.

**Time Needed for Reply:** Up to three weeks.

**Advice for Authors:** Gennera, Knab in interested in seeing the best work that writers can produce, regardless of medium or assignment. The company actively pursues the best writing talent.

# GOLDSHOLL DESIGN & FILM, INC.
**420 Frontage Road**
**Northfield, Illinois 60093**
**(708) 446-8300**

**Contact Person:** Harry Goldsholl, President.

**Types of Material Purchased:** Scripts for a variety of projects and productions.

**Audience:** Corporations, institutions, and governmental bodies.

**Recent Titles Produced:** Educational and promotional films for corporations and trade associations.

**Current Needs:** To be discussed with appropriate writer.

**Author Writes on Speculation or Assignment?** Assignment.

**Payment Information:** Negotiable.

**Rights Policy:** Buys all rights; author writes on a work-for-hire basis.

**How to Contact:** Send query, resume, and writing samples.

**What Not to Do:** Phone.

**Time Needed for Reply:** Indefinite; the company keeps materials on file and replies only when an appropriate assignment becomes available.

**Advice for Authors:** Since Goldsholl Design & Film attempts to match the writer to the project as closely as possible, writers should be certain to state their professional background and experience as fully and precisely as possible in their query letters and resumes.

# STEVE KALSOW PRODUCTIONS, INC.

**1425 Holmes Road**
**Elgin, Illinois 60123**
**(708) 888-1260**                    **Established: 1983**

**Contact Person:** Steve Kalsow, President.

**Types of Material Purchased:** Scripts for marketing/training videos.

**Audience:** Prospects, customers, employees, dealers, general public.

**Recent Titles Produced:** Product/corporate promotional and training videos.

**Current Needs:** Contact firm for current needs.

**Author Writes on Speculation or Assignment?** Assignment.

**Payment Information:** Negotiable.

**Rights Policy:** Buys all rights; author writes on a work-for-hire basis.

**How to Contact:** Send query.

**What Not to Do:** Phone.

**Time Needed for Reply:** Indefinite; firm keeps materials on file and replies only when an appropriate assignment becomes available.

**Advice for Authors:** Steve Kalsow Productions is a custom house, creating work to match specific client needs.

# JACK MORTON PRODUCTIONS, INC.

**680 N. Lake Shore Drive, Suite 1300**
**Chicago, Illinois 60611**
**(312) 440-9700**

**Contact Person:** Bill Bunkers, Vice President and Director of Production.

**Types of Material Purchased:** All forms of business communication: audio-visual and multimedia scripts; interactive media; training; theatrical skits for sales presentations; new product information; exhibits; also instructors' manuals, participant workbooks, and other reference materials.

**Audience:** Business and industry.

**Recent Titles Produced:** Interactive sales presentation for a healthcare provider; also standard employee communications.

**Current Needs:** To be discussed with appropriate writer.

**Author Writes on Speculation or Assignment?** Can be either.

**Payment Information:** Varies.

**Rights Policy:** Buys all rights; author writes on a work-for-hire basis.

**How to Contact:** Send resume, list of specific credits, and brief sample of proposal writing; may also phone.

**What Not to Do:** Drop in without an appointment.

**Time Needed for Reply:** Indefinite; company keeps promising resumes on file and replies only when an appropriate assignment becomes available.

**Advice for Authors:** Jack Morton Productions, Inc., is interested in hearing from writers who understand business and the use of media in communicating business issues.

# MOTIVATION MEDIA, INC.

**1245 Milwaukee Avenue**
**Glenview, Illinois 60025**
**(708) 297-6829**

**Contact Person:** Kevin Kivikko, Creative Director; Ken Lewis, Creative Director; Marty Rosenheck, Manager of Training and Multimedia Development.

**Types of Material Purchased:** Training programs, proposals, creative concepts for a wide range of corporate communications, speeches and scripts for live and recorded presentations, scripts for interactive multimedia and industrial theater, and copywriting for printed materials.

**Audience:** Internal and external corporate audiences (generally nonconsumer).

**Recent Titles Produced:** Video tapes, training programs, interactive multimedia, and print materials for business meetings.

**Current Needs:** Writers who are very experienced in corporate communications.

**Author Writes on Speculation or Assignment?** Assignment, generally.

**Payment Information:** Agreed-upon fee within 30 days of billing.

**Rights Policy:** Retains all rights.

**How to Contact:** Send resume, cover letter, list of credits, and writing sample (photocopies only) for the company's files.

**What Not to Do:** Phone.

**Time Needed for Reply:** Three to six weeks.

**Advice for Authors:** Motivation Media consistently hires writers who work well on a team, able to play a leadership role in the creative brainstorming process and craft a document that amplifies and clearly communicates the collective concepts. Writers should also be able, along with the rest of the team, to present ideas to clients.

# BURT MUNK AND COMPANY
**666 Dundee Road, Suite 501/502**
**Northbrook, Illinois 60062**
**(708) 564-0855**

**Contact Person:** Burton Munk, President.

**Types of Material Purchased:** Material for business communications, sales training, product information, and education; also video tapes, booklets, movie presentations, and software.

**Audience:** Client companies, employees, dealers, and the general public.

**Current Needs:** Contact the company for current projects.

**Author Writes on Speculation or Assignment?** Assignment.

**Payment Information:** Negotiable.

**Rights Policy:** Buys all rights; author writes on a work-for-hire basis.

**How to Contact:** Send query and resume.

**What Not to Do:** Phone.

**Time Needed for Reply:** Indefinite; company keeps promising resumes on file and replies only when an appropriate assignment becomes available.

**Advice for Authors:** Burt Munk and Company is a custom house. It prepares all work to order for specific client needs.

# NYSTROM

**Division of Herff Jones**
**3333 Elston Avenue**
**Chicago, Illinois 60618**
**(312) 463-1144**

**Contact Person:** Pat McKeon, Vice President—Marketing.

**Types of Material Purchased:** Scripts for videos, cassettes, worksheets, multimedia, CD-ROMs, and readers' and teachers' guides in the fields of social studies and science.

**Audience:** Students in kindergarten through 12th grade.

**Recent Titles Produced:** "Student Desk Atlas"; "The Physics of Flight" (CD-ROM); "Math Sleuths" (CD-ROM).

**Current Needs:** To be discussed with appropriate writer.

**Author Writes on Speculation or Assignment?** Assignment.

**Payment Information:** Rates vary according to the type of material and level; the company generally pays at the end of the assignment.

**Rights Policy:** Buys all rights; author writes on a work-for-hire basis.

**How to Contact:** Send query with resume and samples.

**What Not to Do:** Phone.

**Time Needed for Reply:** Varies according to the urgency of the project and the suitability of the writer to a particular project.

**Advice for Authors:** Writers should have a strong background in education and, preferably, substantial teaching experience.

# ONEONONE COMPUTER TRAINING

**Division of Mosaic Media, Inc.**
**2055 Army Trail Road, Suite 100**
**Addison, Illinois 60101**
**(708) 628-0500**                                    **Established: 1976**

**Contact Person:** Natalie Young, Editorial Manager.

**Types of Material Purchased:** Primarily audio scripts for step-by-step training in the use of computer hardware and software.

**Audience:** Business and industry.

**Recent Titles Produced:** Various "How to Use . . . " audio courses with quick-reference guides for employees learning popular business software; also software documentation.

**Current Needs:** To be discussed with appropriate writer.

**Author Writes on Speculation or Assignment?** Assignment, mostly.

**Payment Information:** Varies depending on project.

**Rights Policy:** Buys all rights; author writes on a work-for-hire basis.

**How to Contact:** Send query, resume, and brief writing sample.

**What Not to Do:** Phone.

**Time Needed for Reply:** Two to four weeks.

**Advice for Authors:** OneOnOne wants writers with instructional design experience and, preferably, with access to personal computer hardware and software.

# PILOT PRODUCTIONS

**2123 McDaniel Avenue**
**Evanston, Illinois 60201**
**(708) 328-3700**                    **Established: 1941**

**Contact Person:** Chris Isely, President.

**Types of Material Purchased:** Writing for desktop and audio-visual services. Most writing, however, is done in-house.

**Audience:** Business and industry.

**Recent Titles Produced:** Marketing and training presentations.

**Current Needs:** To be discussed with appropriate writer.

**Author Writes on Speculation or Assignment?** Assignment.

**Payment Information:** Fee of variable rate paid in increments of thirds or halves.

**Rights Policy:** Buys all rights; author writes on a work-for-hire basis.

**How to Contact:** Send resume.

**What Not to Do:** Drop in without an appointment.

**Time Needed for Reply:** Indefinite; the company keeps materials on file and replies only when an appropriate assignment becomes available.

**Advice for Authors:** Pilot Productions values business-oriented writers who have the ability to understand the client's material, write clearly, and explain concepts well. Writers must be able to identify quickly both the audience and the purpose of the film— from the client's point of view—and harness his/her creative energies to achieve that purpose.

# SHEPPARD PRODUCTIONS, INC.

**1741 Green Bay Road**
**Highland Park, Illinois 60035**
**(708) 926-0060**

**Contact Person:** Julie Seedorf, Producer; Jim Owcarz, Executive Producer.

**Types of Material Purchased:** Primarily scripts for video presentations but also for some motion-picture and industrial theater projects.

**Audience:** Business and industry.

**Recent Titles Produced:** Video tapes of all sorts for industrial clients. Tapes are used for corporate marketing activities, sales meetings, and technology conference programs.

**Current Needs:** To be discussed with appropriate writer.

**Author Writes on Speculation or Assignment?** Assignment, usually.

**Payment Information:** Fee varies according to writer and assignment. Payment is usually made upon completion of the assignment, but the company will make partial payments with assignments of long duration.

**Rights Policy:** Buys all rights; author writes on a work-for-hire basis.

**How to Contact:** Send query with resume and writing samples (portions of scripts); may also phone.

**What Not to Do:** Drop in without an appointment.

**Time Needed for Reply:** Sheppard Productions does not acknowledge unsolicited queries and resumes. It keeps appropriate materials on file and contacts writers when suitable projects become available.

**Advice for Authors:** Creativity is the most important quality Sheppard Productions seeks in a writer. Other essentials include the ability to produce what the client wants, to assess the needs of the audience, and to write material that lends itself to easy visualization.

# RICK SIMON & COMPANY

**720 N. Franklin Street**
**Chicago, Illinois 60610**
**(312) 951-7275**

**Contact Person:** Rick Simon, President; Sandy Tanner, Executive Producer.

**Types of Material Purchased:** Videos in the areas of marketing, public relations, and sales training.

**Audience:** Businesses and trade associations.

**Recent Titles Produced:** Marketing, image, and training videos.

**Current Needs:** To be discussed with appropriate writer.

**Author Writes on Speculation or Assignment?** Assignment.

**Payment Information:** Fee of variable rate; the company generally pays in increments throughout project development.

**Rights Policy:** Buys all rights; author writes on a work-for-hire basis.

**How to Contact:** Send query with resume and either strong corporate video script samples or portions of proposals; may also phone.

**What Not to Do:** Drop in without an appointment.

**Time Needed for Reply:** Two weeks maximum.

**Advice for Authors:** Rick Simon & Company is looking for three things in a writer: imagination, reliability, and an ability to do solid research. The firm's production is oriented toward business.

# TRITEL PRODUCTIONS, INC.
**53 W. Seegers Road**
**Arlington Heights, Illinois 60005**
**(708) 952-0020**

**Contact Person:** Terry Thiry, Office Manager.

**Types of Material Purchased:** Scripts for video, slide, and multi-image presentations.

**Audience:** Tritel works with the marketing/communications departments of client companies. It is also involved in meeting planning for business and industry.

**Recent Titles Produced:** Produced a video providing a company overview for a local building contractor; also planned a sales meeting in Puerto Rico.

**Current Needs:** Script writers for various projects.

**Author Writes on Speculation or Assignment?** Assignment.

**Payment Information:** Fee paid on a contractual, per-job basis.

**Rights Policy:** Buys all rights; author writes on a work-for-hire basis.

**How to Contact:** Send query and writing samples.

**What Not to Do:** Phone or drop in without an appointment.

**Time Needed for Reply:** Indefinite; the company keeps materials on file and replies only when a suitable project becomes available.

**Advice for Authors:** Tritel Productions is looking for writers who possess both creativity and a strong knowledge of business.

# UNITED LEARNING

**6633 W. Howard Street**
**Niles, Illinois 60714**
**(708) 647-0600**                              **Established: 1969**

**Contact Person:** Ron Reed, President; Gayle Schaffer, Production Manager.

**Types of Material Purchased:** Scripts for educational videos and cassettes; also teachers' guides, study sheets, and blackline master activities. Authors supply photos for some projects.

**Audience:** Students from kindergarten through 12th grade; also adults.

**Recent Titles Produced:** "The Desert's Struggle for Survival" (science); "The Sentencing of Bill Thomas" (guidance); "Judaism: The Religion of a People" (social studies).

**Current Needs:** To be discussed with appropriate writer.

**Author Writes on Speculation or Assignment?** Assignment.

**Payment Information:** Standard fee for educational audio-visual scripts.

**Rights Policy:** Buys all rights.

**How to Contact:** Send query with a brief outline.

**What Not to Do:** Phone or drop in without an appointment.

**Time Needed for Reply:** Usually four weeks.

**Advice for Authors:** United Learning wants writers who know both the educational and audio-visual markets. A teaching background is helpful but not necessary.

# WILLIAMS/GERARD PRODUCTIONS, INC.
420 N. Wabash Avenue
Chicago, Illinois 60611
(312) 467-5560                              Established: 1976

**Contact Person:** Janet Hansen, Vice President—Production; Drew Suss, Creative Director.

**Types of Material Purchased:** Scripts for executive speeches, videos, proposals, training programs, interactive computer programs, electronic presentations.

**Audience:** Fortune 1000 companies and their employees.

**Recent Titles Produced:** Product introductions, training programs, interactive CD-ROM programs, marketing videos, touring meetings, sales meetings.

**Current Needs:** Contact the firm for current needs.

**Author Writes on Speculation or Assignment?** Can be either.

**Payment Information:** Negotiable.

**Rights Policy:** Buys all rights; author writes on a work-for-hire basis.

**How to Contact:** Send query, list of credits, and current writing sample.

**What Not to Do:** Phone.

**Time Needed for Reply:** Three to four weeks.

**Advice for Authors:** Williams/Gerard Productions uses freelancers on a regular basis, looking in particular for those with creativity and experience in the business who possess strong credentials in a wide range of areas. Writers should also have presentation skills and the ability to take direction and work quickly.

# EDITORIAL SERVICES

# LIGATURE, INC.
**165 N. Canal Street**
**Chicago, Illinois 60606**
**(312) 648-1233**

**Contact Person:** Constance Rajala, Editorial Director.

**Types of Material Prepared:** All services—manuscript preparation, editing, and analysis; rewriting; picture searches; etc.—involved in the creation and production of elementary and high school textbooks.

**Client Base:** Educational publishers.

**Recently Produced Materials:** Mathematics program for grades K-6; English grammar and composition textbooks for grades 7-12; 8th grade U. S. history textbook; biology ancillaries; multimedia language arts program for grades 6-8.

**Current Needs:** Writers, editors, copyeditors, and proofreaders; also designers and production people who are familiar with Quark.

**Author Writes on Speculation or Assignment?** Assignment.

**Payment Information:** Negotiable.

**Rights Policy:** Buys all rights; author writes on a work-for-hire basis.

**How to Contact:** Query with resume.

**What Not to Do:** Phone, send manuscript, or drop in without an appointment.

**Time Needed for Reply:** One to two weeks.

**Advice for Authors:** Because Ligature's primary business is providing publishing services for educational publishers, the company wants people who have a teaching background to work on its various projects.

# MOBIUM

**Subsidiary of R. R. Donnelly**
**414 N. Orleans Street, Suite 610**
**Chicago, Illinois 60610**                    **Established: 1978**

**Contact Person:** Lisa Cluver, Editorial Supervisor.

**Types of Material Prepared:** Large database-driven catalogs and technical materials; also software documentation and computer template projects.

**Client Base:** Business and industry, including the medical and computer fields.

**Recently Produced Materials:** Catalogs for makers of catheters, office supplies, industrial/construction tools, and medical instruments.

**Current Needs:** Ongoing need for editors, proofreaders, and data-entry people.

**Author Writes on Speculation or Assignment?** Assignment.

**Payment Information:** Negotiable.

**How to Contact:** Send resume; then follow up with a phone call.

**What Not to Do:** Drop in without an appointment.

**Time Needed for Reply:** One week.

**Advice for Authors:** Mobium does not usually have a need to hire writers, and most editorial work is done on-site. Good computer skills are a plus; so is a background in the preparation of technical materials.

# NAVTA ASSOCIATES, INC.

**932 W. Wolfram**
**Chicago, Illinois 60657**          **Established: 1985**

**Contact Person:** Tom Navta, President.

**Types of Material Prepared:** Textbooks and ancillaries, software and videos for all grade levels.

**Client Base:** Educational publishers and software/video producers, including Addison-Wesley, Harcourt Brace Jovanovich, Macmillan/McGraw Hill, Prentice Hall, Scott Foresman, Simon and Schuster, and World Book/Childcraft.

**Recently Produced Materials:** General math text and ancillaries; yearbook supplement for children's encyclopedia; economics data bank and workbook masters; tutorial and applications for Microsoft Works 3.0.

**Current Needs:** Writers, editors, copyeditors, proofreaders, designers, production people.

**Author Writes on Speculation or Assignment?** Assignment.

**Payment Information:** $20-$25 per hour for writing and editing; $10-$15 per hour for copyediting, proofreading, and production work; project fee for design work.

**Rights Policy:** Buys all rights.

**How to Contact:** Send resume.

**What Not to Do:** Drop in without an appointment.

**Time Needed for Reply:** One or two weeks.

**Advice for Authors:** Navta Associates, with offices in New Jersey and Pennsylvania, launched its Chicago office in 1994. It has a wide range of needs for talented individuals in the educational publishing, software, and video fields.

# PUBLISHERS SERVICES, INC.
**Division of Black Dot Graphics**
**1331 Business Center Drive**
**Mount Prospect, Illinois 60056**
**(708) 390-9890**

**Contact Person:** Gene Malecki, Vice President.

**Types of Material Prepared:** The company provides manuscript evaluation and development, editing, design, production, art, and project management services for publishers.

**Client Base:** Educational publishers.

**Current Needs:** Project managers.

**Author Writes on Speculation or Assignment?** Assignment.

**Payment Information:** Negotiable.

**Rights Policy:** Buys all rights; author writes a on work-for-hire basis.

**How to Contact:** Send resume.

**What Not to Do:** Phone.

**Time Needed for Reply:** One week.

**Advice for Authors:** Freelancers who work for Publishers Services must adhere to very strict deadlines. Those seeking project manager positions should possess book production experience.

# THE QUARASAN GROUP, INC.
214 W. Huron Street
Chicago, Illinois 60610
(312) 787-0750                    Established: 1982

**Contact Person:** Randi Brill, President (for art, design, and production queries); Suzanne Tighe, Editorial Director (for writing and editing queries).

**Types of Material Prepared:** The company prepares core educational products and ancillary materials for textbook publishers. It also field tests and checks facts.

**Client Base:** Educational publishers.

**Recently Produced Materials:** Materials in all curriculum areas of science, language arts, reading, and history for students in grades K-12.

**Current Needs:** Writers, editors, and project managers.

**Author Writes on Speculation or Assignment?** Assignment.

**Payment Information:** Payment is usually on a contract-for-assignment, work-for-hire basis.

**Rights Policy:** Buys all rights; author writes on a work-for-hire basis.

**How to Contact:** Send resume.

**What Not to Do:** Phone.

**Time Needed for Reply:** The company keeps resumes on file in its databases and, as the need arises, selects freelancers whose abilities match a particular project.

**Advice for Authors:** The Quarasan Group requires its writers and editors to have elementary/high school teaching experience and/or educational textbook development experience.

# SYNTHEGRAPHICS CORPORATION

**33 Green Bay Road**
**Highland Park, Illinois 60035**
**(708) 432-7699**                    **Established: 1972**

**Contact Person:** Richard Young, President.

**Types of Material Prepared:** Complete editorial and graphic services—including copyediting, design and layout, illustrations, proofreading, typesetting, indexing, and printing—for book publishers.

**Client Base:** Publishers.

**Recently Produced Materials:** Materials produced and services performed for Scott Foresman; Little, Brown; Encyclopaedia Britannica; World Book; Science Research Associates; and Garrett Educational Corporation.

**Author Writes on Speculation or Assignment?** Assignment.

**Payment Information:** Varies depending on assignment.

**Rights Policy:** Buys all rights; author writes on a work-for-hire basis.

**How to Contact:** Phone.

**What Not to Do:** Drop in without an appointment.

**Time Needed for Reply:** Within a week.

# THE WHEETLEY COMPANY, INC.

**3201 Old Glenview Road, Suite 300**
**Wilmette, Illinois 60091**
**(708) 251-4422**                    **Established: 1986**

**Contact Person:** Neysa Chouteau, General Manager.

**Types of Material Prepared:** The company provides a full range of publishing services: planning, market research, writing, editing, art, design, and production.

**Client Base:** Publishers of educational and professional materials.

**Recently Produced Materials:** *Personal Selling; Estrellas De La Literatura Teacher's Edition, Grade 5; Glencoe Geometry* (TE and ancillaries); *Macmillan-McGraw Hill Science* (TE and ancillaries); *Documents in British History.*

**Current Needs:** Content editors, copyeditors, proofreaders, designers, and production people.

**Author Writes on Speculation or Assignment?** Assignment.

**Payment Information:** Fee on a contractual basis; can be based on either an hourly or project rate.

**Rights Policy:** Buys all rights; author writes on a work-for-hire basis.

**How to Contact:** Phone first to determine needs; then send resume.

**What Not to Do:** Drop in without an appointment.

**Time Needed for Reply:** Ten to fifteen days.

**Advice for Authors:** The Wheetley Company prefers, but does not require, the freelancers it hires to have a teaching background.

# OTHER FREELANCE MARKETS

# GALLANT GREETINGS CORPORATION
**2654 W. Medill Street**
**Chicago, Illinois 60647**
**(312) 489-2000**

**Contact Person:** Carolyn McDilda, Editorial Coordinator.

**Types of Material Purchased:** Greeting cards—informational, conventional, humorous, seasonal, inspirational.

**Current Needs:** Copy (verse or prose) and artwork, either together or separately.

**Policy on Seasonal Pieces:** Six to nine months in advance.

**Author Writes on Speculation or Assignment?** Speculation.

**Payment Information:** Variable fee, paid on acceptance.

**Rights Policy:** Buys worldwide greeting card rights for copy, one-time rights for photographs.

**How to Contact:** Submit ideas on no more than 20 3x5 cards.

**What Not to Do:** Phone.

**Time Needed for Reply:** Ten to twelve weeks.

**Advice for Authors:** Before submitting card ideas, request a copy of the company's writer's guidelines; enclose a self-addressed, stamped envelope with request.

# INNOVISIONS, INC.

**P. O. Box 3361**
**Chicago, Illinois 60654**
**(312) 755-1070**

**Contact Person:** Richard McGinis, Copyeditor.

**Types of Material Purchased:** Greeting cards—adult humor, mostly woman-to-woman; a small risque section.

**Current Needs:** Humorous birthday cards.

**Author Writes on Speculation or Assignment?** Speculation.

**Payment Information:** $75 per card to start.

**Rights Policy:** Buys all rights.

**How to Contact:** Send ideas typed on 3x5 index cards; enclose a self-addressed, stamped envelope.

**What Not to Do:** Phone or send cartoons or other illustrations with card ideas.

**Time Needed for Reply:** Two to three weeks.

**Advice for Authors:** Send for the company's free writer's guidelines and sample cards; enclose a self-addressed, stamped envelope. The company is not interested in cute, sentimental, or offensive concepts and copy.

# ILLINOIS THEATER CENTER (ITC)

**400A Lakewood Boulevard**
**Park Forest, Illinois 60466**
**(708) 481-3510**                    **Established: 1976**

**Contact Person:** Steve Billig, Artistic Director.

**Types of Material Purchased:** Original plays with small casts, suitable for all audiences; also small-cast musicals.

**Audience:** Adults and children.

**Recently Produced Materials:** "The African Company Presents 'Richard III'"; "Separation"; "Scotland Road"; "Don't Dress for Dinner"; "Love Comic" (musical).

**Current Needs:** Small-cast musicals.

**Author Writes on Speculation or Assignment?** Speculation.

**Payment Information:** Negotiable.

**Rights Policy:** Negotiable.

**How to Contact:** Send complete manuscript with cover letter; enclose a self-addressed, stamped envelope.

**What Not to Do:** Phone, send query, or drop in without an appointment.

**Time Needed for Reply:** Eight to ten weeks.

**Advice for Authors:** ITC is interested only in full-length plays and musicals.

# NEW TUNERS THEATRE AND WORKSHOP
1225 W. Belmont Avenue
Chicago, Illinois 60657
(312) 929-7367

**Contact Person:** Allan Chambers, Artistic Coordinator.

**Types of Material Purchased:** New musicals with casts of 15 or fewer.

**Audience:** Adults (cross-section of young urban and suburban adults).

**Recently Produced Materials:** "Ten-Minute Musicals"; "Trask & Fenn"; "Hans Brinker and the Silver Skates"; "Charlie's Oasis"; "Tickle Cakes."

**Current Needs:** Musicals, especially those involving a younger (i.e., 35 and under) ensemble of actors and actresses.

**Author Writes on Speculation or Assignment?** Speculation.

**Payment Information:** Flat fee plus a percentage of the gross.

**Rights Policy:** Buys first-time rights to original material.

**How to Contact:** Send synopsis and cassette with four songs.

**What Not to Do:** Phone or drop in without an appointment.

**Time Needed for Reply:** Three months.

**Advice for Authors:** Although New Tuners Theatre and Workshop is interested in traditional forms of musical theater, it is also willing to consider more innovative styles as well as new voices from composers and authors. It is less interested in operetta and operatic works. The company looks primarily for authors who want to develop their work through New Tuners' three-step workshop, rehearsals, and production.

# NORTHLIGHT THEATRE
**c/o National-Louis University**
**2840 Sheridan Road**
**Evanston, Illinois 60201**

**Contact Person:** Brian Russell, Artistic Associate.

**Types of Material Purchased:** New plays, translations, and adaptations from other literary forms.

**Audience:** College age and older.

**Recently Produced Materials:** "Betrayal"; "My Other Heart"; "The Lonely Planet."

**Current Needs:** Contemporary works for a one-set show with a cast size of eight or fewer characters.

**Author Writes on Speculation or Assignment?** Speculation.

**Payment Information:** Negotiable.

**Rights Policy:** Negotiable.

**How to Contact:** Send synopsis: description of plot, themes, and production requirements; include number of characters and who they are.

**What Not to Do:** Phone or drop in without an appointment.

**Time Needed for Reply:** Two months.

**Advice for Authors:** Plays may vary in genre and topic, but commercial work or dinner theater material is not appropriate for Northlight Theatre's audience. Submit work that speaks to the human condition.

# THE RIVERSIDE PUBLISHING COMPANY
**Subsidiary of Houghton Mifflin Company**
**8420 W. Bryn Mawr Avenue, Suite 1000**
**Chicago, Illinois 60631**
**(708) 714-7000**

**Contact Person:** Lori Carr, Human Resources Associate.

**Types of Material Purchased:** Instructional materials for elementary school and high school curricula; also standardized educational, clinical, and psychological tests.

**Audience:** Students from kindergarten through 12th grade.

**Recently Produced Materials:** Standardized norm-referenced test materials and customized state contract materials.

**Current Needs:** Educational item writers, copyeditors, proofreaders, graphic artists, individuals familiar with electronic desktop (Mac) publishing.

**Author Writes on Speculation or Assignment?** Assignment.

**Payment Information:** Varies according to assignment.

**Rights Policy:** Buys all rights.

**How to Contact:** Send query and resume with writing samples.

**What Not to Do:** Phone.

**Time Needed for Reply:** One to three months.

**Advice for Authors:** The Riverside Publishing Company almost always requires that writers have classroom teaching experience in the fields in which they intend to write test items.

# SCHOLASTIC TESTING SERVICE

**480 Meyer Road**
**Bensenville, Illinois 60106**
**(708) 766-7150**

**Contact Person:** Dr. John Kauffman, Vice President.

**Types of Material Purchased:** Ability tests, achievement tests, readiness tests, creativity tests, special education tests, and career guidance tests.

**Audience:** Primarily elementary through high school students; some college and adult students as well.

**Recently Produced Materials:** Fine-arts tests; health and physical development tests; new versions of "Education Development Series," "The Coping Inventory," and "The Human Information Processing Survey."

**Current Needs:** Test items (i.e., questions) for math, reading, social studies, science, and sometimes for vocabulary.

**Author Writes on Speculation or Assignment?** Assignment.

**Payment Information:** Variable fee on a per-item basis.

**Rights Policy:** Buys all rights; author writes on a work-for-hire basis.

**How to Contact:** Send resume and samples; may also phone.

**What Not to Do:** Send manuscript or drop in without an appointment.

**Time Needed for Reply:** Two to four weeks.

**Advice for Authors:** Scholastic Testing Service can use writers who possess general background knowledge in many fields and who are willing to learn how to write test items. In addition, the company is always looking for people who have special knowledge in the areas of science, math, social studies, and reading education as well as for people with experience in writing test materials.

# TPC TRAINING SYSTEMS
**Division of Telemedia, Inc.**
**750 Lake Cook Road**
**Buffalo Grove, Illinois 60089**
**(708) 808-4000**                    **Established: 1968**

**Contact Person:** Edward J. Amrein, Editor-in-Chief.

**Types of Material Purchased:** Training manuals for supervised self-study in technical skill areas.

**Audience:** Plant personnel, many of whom have limited educations.

**Recently Produced Materials:** "Process Control Instrumentation"; "Robotics"; "Electronics"; "Microprocessors"; also instructor guides.

**Current Needs:** Technical writers for new and revised materials.

**Author Writes on Speculation or Assignment?** Assignment.

**Payment Information:** $600 for a complete lesson, including objectives and test questions; fee paid on acceptance.

**Rights Policy:** Buys all rights.

**How to Contact:** Send query with resume.

**What Not to Do:** Phone.

**Time Needed for Reply:** One to two weeks.

**Advice for Authors:** Authors for TPC Training Systems must have a technical background, preferably an engineering degree or equivalent. The company expects authors to supply sketches as the basis for developing finished artwork.

# UNIVERSAL TRAINING SYSTEMS COMPANY

**255 Revere Drive**
**Northbrook, Illinois 60062**
**(708) 498-9700**

**Contact Person:** John Doyle, Senior Consultant and Principal.

**Types of Material Purchased:** Custom training programs involving print, audio, video, multimedia CBT, and sometimes motion pictures. Some programs combine print and other media; others use printed matter only—e.g., self-instructional texts.

**Audience:** Primarily Fortune 1000 companies: financial services, manufacturers, automotive, and retail industries,

**Recently Produced Materials:** Program about credit collection skills.

**Current Needs:** Instructional designers skilled in technical writing, data processing, health care, and sales skills.

**Author Writes on Speculation or Assignment?** Assignment.

**Payment Information:** Varies depending on client and program.

**Rights Policy:** Buys all rights; author writes on a work-for-hire basis.

**How to Contact:** Send resume with samples of previous work in relevant area; may also phone.

**What Not to Do:** Drop in without an appointment.

**Time Needed for Reply:** Within one month.

**Advice for Authors:** Universal Training Systems Company wants people who have experience writing training programs for business and industry—particularly Fortune 1000 companies. Writers must be able to work with and meet the needs of the clients. Experience with customer service, sales, management/franchisee development, or policy/procedures manuals is especially valuable.

# INDEX

## of Publishers and Publications

Abbot, Langer & Associates, 2
Academy Chicago, 3
ACTA Publications, Inc., 4
Advanstar Communications, 216
Advertising Age, 172
African American Images, 5
AGS & R Communications, 288
AIM: America's Intercultural Magazine, 80
AIM: Liturgy Resources, 149
Aim Publications, 80
Air Waves, 81
American Association of Individual
    Investors, 185
American Bar Association, 6, 176, 195, 209
American Catholic Press, 7
American Clean Car, 210
American Coin-Op, 211
American Drycleaner, 212
American Field, 82
American Hospital Publishing, Inc., 8, 242,
    246
American Laundry Digest, 213
American Libraries, 173
American Library Association, 9, 173
American Marketing Association, 201
American Medical Association Alliance, 191
American Nurseryman, 214
American Nurseryman Publishing Company,
    214, 243
American Planning Association, 204
American Printer, 215
American Society of Church History, 157
American Technical Publishers, Inc., 10
American Trade Magazines, 210, 211, 212,
    213
America's Network, 216
Ammark Publishing Company, 222
Amoco Jobber, 248
Amoco Oil Company, 248
Anglican Advance, 150
Another Chicago Magazine, 136
Another Chicago Press, 11
Antiques & Collecting Magazine, 83
Appliance Service News, 217
Argus Business, 192, 197
Art Institute of Chicago, The, 12
Assembly, 218
Auto Racing Digest, 84
H. H. Backer Associates, Inc., 241, 253
Baha'i Publishing Trust, 13

Bank Administration Institute, 174
Bank Fraud, 174
Bank Management, 174
Bar Examiner, The, 175
Barrington Area Arts Council, 148
Barrister, 176
Baseball Digest, 85
Basketball Digest, 86
BCR Enterprises, Inc., 223
Billiards Digest, 219
Black Dot Graphics, 309
Bolingbrook Metropolitan Newspapers, Inc.,
    264
Bonus Books, 14
Bowlers Journal, 220
Bowling Digest, 87
Boxboard Containers, 221
Brewers Digest, 222
Brigade Leader, 151
Bulletin of the Atomic Scientists, The, 88
Business Communications Review, 223
Business Insurance, 177
Business Marketing, 178
C & D Debris Recycling, 224
Cade Communications, 132
Cahners Publishing Company, 207, 230, 236,
    244, 258
Campus Life, 89
Career World, 90
Catholic Church Extension Society, 160
Center for Neighborhood Technology, 202
Century Publishing Company, 84, 85, 86, 87,
    109, 112, 115, 129
CES Associates, 15
Chef Magazine, 225
Chicago, 91
Chicago Advertising and Media, 179
Chicago Computers and Users, 92
Chicago Daily Law Bulletin, 180
Chicago Film & Video News, 181
Chicago Historical Society, 93
Chicago History, 93
Chicago Lawyer, 182
Chicago Life, 94
Chicago New Art Association, The, 121
Chicago Parent Newsmagazine, 95
Chicago Purchasor, 183
Chicago Reader, 265
Chicago Reporter, The, 96
Chicago Review, 137

Chicago Review Press, 16
Chicago Schools, 97
Chicago Sports Resources, Inc., 134
Chicago Studies, 152
Chicago Sun-Times, 266
Chicago Tribune Magazine, 267
Childrens Press, 17
Chiron Publications, 18
Christian Century, The, 153
Christian Century Foundation, The, 153, 156
Christian Ministry, The, 156
Christian Service Brigade, 151, 169
Christianity & the Arts, 154
Christianity Today, 89, 155
Church History, 157
Civitas Dei Foundation, 152
Clapper Communications Company, 100
Clark Boardman and Callaghan, 19
Clearvue/eav, Inc., 289
Commercial Investment Real Estate (CIRE) Journal, 184
Complete Woman, 98
Computerized Investing, 185
Concordia University, 200
Concrete Products, 226
Confetti, 186
Consumer Guide$^R$ Publications, 57
Consumers Digest, 99, 135
Contemporary Books, 20
Control, 227
David C. Cook Foundation, 161
Corporate Legal Times, 187
Corporate Legal Times Corporation, 187
Covenant Companion, The, 158
Covenant Publications, 158
Crafts 'n Things, 100
Crain Communications, Inc., 101, 172, 177, 178, 203, 268
Crain's Chicago Business, 268
Crain's Small Business, 101
Creative Woman, The, 138
Critic, The, 139
Crossroads Books, 21
Crossway Books, 22
CTI Publications, Inc., 155, 167
Curriculum Review, 188
Daily Herald, 269
Darby Media Group, 290
Dartnell Corporation, The, 23, 102
Daughters of Sarah, 159
DBI Books, Inc., 24
Dearborn Financial Publishing, 59
Ivan R. Dee, Inc., 25
DePaul University, 143
Des Plaines Publishing Company, 270
Distributor, 228
Dog World, 103
R. R. Donnelly, 307
Down Beat, 104
DuPage Business Ledger, 271
Ebony, 105

Editor & Publisher, 189
Educational Foundation for Nuclear Science, 88
Electronic Packaging & Production, 229
Elks Magazine, The, 106
Employee Benefit Plan Review, 190
Employee Services Management, 107
Encyclopaedia Britannica, Inc., 26
Energy Focus, 230
Episcopal Diocese of Chicago, 150
Evangelical Lutheran Church in America, 163
Evanston Publishing, Inc., 27
Everyday Learning Corporation, 28
Extension, 160
Extra Bilingual Community Newspapers, 272
Facets, 191
Family Safety and Health Magazine, 108
Fancy Food, 231
J. G. Ferguson Publishing Company, 29
Fire Chief, 192
Fleet Equipment, 232
Food Business, 233
Food Industry News, 234
Food Processing, 235
Foodservice Equipment & Supplies Specialist, 236
Foodservice Publishing Company, 234
Football Digest, 109
Forest House Publishing Company, Inc., 30
Forum Press, Inc., 33
Futures Magazine, 193
Gallant Greetings Corporation, 314
Gamit Enterprises, Inc., 217
Gas Industries, 237
Gay Chicago Magazine, 110
General Learning Corporation, 90
Gennera, Knab & Company, 291
Gernhardt Publishing, Inc., 110
Giant Steps Publishing Corporation, 196
Global Telephony, 238
Go Chicago Travel Guide, 111
Goldsholl Design & Film, Inc., 292
Good Cents, 239
Goodheart-Willcox Company, Inc., 31
Good News Publishers, 22
Great Quotations Publishing Company, 32
Grocery Distribution, 240
Grocery Market Publications, 240
Groom & Board, 241
Hadley School for the Blind, The, 123
Harlan Davidson, Inc., 33
HarperCollins Publishers, 60
Healthcare Financial Management, 194
Healthcare Financial Management Association, 194
Health Facilities Management, 242
Herald Newspapers, Inc., 273
Herff Jones, 297
HispaniMedia L. P., 272
Hitchcock Publishing Company, 218

Hockey Digest, 112
Hollingsworth Group, The, 206
Houghton Mifflin Company, 319
Hoyt Publishing, 256
Human Rights, 195
Hunter Publishing Company, 249, 261
Hyde Park Herald, 273
Illinois Entertainer, 113
Illinois Legal Times, 196
Illinois Theater Center, 316
Industrial Fire Chief, 197
Inland Architect, 198
Innate Graphics, Inc., 114
Innovisions, Inc., 315
InQ Publishing Company, 34
Inside, 274
Inside Publications, 274
Insider, 114
Inside Sports, 115
Institute of Real Estate Management, 199
Interlit, 161
Interior Landscape, 243
Intertec Publishing Corporation, 238, 260
InterVarsity Press, 35
In These Times, 116
Richard D. Irwin, Inc., 36, 37
Irwin Professional Publishing, 37
JB Communications, 81, 92, 97, 111, 179
Jewish Federation of Metropolitan Chicago, 162
Johnson Publishing Company, Inc., 105
Journal of Property Management, 199
JUF News, 162
Steve Kalsow Productions, Inc., 293
Kazi Publications, Inc., 38
Charles H. Kerr Publishing Company, 39
Key This Week in Chicago, 117
Kidsbooks, Inc., 40
Kona-Cal, Inc., 259
Lakeland Boating, 118
Lakeland Publishers, Inc., 275
Lake View Press, 41
Law Bulletin Publishing Company, 180, 182
Leader Papers, Inc., 276
Ledger Publications, Inc., 271
Leigh Communications, Inc., 130
Lerner Communications, Inc., 277
Life Newspapers, 278
Ligature, Inc., 306
Lightner Publishing Corporation, 83
Lion Magazine, The, 119
Lions Club International, 119
Loyola University Press, 42
Luby Publishing, 219, 220
Lutheran, The, 163
Lutheran Education, 200
Luxury Homes, 244
Maclean Hunter Publishing Company, 103, 221, 226
McDougal, Littell & Company, 43
Maher Publications, Inc., 104, 250

Manufactured Home Merchandisers, 245
Maple Publishing, 232
Marketing Research, 201
Materials Management in Health Care, 246
George S. May International Company, 247
May Trends, 247
Merchandiser, 248
Midwest Outdoors, 120
Midwest Outdoors, Ltd., 120
Mobium, 307
Modern Poetry Association, 142
Moody Press, 44
Morton Productions, Inc., Jack, 294
Mosaic Media, Inc., 298
Mosby-Year Book, Inc., 45
Motivation Media, Inc., 295
Motor Service, 249
Burt Munk and Company, 296
Murphy-Richter Publishing Company, 257
Music Inc., 250
National Assembly of Religious Women, 165
National Conference of Bar Examiners, 175
National Employee Services and Recreation Association, 107
National-Louis University, 318
National Provisioner, 251
National Safety Council, 108
National Spiritual Assembly of the Baha'i's of the United States, 170
National Women's Christian Temperance Union, 171
Navta Associates, 308
Neighborhood Works, The, 202
Nelson-Hall Publishers, 46
New American Writing, 140
New Art Examiner, 121
New City, 279
New Product News, 252
New Tuners Theatre and Workshop, 317
Noble Press, Inc., The, 47
Northlight Theatre, 318
North Shore, 122
Northwestern University, 147
Northwestern University Press, 48
NTC Publishing Group, 49
Nystrom, 297
O'Meara-Brown Publications, Inc., 118
OneOnOne Computer Training, 298
Orbit, The, 123
Original Art Report, The, 124
Oster Communications, 193
Other Voices, 141
Paddock Publications, Inc., 269
Palmer Publishing Company, 228, 229, 239
J. S. Paluch Company, Inc., 149
Paper Industry Management Association, 254
Path Press, Inc., 50
PB Communications, 122
F. E. Peacock Publishers, Inc., 51
Pensions & Investments, 203

Pet Age, 253
P-Form: Performance Art Magazine, 125
Pilot Productions, 299
PIMA Magazine, 254
Pioneer Clubs, 164
Pioneer Clubs' Perspective, 164
Pioneer Press, Inc., 280
Pizza & Pasta, 255
Planning, 204
Planning Communications, 52
Playboy, 126
PlusVoice, 127
Poetry, 142
Poetry East, 143
Polychrome Publishing Corporation, 54
P-O-P Times, 256
P. O. Publishing Company, 53
Press Publications, 281
Primavera, 144
Printing News Midwest, 205
Probe, 165
Probus Publishing, 55
Progressive Railroading, 257
Proteus Enterprises, Inc., 56
Publications International, Ltd., 57
Publishers Services, Inc., 309
Purchasing Management Association of Chicago, 183
Putman Publishing Company, Inc., 227, 233, 235
Quarasan Group, The, 310
Quintessence Publishing Company, Inc., 58
Quoin Publishing, Inc., 205
Ragan Communications, Inc., Lawrence, 188
Rambunctious Review, 145
Randall Publishing Company, Inc., 186
Real Estate Business, 206
Real Estate Education Company, 59
Real Estate News Corporation, 181, 198
Regional News, 282
Regional Publishing Corporation, 282
Remodeled Homes, 258
Reporter Newspapers, The, 282
Reporter/Progress Newspapers, 283
Restaurants & Institutions, 207
Rhino, 146
Riverside Publishing Company, The, 319
RLD Group, Inc., 245
Roberts Publishing, Inc., 113
Rotarian, The, 128
Rotary International, 128
Russell Publications, Inc., 284
Scholastic Testing Service, 320
Scott Foresman & Company, 60
Screen Enterprises, Inc., 208
Screen Magazine, 208
Sentinel, The, 166
Sentinel Publishing Company, 166
Harold Shaw Publishers, 61

Sheppard Productions, Inc., 300
Signature Group, The, 132
Rick Simon & Company, 301
Soccer Digest, 129
Sourcebooks, 62
Charles D. Spencer & Associates, Inc., 190
Stagnito Publishing Company, 251
Star Publications, 285
Student Lawyer, 209
Successful Dealer, 259
Surrey Books, Inc., 63
Synthegraphics Corporation, 311
Talcott Communications Corporation, 225, 231, 255
TAPP Group, The, 138
Telemedia, Inc., 321
Telephony, 260
Theosophical Publishing House, 64
Third Side Press, Inc., 65
Third World Press, 66
Thorntree Press, 67
3X/400 Systems Management, 261
Thunder & Ink Publishers, 68
Tia Chucha Press, 69
TMA, 139
Today's Chicago Woman, 130
Today's Christian Woman, 167
TPC Training Systems, 321
Transport Fleet News, 262
Transport Publishing Company, 262
TravelHost, 131
Trend Publishing, Inc., 252
TriQuarterly, 147
Tritel Productions, Inc., 302
Triumph Books, 70
Tyndale House Publishers, 71
United Learning, 303
Universal Training Systems Company, 322
University of Chicago, 72, 137
University of Chicago Press, 72
University of Illinois at Chicago, 141
Urban Ministries, Inc., 168
Urban Research Press, 73
Vantage, 132
Vegetarian Times, 133
Venture, 169
Victor Books, 74
Waveland Press, 75
Wednesday Journal, Inc., 95, 286
Wheetley Company, Inc., The, 312
Whetstone, 148
Albert Whitman and Company, 76
Williams/Gerard Productions, Inc., 304
Windy City Sports Magazine, 134
Woodall Publishing Company, Inc., 77
World Book, Inc., 78
World Order, 170
Young Crusader, The, 171
Your Money, 135